Steps on a Mindful Journey
Person-centred expressions

Godfrey T. Barrett-Lennard

PCCS BOOKS
Ross-on-Wye

First published in 2003

PCCS BOOKS
Llangarron
Ross-on-Wye
Herefordshire
HR9 6PT
United Kingdom
Tel (01989) 77 07 07
website www.pccs-books.co.uk
email   contact@pccs-books.co.uk

Steps on a Mindful Journey: Person-centred expressions

ISBN 1 898059 58 6

Cover design by Old Dog Graphics
Printed by Biddles Ltd., Guildford, United Kingdom

Contents

Preface

My choice of title for this book invites some explanation of the guiding idea and scope. Each chapter, distinct in its topic, is grounded in thought that originated at a different point in my professional-personal journey. Extending the metaphor, each can be considered a step in this journey. But why the term 'mindful'? Although one of my aims was to make this volume accessible to a broad range of readers, each idea and passage has been a focus of careful reflection, yielding textured meanings that I have tried to capture rather precisely but without undue verbiage. Even when my language is quite informal the content is mindful — my mind reaching out to your thinking self, as reader.

My first idea for this book and a companion volume was to bring together a connected selection of my unpublished and limited-circulation papers. I worked away patiently at this project for a considerable time, gradually finding myself drawn to much more rewriting and extension of thought than I had first envisaged. Finally, it became clear to me that two complementary books would work better than one, each complete and distinct with its own concept.

The territory of *this* volume is largely within the counselling sphere and the chapters, while representing my own thought, have person-centred anchorage in style and idea — in keeping with the book's subtitle. Some of the material has been published, or distributed privately; other parts are newly shaped or presented here for the first time. All chapters are at the least revised, reframed or updated from any earlier form, and I believe that even those readers who know my work quite well will find much that is not familiar to them.

In varied ways, themes regarding the self and relationships between selves course throughout this book. The nature, growth and healing of self through therapy and life experiences is a major strand. I have sought to illuminate how relationships work between therapist and client, in developmental groups and in families. The nature of listening and processes of empathy in human life are particular foci in at least three chapters. Description, illustration, theory and systematic study follow each other with varied emphasis, according to the topic. My sharing in some parts of the book, especially within the appendices, is more to evoke meaning than to pin it down.

John Shlien and probably others have argued that (good) theory is autobiography, that it comes out of life experience, including personal observation. Be that as it may, this book includes both frankly and implicitly autobiographical elements. I have ventured to speak directly about aspects of my own journey in the Appendix, to include a selection of my poems (on self and relationship themes) after that, and to acknowledge in other places how I came to focus on particular topics and issues. The final chapter includes a preview of the distinctive concern and direction of my other manuscript book, presently titled *The primacy of relationship: Healing revisited in an altered world.*

Closer introduction to the background or specific content of this work seems unnecessary, especially since each of the ten chapters begins with an informal mini-preface about how it came to be 'born' and grew to its present form, with hints as to the nature of this offspring of thought. Each chapter (and appendix) of this book is sufficiently self-contained that you as reader could readily choose to take its content in a different order than arranged. If you are formally studying the book, and are relatively new to its subject matter, there may be something to be said for staying more or less with the given sequence.

Finally, I hope that this book can be educational in the best sense, that it can inform, stimulate and provoke and, above all, truly engage you as reader — whether formally a student, teacher or researcher, or a curious and inquiring person simply following your interest. Whether you are in this latter category or an official student I naturally hope that there will be many fellow-readers, and that you find opportunity for contact and discussion with some one or more of them. Should you wish to be in touch with me my present Email address is <G.Barrett-Lennard@Murdoch.edu.au>.

Bon voyage, as companion in this shared 'mindful journey'.

Godfrey Barrett-Lennard

Chapter 1

Qualities of the helping interview

This analysis has its roots within a much longer contributed chapter 'The client-centred system unfolding' (in Turner, 1979). It later evolved into a separate article for the British Journal of Hospital Medicine *(in 1985), from which this present version is revised. I have kept to its previous style and scope but amended many specifics of content and updated the references. As I reviewed my earlier text, I was happy with the direction but not with the exact framing. Wanting to amend some elements should not surprise me since the 1985 version was edited for a particular journal context and, especially, since 18 years and a large part of the writing of my 1998 book have intervened.*

Unlike Rogers, who rarely revised or altered a paper once it had received any circulation, I often live with provisional drafts or versions for some time, and tend to take opportunities for revision even after initial publication. In the present case, I like the scope and economy of the statement and am glad to have revisited it again, with opportunity for refinement. The chapter brings into live view a perspective that the remaining chapters of Part 1 further unfold. There are nuances that I suspect are unique to this 'introductory' statement, and I am pleased to be sharing it with fresh readers.

During and following World War II radical innovations in the study and development of the helping interview took place. These innovations were most fully expressed in what came to be known as client-centred therapy (Rogers and Wallen, 1946; Rogers, 1949, 1951, 1961a, 1966), but have influenced almost all forms of therapy and helping encounter. The new approach was visibly launched by a book concerned with its philosophy and, most vividly, its distinctive practice (Rogers, 1942). This work includes the first published transcript of the total verbal exchange between a counsellor and client, from the initial meeting to the conclusion of therapy, eight interview hours and 170 pages later!

Any approach to personal helping involves assumptions about human nature or personality. A key assumption in the present case is that tendencies toward growth, development of individual and species potentialities, and integrated or organismic functioning, occur normally or 'by nature'. However, their expression can be blocked or even warped by chronic deprivation of the nutrients for growth or by sustained stress. In this viewpoint an effective helping relationship provides the conditions that release and nourish inbuilt recuperative and actualising tendencies (Rogers, 1961a, 1962a). True emotional healing and growth cannot be induced and directed, a view taken so seriously that the approach was first called non-directive therapy (Rogers, 1942). As I would now put it, *attempts to instil a new pattern may alter behaviour but cannot produce wellness, since wellness is a fruition of being not a rendered shape or adjustment.* Recovery and growth flow from the nature of living beings in a favourable environment. The challenge of therapy is the discovery and creation of such an environment. Each therapy partner plays a crucial part but my main focus here is on the therapist-helper's contribution.

Primary qualities of helper response

The client-oriented helper relies on far more relevant and powerful 'tools' than advice, external judgement, verbal reassurance, or the teaching of solutions to problems in living.

- He/she listens, with as much empathy as can honestly be brought to bear, such that the client has the experience of being deeply heard and, through this, of coming to new quality of inner listening and connection. Finding that the helper knows, at least at this moment and in glimpses, 'how it is to be me', can be at once profoundly reassuring, clarifying and freeing (Barrett-Lennard, 1963, 1981; Rogers, 1961a [Chapter 3], 1975). Individuals are isolated by intensely felt experience that has not been both expressed *and* received. Genuine, communicated empathic understanding is like oxygen to the living self within.

- There is no attitude on the helper's part of judging the person in need, but a caring, accepting compassion for a fellow human who is injured, sick, buffeted, or deprived. Acceptance does not imply agreement with the other's behaviour or attitude but, at best, an unqualified responsiveness to their experiencing self, including their own sense of who they are, and where in pain, stuck or free.

- The helper's response ideally is totally lacking in affectation or phoniness. It has no performing quality, elusiveness, or hidden calculation. The helping partner is congruent in the interaction, transparent in showing how s/he is genuinely responding at that time — even when non-empathic or inclined to judge. In a person who is open, real, and unencumbered by a need to appear infallible, occasions of such discomfort are allowed to show visibly. The message of strength and trust conveyed by such congruency aids the client in also letting down his or her guard and being true to self.

These qualities of experienced helper response, refined in theory and systematically measured, have been a focus of extensive research (Barrett-Lennard, 1998, Chapter 13). Examination of the therapist-client relationship in differing therapy approaches is included within this research. Generally, the findings support the practical importance for effective therapy of these relationship qualities, first advanced by Rogers but also under continuing refinement.[1] The focus of this chapter, however, is not on research but on the process qualities of a helping interview in action, in keeping with the principles outlined.

The helping interview process

For convenience, the discussion that follows is arranged to highlight a number of process features which, in practice, are interwoven in a single dynamic tapestry. T refers to the *therapist* (or social caseworker, pastoral or physician counsellor, psychiatric nurse, or other personal helper) and C to the *client* (or patient-counsellee or other aided person).

Sharing responsibility in the interview

Initiative for the main topical content of the communication lies with the client. The helping conversation largely follows his or her agenda. On the other hand, the nature of the relationship and process of communication between T and C is equally or more in T's hands. The balance of initiatives partly reflects the differing intentions, expectations and resources of the participants within the helping engagement. C knows best where s/he is hurting, in conflict, or wanting to move beyond some present quality of functioning. T has experiential knowledge of how to respond and relate to C in potentially helpful ways. 'Applying' this knowledge is not so much a technical exercise as it is an authentic living of the therapy conditions outlined, in relation to the client.

T's range of initiative expands further with withdrawn or deeply troubled

---

[1] Refinements were already occurring in the 1980s (Barrett-Lennard, 1981; Lietaer, 1984) and later accelerated, culminating in the rich array of thought advanced in a multi-volume series (Wyatt, 2001; Haugh and Merry, 2001; Bozarth and Wilkins, 2001; Wyatt and Sanders, 2002).

persons — as described, for example, by Gendlin (1962, 1964, 1967), Rogers (1962b, 1967) and Shlien (1961) in their work with schizophrenic clients. This also is often true with children and younger adolescents. However, such initiatives are an active offering of relationship, direct indications of the attentive presence and personhood of the therapist, and at times a congruent sharing of immediate thought and feeling about what C and T might fruitfully do together. T's initiatives and self-expression in such contexts are simply conveyed, openly suggestive but non-impositional in quality, and consistent with continued empathic listening.

The focus on presently felt experience

The interview tends to focus on immediate feelings and personal meaning, often with mention of outside contexts but without description of events taking centre stage. T's responses have an experiential quality (Gendlin, 1968). They imply and support a focus on felt meaning, and do not refer to feelings in a disembodied way as external events. This means that T rarely responds in observational mode, or in a way that washes out the emotion from C's communication. To the contrary, the therapy partners' communication tends to carry the full coloration and life of inner feeling.

The experiential mode also has the quality of immediacy. The client tends to communicate felt meanings that surface in words and non-verbal expressions as s/he goes along. Effectively, T is doing this too. Such communication cannot be rehearsed, or even premeditated in its specifics; in many ways, it is the opposite of planned reporting or calculating intervention. Much of the familiar terrain of C's construed world of experience and meaning is allowed to recede as s/he gains security and mobility in the helping endeavour and relationship, engaging in a process of experiential inquiry and growth with a companion who encourages and aids this search but does not conduct it. The interview excerpts to come are expressive of these and other mentioned qualities.

Active empathic listening

The helping listener tries, in Rogers' words, to 'hear the sounds and sense the shape of the other person's inner world'. She asks herself 'Can I resonate to what he is saying, can I let it echo back and forth in me, so deeply that I sense the meanings he is afraid of yet would like to communicate, as well as those meanings he knows?' (Rogers, 1969, p. 223). For C, the impact of such understanding may be so powerful that it is 'as though something that had stopped inside him has begun to move and live again, that some part of his loneliness in a world of imperfect communication and knowing has dissolved, or that some vital connection he had been unable to bring into focus has become suddenly and vividly clear to him' (Barrett-Lennard, 1963). Deeply attentive, sensitive listening and resonation, and expressive empathic responding, may be said to comprise the manifest 'work' of the therapist interviewer (Rogers, 1966).

What T hears is happening within him/herself and influenced by qualities he/she brings to the helping encounter. Client-centred interviewers imply that it is *their own personal consciousness* of the other's experience that is being conveyed in their reflective acknowledgement of their clients' feelings and meaning. The principal features of T's response tend to be most explicit in beginning interviews, and to become more subtle or economical in expression as a helping relationship develops. The following segment began only about 15 minutes after the client and therapist had first met.

T1:   *I guess you mean you want a much more positive feeling, somehow, about being on top of your life, of being able to cope and manage. A sort of expectation that you will, instead of fear (C: Right) perhaps you won't.*

C1:   *It's a little bit wider than that though. You used the word 'to be on top of things'. And I would like to feel that I don't have to be on top of things but that I can just be, you know, kind of equal to them. (C's voice breaks, and tears begin to come.) Right now I feel I have to be on top of them which I don't think is exactly the way everybody — you know, that it's a realistic expectation.*

T2:   *Somehow that touches a feeling that's close to home, for you.*

C2:   *Yes, right (blows nose). (Pause)*

T3:   *'On top' is not the right word — ehr — you, that suggests pushing yourself and having to be better, maybe other things I'm not sure. (Gently) I guess I don't want to push you with a question. It's your immediate feeling that I'm . . .*

C3:   *Well you did hit home there, but I don't know exactly how . . . how that works. (Pause) I mean I would like to feel I don't have to be in control of things in order to survive. It's what I mean about . . . you can't expect always to be on top of things, and I don't think that one should need that feeling in order to survive. Some people manage quite well without having to feel in complete control, all the time, of what's happening . . . So, is that realistic or — ? (T: [At once, softly] I don't know.) Do most people feel they have to be on top? I don't know whether you know either.*

T4:   *I don't really know. But, I'm trying to sense your feeling, I'm not sure how close I am, but it's — and I would like you to correct me — but you would like to be able to take things more as they come, somehow.*

>   *Does the expression 'rolling with the punches' — are you familiar*
>   *with that?*
>
> C4:   *Yes. Yes, I would like to have that capacity.*
> T5:   *I guess my sense is that something kind of hurts you about the way —*
>   *some way — that you push yourself or feel that you have to try to be.*
> C5.   *Right. I always feel like . . . ahm, like if I just (voice quivers and breaks),*
>   *just forget to try, everything would sort of collapse and I'm just tired of*
>   *always trying (takes another cigarette and lights it with the previous*
>   *one). I ran out of matches.*
>   *(After a brief interlude, the client is speaking again, re-entering and*
>   *elaborating her feeling with strong example.)*
> C6:   *When I'm in a plane I'm convinced when we finally land that it was*
>   *just me holding it up there. Not really, but emotionally when I'm up*
>   *there if I'm not just thinking about it staying up all the time (voice*
>   *breaks again) I'm convinced we're going to crash. I'm just bringing*
>   *that up symbolically — I think that holds for just about everything.*
> T6:   *I don't know, I just have the image that it must be so exhausting for*
>   *you to carry that load, to carry that weight! (T leans back, involuntarily*
>   *miming the strained holding or pressing up of a heavy weight.)*

In T1 of this excerpt, the therapist is approaching but not yet fully tuned to the client's meaning. His response and choice of words effectively provide an opening for C to clarify something that she feels deeply and sees as an important part of her problem. T2 is true to what C is implying but does not advance it. The therapist is openly trying to connect more closely in T3 and T4, and is moving toward the deeper sense and expression of empathic contact conveyed in T5 and T6. In this illustration, the message that T's communicated understandings are an expression of him as well as of C is openly conveyed or transparently implied. The interaction is an encounter between persons, albeit with distinctive aims. Much less is taken for granted in such a helping encounter than in most life interactions, and accurate or close understanding by T usually is not assumed in advance of verifying signs by C. To the extent that this understanding is faulty or incomplete, T wants to be put right by C, or else to listen and try again until clearly in touch with C's felt experience and meaning.

Beyond explicit content

Through empathic listening and experiential responding, T may go significantly beyond C's directly expressed messages. While staying with the client's experienced world it is not the case, in Rogers' words (1966), that the helper 'responds only to the obvious in the phenomenal world of the client. If that were so, it is doubtful that any movement would occur . . . Instead the . . .

therapist seems to dip from the pool of implicit meanings just at the edge of the client's awareness' (p. 190). In the same passage, Rogers alludes to the similarity between this quality in the client-centred therapy interview and the aspect of skilled analytic interpretation as characterised by Fenichel (1945), who stresses that 'effective interpretations can be given only at one specific point, namely, where the patient's immediate interest is momentarily centred' and some new awareness 'is striving to break through'.

The value of responsive imagery, metaphor or other figurative language has been a topic of discussion and advocacy in client-centred circles (Butler, 1974; Rice, 1974). Images tend to reflect lively engagement by the therapist and can carry messages of empathic awareness. They may go far beyond the client's explicit communication and are not either reflective or reducible to interpretation. However, the more that T departs from C's explicit or transparently implied messages, the more it is *possible* that T has moved away from 'the edge of the client's awareness', and is not furthering inner illumination and easing on the client's part. It is also very possible that the contact has become deeper and, providing the therapist also checks with sensitive insistence against the client's experience and frame of reference, responsive sharing by T of intuitive sensings and images may potently further the helping relationship and process.

The brief episode that follows is from a fourth interview in an evolving helping alliance. The therapist's metaphorical expression and other (empathic) clarification and acknowledgement of her feeling, is associated with a qualitative shift in the client's experiencing and communication. C has just been speaking of extreme feelings of jealousy that easily spring up in her, but describing her reaction almost as an observer rather than from inside immediate or deeply felt experience.

> T: *A little thing — it's like pulling a trigger (C: Right) — can set off a very big bang in you.*
>
> C: *Right. And in my past — this is what also worries me right now — is that with Julian, and with another very important person, the only way I could handle these feelings when they got out of bounds was to consciously go out of my way to stop having them, and to terminate the whole relationship (client's voice breaks. Pause).*
>
> T: *You mean your feeling was so overpowering and unbearable that somehow you had to get right out of the relationship to go on.*
>
> C: *(Speaking softly through tears) Right.*
>
> T: *(Gently) I guess that brings back a lot of feeling right now (C moves at once to a focus directly on present intensely felt experience in relation to her husband).*

Caring acceptance, and trust

In the helping interview situation, C is in a position of acknowledged or implied need as a person. This need provides occasion for the association with T, and is behind the unusually direct or persistent focus on self-related experience and behaviour. Generally, C both desires *and* fears to show and explore the sensitively charged territory of his/her feeling life. Trust in T is a necessary condition for significant sharing and exploration. Such trust seldom springs full-blown but grows through experience of the helping interview qualities described.

As mentioned above, and especially for a person who is anxious or under other stress, it can be enormously reassuring and easing 'simply' to feel heard and known in some immediate acute region of experience. One effect is to hear or see oneself in sharpened focus or differing light. To a troubled person desiring change such awareness is vital in taking the next step — with strengthened confidence that the helper can safely assist in the difficult uncertain process of personal search and becoming.

Another basic source of trust is the experience of human warmth or caring, especially of a non-possessive no-strings-attached kind. In the client-centred interview, personal detachment or distance is seen as mitigating against the helping process. Feelings of compassion, warmth, respect, interest or liking that may arise in T are allowed to show sensitively as seen, for example, in Rogers' interview with 'Gloria' (1965c). The aspect of non-judgemental acceptance finds strong expression in valuing the other person no-matter-what, of 'prizing' them (Butler, 1958), of respecting or caring for them unconditionally (Lietaer, 1984). One reason for the importance of unconditionality of regard is that, in its presence, motivation to change or resolve difficulties stays within the client — and may grow further there. More broadly still, if in seeming paradox, the helper can be of greatest assistance when s/he is not trying to change the other (an issue closely explored in Chapter 5). Active conscious effort to change the other person is not compatible with other emphasised features of helper attitude and response.

Conclusion

Ideally, T is completely present in the helping interview, for the process of deeply attending to the experience of another person is one of the very fullest engagements of self. In practice, this deeply receptive attention is not likely to be unwavering and continuous, with constant high empathy. It does entail an unusual and special quality of openness, of being expressively in touch both with elements that are clearly present and those that are barely implicit, and of being there in a way that all sides of T's activity in the relationship are aspects of one unhidden whole. A contrary state would be that of presenting a contrived, cultivated but non-integrated role or part of oneself. At best, T either is fully and deeply attentive, listening to and beyond the words and gestures of the other, with accepting regard and empathy, or else is transparently not responding in these ways. This transparency, although not at the time and of its nature calculated, tends to unblock or keep open the way for T to be fully present again in his or her non-judgemental listening and other enabling ways of being with C.

The helping interview portrayed contains no elements that set it completely apart from everyday life relationships, especially, between close friends, lovers, family members and intimate colleagues. When qualitatively similar interaction does occur in life relationships typically it happens in briefer episodes (such, for example, that a strong momentum of personal exploration would not build) and between partners who are more interdependent and therefore less consistent in their interchange relative to 'formal' helping interviews. Thus, the helping relationship is not of a distinctly different species than other significant life relations. Its existence and importance are seen as resulting from unavailability, or the chronic absence for many people, of personal life relationships with the necessary concentration of qualities — especially under conditions of stress or personal transition. This frequent lack points beyond the individual to a widespread deficit on a societal plane — as further discussed in later chapters and another new book (Barrett-Lennard, 2003). A growing number of individuals with the ability and priorities to engage in helping relationships with the qualities outlined here would be a counterbalancing resource in our culture, not only for 'others' but for most of us at some stage in our own journeys.

Chapter 2

The listening process
in everyday and helping modes

This chapter had its beginning in an invited talk to the members of a school Guidance Workshop in Ontario, not long after I joined the faculty of the University of Waterloo in 1966. A transcription of the talk lay in my files for many years and was the point of departure for the rewritten and much developed version that appeared in the Person-Centered Review *(1988, 3, 410–25). Carl Rogers and I had been in frequent and close contact at the time of my original talk, and I played tape-recorded passages from a lecture he gave early in 1965 (in Sydney, Australia — see Appendix 1). I wanted to retain connection with that episode when I began reworking my talk for publication around the time of Rogers' death in February 1987. David Cain, as editor of the* Review, *suggested numerous amendments in detail to the text I submitted, which usefully contributed to my own further editing. However, a few late adjustments I did not see, and uncorrected printer errors mar some passages in the journal version. This chapter follows the previous publication in structure and scope, with corrections and amendments in presentation. It appeared before under the one-word title 'Listening'.*

I think the component that was most satisfying to work out is the section outlining seven general properties of listening as it occurs in everyday life. Each of these features is encapsulated in a briefly stated proposition then discussed or amplified. This exploration establishes a distinctive context for a focus on sensitive empathic listening, considered as a special case within a broader sphere. Finally, four potential effects of sensitive listening are examined: personal healing and growth, relationship enrichment, tension reduction and problem-solving, and advancement of knowledge. One reason that I like this piece is that it includes careful distinctions woven into a whole cloth of meaning but with very little recourse to usual theoretical language. I am glad to give this statement a voice again, and would be pleased to hear from any reader for whom it triggers fresh thought.

Listening to others is a universal activity. The extent of our practice might suggest that little could be said on the topic that is not already a part of common human experience and reflection. Although it seems that human problems typically involve disturbed relationships and faulty communication, a focus on listening might seem too simple to be useful as we work to understand and resolve these problems. I think otherwise. It is my own view that we get into and out of difficulties with each other to a large extent by the *way* we listen and by what we hear, mishear, and fail to hear. Further, the topic is far from simple. It is many-sided and a continuing challenge to our understanding.

It may help to clarify my terms a little at this point. In ordinary language, listening to another person refers essentially to the process of attending to his or her communication. While at times a passive response, listening clearly can also be very active, as we tune into and actually engage with the other's felt experience and meaning. In active listening, we may have all our 'antennae' out, with the concern and aim of receiving the whole range of signals the other is using, reading the other's central meaning, sensing their feeling, and being in touch with their listening and response to us. Hearing is the product of our listening. It may include not only what the other is pointing to — their overt, content message — but where the other is pointing from inside: their feelings, attitude, outlook. Such depth listening and hearing can and sometimes does happen, but in the great range of everyday communication it is the exception.

General properties of listening

What can be said about listening that is true generally? What properties apply over a very wide range of contexts, purposes and sensitivity in listening? In careful outline, the seven general features that have occurred to me are as follows:

1. *Listening is always selective and incomplete in relation to the potential meanings in the speaker's expression.* Yes, for practical purposes, I do mean 'always'. Either we do not pick up all of the verbal and non-verbal communication signals or we do not read and resonate to these signals in a manner that allows their whole spectrum of meaning to come alive in us. Rarely, if ever, does this meaning have only one element. Typically, it includes messages on more than one level that unfold as we tune in to them. Even where it is produced spontaneously and quickly the meaning expressed results from a complex process in a unique individual communicating in a particular situation. It is almost a truism that different listeners hear different specific messages and overtones of meaning when confronted with the same total expression. Thus the message sent is not the same as the message received. The two may be close, different but overlapping, far apart or even opposite.

2. *Qualities of the listener and of the immediate relationship or context, as well as the signals sent, govern what is heard.* More specifically, what we hear is conditioned by our own interests and what we want at the time, our expectations in the situation, our own fears or conflicts, and by other conditions that stem from our view of the speaker and our relationship. Our response is

an outcome of experience in many communication situations moderated or shaped by the ambience and personal meaning of this relationship, of relations with third persons who may be present or in our thoughts, and by the particular interplay of contexts on this occasion. I will give a partial illustration.

In a classroom teaching situation, different intentions, expectations, attitudes, and personal needs may operate, for any one of us, than those that would apply in our family situation. If our own child shows, in a family context, that he or she is feeling overlooked, unhappy, or humiliated, there is a good chance we will 'hear' the gist of their felt message. In a classroom, or a social situation outside the family, we may easily overlook such a feeling message, or choose to ignore it. Sometimes we confuse another person because we pick up what they are telling us at one time but completely fail to register the same message on another occasion. Underlying this discrepancy is the influence of context on what we are open to, and on how we read the 'same' signals.

3. We seldom if ever distinguish or express all that registers in us while exposed to another's communication. I think that we do register at some level more than comes to mind consciously, and certainly more than we express. In the moment of encounter with another person we seldom notice, integrate, and have at the tip of our tongue all the impressions we are getting from that person. Sometimes, a strong sense of what the other person was really conveying comes to us later, after the interchange. For example, we might say, as we reflect afterwards, '*That* was what he was trying to tell me.' Or we might recognise a person's mood that we hadn't formulated to ourselves at the time. Without realising it, we had registered information or cues that took shape afterwards to give us a more powerful impression of the meaning of the other person's communication or experience.

In practice, often we are unable to lift the full meaning from what we do notice or recall. We might sense that there is something unmanageable or threatening there, while protecting ourselves from having to deal with it. Or we might just be preoccupied with some other ongoing activity and concern that doesn't leave room at the time for full attention to what the other person is expressing. Or we may have a rather fixed view of that person, which permits some meanings to surface but not others. In these and countless other ways, information can be passed over or not processed. Our response typically reflects only part of what we have in some sense heard. Thus a fuller awareness of another's experience and meaning than we realise and articulate is within our reach.

4. What we hear affects and can profoundly influence the other person's further communication. Usually, we give some clues to the other person about what it is we are hearing and the extent to which we have taken in and heard what was meant. Our response may also add to the other's impression of what we generally listen to, listen for, and hear. Frequently, when a person is trying to communicate something, we tune in to the outward content only (what the person is pointing to) and miss the person's feelings, or we may fail to sense the other's personal involvement with his or her ideas. If one disagrees with the other, without this awareness of them (perhaps only meaning to dispute the expressed idea or reasoning), the other person may feel rejected and not fully heard. If, on the other hand, we first acknowledge our understanding of the other's meaning and sense of their attachment to this meaning, we may then place our differing view beside theirs with helpful effect.

5. *To a point, we cannot help listening. It is not possible to hear nothing while exposed to another person's communication.* It is often difficult to tune in accurately but is awfully hard, as well, to tune out totally, completely ignoring the other person's signals and message. We may try to do this, perhaps to avoid a (perceived) demand with which we feel we cannot cope at the time, or because we want to focus our attention elsewhere. However, I think that such attempts to avoid receiving another individual's messages only partially shield us from them. The other person tries harder to get through or makes stronger or more persistent demands on our attention. He or she may, for example, resort to non-verbal actions that sharply express feelings of hurt, rejection, or resentment. When we try hard to tune out or evade the other's communications, we are really still responding to them, and conveying a message. Someone has said, wisely, that we cannot not communicate. If we are in any kind of encounter with another person, what we don't do as well as what we do will have meanings to that person. Thus it is also true that one 'cannot not listen' in any first-hand encounter, even if one's impressions are fragmentary or grossly inaccurate.

6. *Listening in everyday interchange is, as a rule, accompanied by an evaluative reaction to what is heard.* Often, we attend to the other with the conscious purpose to assess, compare, or judge. Even if this is not a conscious aim, rarely is our response in a listening situation without elements of approval-disapproval, agreement-disagreement, distaste or appreciation. Typically, we do not simply register what the other conveys, but sift, judge, translate, label or refashion the other's communication in a way that says as much about ourselves as about the other's meaning. To the extent that we openly receive and allow the other's melody to play in us before forming an opinion of it, there is the possibility of enrichment — on the other's part, our own, and in the relationship.

7. *People need to hear others and to be heard by them.* We need the effects of hearing other people as well as the fruits of their hearing us. Although some of us can survive in relative isolation, most of us hunger for connection with our own kind, and depend on being in close or intimate contact with *at least* one other person (Barrett-Lennard, 1986; 2003, Chapter 8). Basic to such connection and close contact is a sense of being known and experiencing companionship in one's own right; and of reaching out and being there for the other, with awareness of the other. Such mutual, informed relationships cannot develop without listening, hearing, and being heard.

This completes my outline of listening in general. As another bridge to the thought that follows, I wish to share excerpts from a talk by Carl Rogers (1965b), given in Australia. These passages are as transcribed from the live recording.[1]

> The first simple feeling that I want to share with you is my enjoyment when I can really hear someone. I guess perhaps this is telling a long-standing characteristic of mine. I can remember, even in my very early school days, a child would ask the teacher a question and the teacher would give a perfectly good answer to a question that hadn't been asked — a kind of miscommunication that is so extremely frequent. A feeling of pain and distress would always strike me in that situation. My reaction was: 'But you didn't hear him.' I felt a kind of childish despair at the failure of communication that is so very common.
>
> I think I know why I'm satisfied to hear someone. When I can really hear someone it puts me closely in touch with him. It enriches my life. It's also true that it's through hearing people that I have learned all that I know about individuals, about personalities, about inter-personal relationships. Then, there is another peculiar satisfaction. I'm not sure I can communicate it — but when I really hear someone there is something in it of listening to the music of the spheres, if that doesn't seem too romantic to you. Beyond the immediate message of the person, no matter what that might be, there is the universal and the general. It is hidden in all the personal communications that I really hear. There seem to be orderly psychological laws, aspects of the awesome order that we find in the universe as a whole. So there is both the satisfaction of hearing this person, and also the satisfaction of feeling ourselves in some sort of touch with what is universally true (Rogers, 1965b).

---

[1] I was present at Rogers' talk, and had played a part in organising it. His presentation, to a large and responsive audience, was audio tape-recorded — a recording that I still have. The passages quoted here are taken from excerpts I used in my talk from which this article grew.

Rogers' eloquent communication continued and, while speaking of the kind of listening he most valued, he recounted the following episode:

> Not long ago, a friend called me long distance on the telephone about a certain matter. We concluded the conversation and I hung up the phone. Then, and only then, did the tone of voice really hit me. I said to myself that behind the subject matter we were discussing there seemed to be a note of distress or discouragement or even despair, which had nothing to do with the matter at hand. I felt this so sharply that I wrote him a letter saying to this effect: 'I may be all wrong in what I am going to say and if so you can toss this letter in the waste basket, but to me after I'd hung up the phone it sounded as though you had been in real distress and pain'. And then I attempted to share with him some of my own feelings about him and about his situation in ways that I hoped might be helpful. I sent off the letter with some real qualms, thinking that I might have been ridiculously mistaken. I very quickly received a reply. He was extremely grateful that someone had heard him. I'd been quite correct in hearing his tone of voice and I felt pleased within myself that I had been able to do so and hence make possible a real communication and a deeper relationship. So very often, as in this instance, the words convey one message and the tone of voice conveys a sharply different one; and this time I had been able to hear both (Rogers, 1965b; see also Rogers, 1980b, pp. 5–26).

While the quality of listening exemplified in this cited episode is unusual, it is not outside the framework I have described so far. Within this broad framework, it is a special kind that I will simply call sensitive listening. I could alternatively have used the term empathic listening — as implied in my next heading.

Sensitive or empathic listening

Sensitive listening refers broadly to listening in which individuals feel that their full communication — and thus potentially their inner self — is heard and understood. Such listening is not only directed to the other's intended verbal messages but also, as Rogers illustrates, to messages that come in other ways, perhaps without clear awareness on the sender's part. In sensitive listening, one is receptive to the full spectrum of the other's experience. The other person feels that you have tuned in, that you have indeed heard him or her, perhaps that you may almost know at this moment how the other's world is to them. Generally this is also accompanied by a feeling of being prized or accepted and trusted. This is so because this particular kind of listening, in its full expression, is rare and implies that the listener is not standing apart but is close to the point of touching with their understanding.

In a related vein, sensitive listening implies giving others an opportunity to be heard on their own terms. It reflects openness to receiving and responding to the internal frame of reference of the other person. Mostly, I believe we want to be heard in the full depth of our experience and meaning, not only in some narrow aspect of our awareness. At best, the listener can pick up and reverberate to any level of communication, and to any content in the other's experience and meaning.

If one can be this way with another individual, in a sustained manner, then it isn't long before the other is likely to begin to disclose aspects of his or her experience that are seldom expressed. And, if the helping relationship is a continuous one, many aspects of the person's inner world, which were previously not in clear consciousness, can now be seen and shared. This, of course, also happens outside a formal helping situation, and is one of the factors that enable people to form deep relationships with each other.

In sensitive listening, judgement of the other person is absent or largely suspended. One is not listening to gain advantage for oneself, or with any ulterior aim. One is listening from genuine interest, from desire to be in contact with the other, and to know the other's reality. The listener does not presume that this reality is fixed and immutable but rather is aware that experience and meaning are living processes that move and change in the flow of open sharing. Thus the deepest listening does not come from conscious and deliberate intention to bring about change in the other. Such change, when it occurs, is a natural by-product of a larger process of self and interpersonal engagement in which deeply perceptive listening is a crucial element.

Listening beyond the other's words means hearing the literal content of those words but, in addition, responding to the other's manner of expression, gestures, and to the other nuances interwoven in the total communication. With such broad and deep listening, we may pick up diverse or conflicting messages, as though from different voices in the other person. If, when we hear the more submerged voice, we neglect the other's spoken words, our listening will have become selective in another way and, to that extent, insensitive. Sometimes, what we hear or sense may go beyond what we feel the other person could bear to have acknowledged. It is as though our sensitivity has made us an intruder in their private world. However, if we truly have heard the other, and are not ill at ease from the impact, then usually it is safe and helpful to let them know what we are aware of — especially if we then continue to listen sensitively.

I would like to quote from another article of mine, written many years ago. In the extract that follows, I am speaking of helping relationships and discussing the crucial part that empathic understanding plays. Such understanding flows from sensitive listening.

> The helping person . . . recognizes or senses what is real and meaningful to the other at any given time. He cares to know how the other person sees things, how he feels about himself, what his own subjective experience is in regard to any aspect of his life process. He is able to sense or infer the . . . feelings and meanings underlying the other's outward communication. In a certain real sense the other person's experience becomes alive in him also, although he does not confuse feelings and perceptions originating in the other with those that originate in himself (Barrett-Lennard, 1963, pp. 223–4).

It is challenging and difficult to maintain a clear distinction between meanings originating in oneself and in the other person. Our concern to avoid such confusion requires the attitude that our 'understanding' is always open to correction and change. Expression of this attitude by checking our sense of the other's meaning with them is a basic, frequent element in sensitive listening.

Effects of sensitive listening

This final section of this chapter offers a distillation of four kinds of outcome of sensitive listening. All of these effects are manifestations of one larger consequence. Sensitive listening fosters knowing. It helps to uncover what is partially hidden and to free experiencing and extend consciousness. It brings about fuller contact and deeper relationships between the listener and the person heard. It can open and enhance communication between groups, and extend our understanding of human nature. Here is a fuller expression of these outcomes:

1. *Personal healing and growth.* Sensitive, non-judgemental, empathic listening, which leads to the experience of being deeply understood, helps to open inner channels and serves as a powerful bridge to others. By being clearly and distinctly heard around some acute but unclear concern, we hear or see ourselves more clearly, and often with less fear. Inner divisions or boundaries tend to dissolve, doors we may have shut on some of our experience begin to open. We may feel freer, more whole, released from some bondage or drain that had been sapping us. We realise we are not alone at the moment of understanding and are freshly aware of what this is like. If this understanding recurs, our sharing can develop a self-propelling quality.

  Just the fact that our experience has made sense to someone else can help it to make sense to us. The experience of acceptance and understanding, especially during relatively unguarded communication, lessens our need to be on guard. Being listened to and heard, particularly in the context of struggle and felt limitation, helps to validate and empower us. We see ourselves in the other's mirror and know our humanity and that we are not alone. We see that our image is many-sided and changing and feel a movement toward new possibilities. Implicit is an element of healing or growth.

Growth on the part of the listener can also flow from sensitive listening. In an earlier paper, Rogers and Farson (1957, p. 4) spoke to this point in the following vein:

> Not the least important result of [active, sensitive] listening is that change takes place within the listener himself. Besides the fact that listening provides more information than any other activity, it builds deep, positive relationships and tends to alter constructively the attitudes of the listener. Listening is a growth experience.

The listener need not be seeking any intrinsic gain. It is a by-product, a bonus in the case of a professional helper. Sensitive listening and contact with the inner life of others is potentially deeply affirming and deeply challenging to any of us, as fellow humans on our own personal journeys. To give nourishment that is freeing to the other can nourish and free us, too. We see ourselves in the other's depth while also discovering a consciousness distinct from our own — which moves as we respond. Our relationship acquires a life and quality that act on us both. To listen and understand deeply is often to walk where we have never been.

2. *Relationship enrichment.* Sensitive listening has a major role in the quality and prospects of an established relationship. Where it falls within the repertoire of both members of a twosome — or each person in a family or other small unit — there is potential for a relationship that is enhancing to the selfhood of each member. Such qualities as respect and caring are enriched, perhaps even made possible, by two-way listening. Where this reciprocal listening is occurring, the dyad is effectively listening to itself. Besides being directly healthful or integrative, such capacity for inner listening gives promise of openness and sensitivity to others.

Sensitive listening can be difficult or impossible to sustain in a relationship where participants have felt deeply hurt or where trust is low. Sometimes, however, a third person who listens very well in interaction with both people can reverse the downhill spiral and open the way for each participant to take in what the other is experiencing, and thereby show that this awareness matters to each. I do not mean to suggest that listening is a panacea in distressed relationships, for it is part of a larger matrix in which the component elements are interdependent. However, if changes in quality of listening do come about, this can work like a motor in propelling communication forward.

3. *Tension reduction and problem-solving.* Personal relationships may deteriorate to the point where any improvement hinges on the contribution of a third party: an informally skilled person or a professional helper. The helper's capacity to hear deeply each person and appreciate his or her reality is likely to be crucial in producing change in the quality of listening in distressed relationships. So, too, with groups in conflict. As Carl Rogers (1965a, p. 7) has pointed out, such opposing groups typically each hold two beliefs: 'I am right and you are wrong', and 'I am good and you are bad'. These attitudes can be stated in many ways. Rogers (1965a, p. 8) offers the following extended expression:

> I am correct and accurate and sound in my view of the situation, my perception of its elements, my interpretation of its meaning. My view is the right and true one. You are unfortunately mistaken and inaccurate in your view of the situation and in your analysis of what it means. Your view is false and wrong, yet you stubbornly hold to it.
>
> I am honest and straightforward and fundamentally good in my approach to our relationship and its problems. Unfortunately, you are none of these things. You are essentially bad and evil and untrustworthy in your approach to the whole situation. My motives are good. Yours are not.

I will presume that the opponents can agree to accept help in trying to get through such an impasse and will sketch the ensuing process in briefest terms. First, the consultant-helper listens very closely to individuals on each side, genuinely taking their concerns and views most seriously. The helper demonstrates that this can happen, that no damage results, and that this step begins to diminish threat. Then, step by step, with the helper's determined and perceptive listening the antagonists who stick with the process each come to see the other's concerns and 'character' in a different light. Finally, with renewed capacity to hear each other and enabling assistance to go further, the parties can converse directly. With each step soundly based, tensions will have been sharply reduced, and the improving communication will have a self-perpetuating quality. Such change could not take place without effective listening playing a vital role.

4. *Knowledge advancement.* A different effect of sensitive listening is that it can be a fertile route to knowledge of human nature, especially the nature of experiencing. Gaining knowledge of how humans, as a species, experience themselves and others, and make sense of their world, has long been of interest in varied fields of study. As is the case of basic knowledge in other fields, many particular applications can flow from such enlightenment about our essential nature. Broad areas of application include the personal helping, interpersonal and group relations and communications fields. Most of what we know stems from observing and listening. The latter can be a kind of closed circuit listening, attuned only to predetermined signals over a limited range, and similarly limited to a band of meanings the listener determines in advance. Such listening can test hypotheses but scarcely generate them. We can't learn anything new and unexpected from it. Open, sensitive listening, on the other hand, releases in-depth communication and contact, minimises filtering and promotes new vision, new hypotheses, and expanded knowledge.

The passage from Rogers' talk, already cited, includes his eloquent testimony on the issue of knowledge-via-listening: 'It's also true that it is through hearing people that I have learned all that I know . . . about interpersonal relationships', and 'there is both the satisfaction of hearing this person and also the satisfaction of finding ourselves in some sort of touch with what is universally true'. Note the phrase 'some sort of touch'. Our best generalisations are not cast in stone but held, perhaps, as first approximations of some larger truth, new dimensions of which we perceive as we work to uncover it and push out the boundaries of what is known. It is in this spirit that I offer the observations and thought presented here.

Conclusions

I began the main part of this chapter by advancing a number of propositions concerning listening in general. Some individual propositions would justify extended discussion and teasing out of component meanings, and no doubt additional generalisations would be possible. My immediate aim relates less to exact theoretical statement and more to the hope that what I have advanced can speak to readers in directly useful ways. It will be a bonus if ideas have been added here that help to spark fresh research into the nature of listening, either in everyday communication or helping relationships.

My intention, in the second part of the article, was to introduce sensitive listening as a special case within the broader framework of listening in general. Looking back now, however, I wonder whether this special listening has been made to seem so unlike the usual variety, so exceptional and powerful, that it stands apart as altogether different in kind. My perspective may become clearer in light of one or two further points. Less than total understanding and knowing of each other, a certain *alone*ness by nature, is a price we pay for individuality and complexity of being. Sensitive listening brings us into each other's full presence. Far from leading us to become copies of one another, it works to protect our distinctiveness. Each of us has his or her continual flow of experience, complex in its origins and modes. We always are in motion in some way, changing even as we learn and conserve. Listening, at its best, results in our meeting in encounters of understanding, but it cannot connect us in a continuous and perfect seam of mutual knowing.

In relation to my third and last focus, knowledge of effects can contribute to the importance we place on sensitive listening and, in this indirect sense, help give rise to it. It is part of my thesis, however, that in action listening cannot just be guided by prior calculation and at the same time be responsively sensitive. The effects I have spoken of are mediated by such listening but flow also from energies and desires brought to the helping situation. Listening takes place in a many-sided context of interest and aim, of relationship, of opportunity and capacity. Such factors vitally influence what is heard and the ensuing communication. Communication runs blind without the eyes of listening, and has full sight to the degree that the listening is sensitive. An authentic process of sensitive listening is deeply absorbing for the listener and a path to connection and fuller consciousness for the parties who are being heard.

Chapter 3

Client-centred therapy: A 'reply' to questions and misconceptions

An invitation to speak in a staff seminar at a psychiatric hospital triggered the idea of a novel approach to sharing my perspective on the helping process. The inspiration I had was to put forward some common misunderstandings and stereotypes about client-centred therapy and then respond to these. In truth, however, the result was not well suited to the original context. My text was over-detailed as a talk and its content went over the heads of many members of my practically oriented participant-audience. The majority, as it turned out, knew very little about Rogers' thought and approach and struggled to relate to the points I was making. As expressed in my poem 'On presenting to an audience' (Appendix 2) I was speaking to a preconceived gathering, my 'eye turned in, to stage and actors set beforehand'. Clearly, there would have been better ways of approaching the session. However, some listeners did tune to particular elements, preparing the paper was a valuable exercise for me, and the approach and content has worked much better for readers choosing to scan or study it reflectively.

Initially, my talk was reworked for publication in one of a series of small books of person-centred readings edited by colleagues in Ireland, books that had a special purpose and were not widely available and visible. Within a couple of years I was privately circulating a slightly amended version, now further edited for this chapter. One change is to revert to 'client-centred' in the title, in keeping with the text and my general preference when speaking of therapy. I have left out the self-introduction that the article previously began with, as well as the ending poem 'A person' — now included in Appendix 2 of this book. There is of course no need to read this chapter, or any other, in the sequence arranged. In positioning my 'reply to misconceptions' near the beginning of the book I was thinking especially of readers who already know something of this approach. If you are new to it, this chapter may have added meaning after sampling the chapters that follow.

⍟•⍟

Some readers will approach this chapter from a background of affiliation or exposure to thought and practice systems rather different from the approach I emphasise. Thus my choice to begin this mission to clarify issues with the question that follows:

Could a person who is substantially influenced by another orientation or system of thought also engage fruitfully with ideas and practice linked to the person-centred approach?

In reply, I will reflect first on my own experience. I have been influenced by other perspectives, psychodynamic, humanistic and even behavioural, although I must admit that Carl Rogers' work and client-centred therapy was an early love of mine, and the whole person-centred approach (as now named) has continued to be pivotal for me. I have not felt hemmed in by any narrow homogeneity of thinking or practice but, to the contrary, have found it a roomy, evolving and responsive system; a system that has always been alive and on the move to me. When I have found myself questioning or in disagreement with the viewpoint of some other exponent, including the founder of the system, Carl Rogers, I have felt quite free to express this difference, to debate it, and to pursue what it leads to.

Aside from my own experience, compelling illustration of the range of interests accommodated within this approach is to be found in its visible products. A striking early example of variety was the edited volume *Innovations in Client-Centered Therapy* (Wexler and Rice, 1974). It includes a short opening chapter by Carl Rogers, concerned with core philosophical principles. The next author, with contrasting style and focus, works to interpret major features of the client-centred approach within an information-processing perspective. Two meaty chapters follow this, each with 'cognitive' in their titles and drawing on mainstream psychological theory. Another chapter blends client-centred and Gestalt therapy approaches and a still further paper focuses on 'the evocative function of the therapist'. One author presents theory and research on the developmental course of intensive *groups*; and another examines 'client-centred and symbolic perspectives on social change'.

A further edited volume (Levant and Shlien, 1984) is also illustrative. One chapter re-explores and updates the concept of unconditional positive regard — 'a controversial basic attitude in client-centered therapy' — and another searches into the basic meaning and forms of expression of empathy in therapy. One of the editors presents a major paper on his 'counter-theory of transference'. A different author than any in the first book wrote under the title 'Person-centered Gestalt: toward a holistic synthesis', and another contributor discusses a well-established programme, blending client-centred and behavioural principles, on 'marital and family relationship enhancement therapies'. My own chapter advances a new way of thinking about the connection between family composition and relational experience and learning in children. A paper on the personal meaning of illness examines 'client-centred dimensions of medicine and health care'. In a concluding chapter, Carl Rogers addresses peace and conflict issues under the heading 'One alternative to future planetary suicide'. Breadth and linking of thought, a search for deeper answers, and a socially urgent quest for wider application, are all reflected in the topics of these volumes *and* in the mounting flow of later books.

One of the earliest and most stubborn stereotypes faced by Rogerian workers grew out of the unique emphasis on a particular kind of therapist-to-client feedback response: reflective acknowledgement and checking of the client's felt meaning, as understood at that point by the counsellor. The stereotype may be briefly framed as follows:

Practitioners of client-centred therapy simply mirror and reflect back what the client or patient expresses.

The first part of this mistaken view is that it is no 'simple' matter to hold a mirror so that the other sees and engages with him/herself in new or clearer ways. 'Mirror', used metaphorically, is a tricky term. The good therapist is an artist whose portrait or part-sketch of the other, via 'reflection', is a characterisation not a photograph, at best a likeness powerfully recognised by the client but going beyond his/her exact words and often beyond previous clear or articulated perception. Reflections in this sense may have great force and value.

The client distinctly recognising an aspect of self in the therapist's reflection or 'mirror', coupled with the therapist's attitude that such recognition by the client is the central test of whether it is accurate, has from the start been a distinctive feature of client-centred therapy. However, the presumed *exclusivity* of reflection in this approach is a second element of misconception. Reflection that is informed by full-bodied empathy remains a primary mode of response in the therapy but not the only mode. Sensitive, skilled and accurate reflection is one crucial and effective way of conveying empathic understanding. No presumption is made that it is the *only* way of conveying deep experiential understanding of another person.

In the person-centred approach, it is the empathy which is considered primary and not, as might have seemed true of therapy interviews half a century ago, the reflective response itself. Images that may form in a therapist's mind, sensitive impressions or hunches that may come together from a number of things the other person has expressed verbally and non-verbally, even inquiries, questions and suggestions *arising from the therapist attunement,* can convey a deep and responsive awareness of what the other person is experiencing. Nowadays, one finds a variety of such channels in the work of therapists who are client-centred, although their perfection of the reflective mode is such that it still occupies a central place.

Client-centred therapists believe in the virtue of therapist genuineness and honesty to the point that everything the therapist thinks or feels with the client should be expressed or made transparent to them.

This stated view is distinctly misleading on two main counts. In the first place, it implies that the client would desire and be able to take in such total expression by the therapist. Any of us filters, transmutes and selectively attends to signals from other people, in varying degree (as I discussed in Chapter 2). An anxious, depressed or agitated client, or any seriously troubled person, may get a general sense of the helper's active presence and concern to understand, but could not possibly be expected to pick up all elements of the counsellor's attitude, thinking and feeling with them. Further, it is the client's hour, their need, their therapy and agenda, which is foremost. It is their need to heal, to become whole, to recover from symptoms tending to isolate them, to face what they deeply fear inside themselves and learn to trust in new ways. Such priorities are not consistent with a therapist's expression of all that flows through his or her thought and feeling.

A second consideration that renders the statement misleading is found in what the therapist *is* doing when occupied with a client. Our attention, as client-centred helpers, is centred on trying to understand what the other is experiencing, what their world is like to them, what the process and content of their perception is, what their struggle is like, how it must be in their shoes, seeing with their eyes, feeling with their senses, concepts, attitudes, presumptions, bearing the weight of their past and the circumstances of their present. My experience and response is that of *wanting* (not demanding) to know the other, of letting their immediate feelings or meaning come to life in me, of gaining a sense of them in their world, of a dawning of shared knowing between us and excitement when I see the other's awareness unfolding in some way before me. It is this whole spectrum arising from my focus and absorption with the other person that is truly and largely the substance of my experience as therapist in company with my client.

The 'misconception' is not entirely wrong. I am, when I think about it, concerned not to *mis*lead the other, and I like to be transparent and immediate in my overt response to them. I mostly offer and share in a present and personal way when I respond, whether the form is a reflection, question, or other mode. Partly because this open personal quality is not calculated, it seems to further the other's trust — providing I *am* sensitive and that products of this sensitivity are central features of my authentic response. I say 'I' without meaning to refer only to myself, but to point from my own experience to what I believe is generally true of helper-therapists within this approach.

Client-centred therapists strive to respond with constant, unwavering positive regard to troubled or damaged human beings. They believe that it is generally possible and always most valuable to respond uncritically and caringly to all that the other does and is.

This further impression and assertion is also partly in error. To be unconditionally responsive to the experiencing person does not mean accepting all of their behaviour and certainly does not imply condoning everything they do. It is not the other's particular actions but their self or personhood that I as client-centred therapist prize. I do not wish to critically judge or evaluate the experiencing self of the other, especially in interaction that has a personal helping goal. This is not to say that I don't warm more to some component self-systems, 'voices' or motivations within the other person than to other voices. However, if I am not to reinforce attempted inner domination of one self and feeling system over another but, instead, to help open and free inner channels and dialogue then I need to be receptive and regardful of all the constituent 'selves' and their feelings.

Client-centred therapists proceed in the working belief that if therapists are empathic and congruent or genuine, and positively and unconditionally regardful of the client/patient, therapeutic change will necessarily occur. No other concepts are involved in any fundamental way in their portrayal of what generates a personal helping or therapy process.
As expressed, this impression is wrong in some respects and misleading in others.

Virtually all client/person-centred therapists would agree that each of the mentioned qualities of therapist response, when properly understood, is of basic importance. On the other hand, no colleague whose thought I know well would accept that the statement as presented summarises everything that is vitally important. It omits what many of us believe to be the most fundamental aspect of all, namely, that it is the *client's experience or perception* of the therapist's empathy, regard and congruence that influences him or her directly. The therapist could appear to an outside judging observer to be very highly empathic and regardfully accepting and authentic, but if the client does not see and feel these qualities, or deeply mistrusts impressions along these lines that arise at some moments, the therapist's accepting and regardful understanding is of little avail. Several elements need to occur together, for example: actual empathic resonation or understanding on the therapist's part, effective communication of this responsive understanding, and the client's capacity to take in this response and to believe that it is real, that it can be and is what it seems.

Another mistaken feature of the statement arises from the fact that further 'necessary conditions' are involved. Rogers originally postulated that the client needs to be vulnerable or anxious for the other conditions to produce change. This has not received much attention in the literature, even in Rogers' own later writing, but has never been lost sight of by the more careful exponents of this viewpoint. It follows, as I see it, that a very highly 'defended' person who is *not* overtly anxious, and whose vulnerability is deeply buried, would not be expected to respond well to client-centred therapy. A person who is already unusually well functioning, or 'fully-functioning' in Rogers' terms, probably would not seek therapy and, in any case, would not find it a uniquely fruitful avenue to personal discovery and growth.

There is one further condition, still, which Rogers sensed was necessary for the sake of completion, although I believe he didn't foresee the application I will mention. He proposed that therapist and client need to be in psychological contact, implying some actual awareness of each other and sense of engagement. Persons in a regressed psychotic state might have nearly lost the capacity for such contact. I believe that people rarely lose it entirely, but if the individual's experience is powerfully dominated by intensely felt beliefs and constructions of 'reality' that are projected outward from repeating signals within themselves, then their capacity for contact can be slim indeed. Without such capacity, the person could scarcely experience responsive empathy or the other conditions.

I have already indicated that the italicised assertion is wrong in that it leaves out some of the vital concepts in client-centred accounts of the therapy relationship and process. I want to add a little more. A study of the literature regarding this approach soon reveals that concepts beyond those already mentioned are important. First, there is the motivational principle of an in-built actualising tendency in humans, implying that healing and growth are prompted from within and do not require external incentives. (The conditions of therapy work as 'nutrients' in re-enabling actualising processes.) Second, the conditions of therapy model alone doesn't address the issue of therapy viewed as an unfolding or developmental sequence. This sequence can be seen to have a characteristic beginning, one which then unfolds into an early working process also with distinctive elements, this in turn evolving further and, finally, culminating in an ending process that differs again. The stages are envisioned in detail in my previous writing (1990; 1998, pp. 104–22) and pictured again within Chapter 9 of this book.

Client/person-centred therapists believe that people are essentially good, trustworthy, growthful or ready to be self-actualised; full of constructive potentials which have only to be released for the individual to move in a positive direction of development.
This impression contains elements of truth but is misleading in its over-simplification. Some part of the responsibility for undue simplification can be laid at Rogers' door. He frequently said and implied that human nature is essentially constructive, that people are inherently good and trustworthy and forward-moving in their development, and that it is necessary only to have the psycho-social nutrients he described present in an important relationship for all these qualities to show themselves and come to fruition. His most systematic writing, however, goes further and deeper than this (and either omits the notion of 'good' or makes a special meaning clear). It carefully articulates the mentioned view that an actualising tendency or growth principle is the primary motivating

force in human life and, for that matter, using the even wider concept of 'formative tendency', in all life and perhaps in all of nature (Rogers, 1963a; 1978).

Some exponents of this viewpoint, however, believe that an actualising tendency is not the sole motivational principle to take seriously into account. In my perspective, it exists side by side with another principle: a tendency toward homeostasis, balance and conservation. Life and behaviour, it seems to me, hinge on both growth and preservation forces. Specific motives or needs can be viewed as varied expressions of the impetus to grow or develop, learn, expand, transcend *or,* the disposition to release tensions, to maintain or restore equilibrium, to heal or recover from damage, to preserve the organism or self intact.

I find it persuasive to regard flagrantly self-destructive and deliberately other-destructive patterns as being acquired, not inborn. Logically, however, the potential for them is inborn; and the problem of evil, or of how cruelty or other extreme destructiveness arises, is not easily disposed of. I think that at base the matter has fairly close parallels with the case of integration. Most would agree that an integrative tendency, an inbuilt push to function all of one piece, is a general property of the human organism (and of other life forms), although we find instances of extreme dissociation and many more cases where individuals are painfully divided or 'out of sync' with themselves. Similarly, a tendency to growth and actualisation could be universal but also vulnerable to being stifled and undercut by some extremes of experience.

There is also another whole angle of view that needs to be taken into account. Any interpersonal relationship, including the therapist-client relation, takes place in the larger context of a network (or 'web', even) of other relational engagements in the person's life. These as a rule vitally include personal and family life relationships but, as well, engagements with groups and teams, with organisations and/or communities, with social, 'class' or ethnic groupings that contribute to the person's sense of identity, and relations with even more encompassing systems in the human and natural worlds. These associations clearly have greatly varied quality and potentialities; ones that might support involvement or gains in therapy, or work in the opposite direction. In a word, although the quality of a therapist's response to his/her client is crucial it can never be the only determinant of outcome for the client.

The person-centred approach had its origin in counselling unhappy, mildly neurotic clients actively seeking help. It is of no demonstrable value with schizophrenic or other severely disturbed patients in whom (for example) delusional features or 'thought disorder' is present.

The first part of this assertion is misleading in its slanting. The second, main element is inconsistent with experience over the last quarter century. It does contain an issue that challenges any psychotherapeutic system.

Client-centred therapy had its *origins* not in the university settings in which it first came into prominence but in the extensive prior clinical experience of its founder, and in the existing psychotherapy approaches he was exposed to. Most influential among these was the 'relationship therapy' innovation of Otto Rank and associated workers (see Taft, 1933; Rank, 1936/1945; references in Rogers, 1939, and Barrett-Lennard, 1998). During the formative development of his approach through World War II, Rogers was as much involved in programmes for servicemen and veterans as he was in student counselling (Rogers and Wallen, 1946). And, his university-based work involved therapy with a diverse range of community as well as student clients. By no means was practice confined to unhappy or 'mildly disturbed' people in the early years of client-centred therapy, and certainly this has not been true since. Perhaps more than other major therapy systems, the approach grew from a broad spectrum of experience and clientele.

Client-centred therapy with persons in a very disturbed or disabled state came strongly into view in the late 1950s to mid-1960s. Less disabled clients, in the early 'acute' stages of psychotic disorder, would no doubt tend to benefit more, and over a shorter period, than clients who had been long hospitalised (as is probably true for most treatment modes). There is some evidence, however, that client-centred therapy can be valuable in resourceful long-term application with 'chronic' patients. There are several sources for these conclusions, which illustrate the application in practice:

1. The earliest case that came to wide attention was the psychotherapeutic treatment of a mute schizophrenic woman by Dr Louis Cholden. Interviews were superbly filmed for use in an educational TV documentary, in the mid-1950s, titled *Out of Darkness*. Cholden was a young psychiatrist who had recently spent a year studying and training with Carl Rogers and colleagues in the University of Chicago Counselling Centre. The film includes, for example, a remarkable sequence in which the client finally was able to borrow and use the therapist's comb. Also filmed was the occasion soon afterward in which she finally broke the 'darkness' of her silence during an interview, and began to speak again.[1]

2. In the late fifties, another pioneering and still-important paper appeared. The author, John M. Shlien, also trained at the University of Chicago Counselling Centre. His report 'A client-centered approach to schizophrenia:

---

[1] The client, who became mute at the point of her psychotic breakdown, had not spoken before during the interviews. Sadly, Dr Cholden was killed driving cross-country to a conference after the series of interviews was filmed. One published paper in my collection, reports his thinking and work on psychotherapy with schizophrenia (Cholden, 1956).

First approximation' was subsequently published in the volume *Psychotherapy of the psychoses* (Burton, 1961). Shlien explores the nature of psychosis from a client-centred perspective, concluding with an original account of the 'psychotic situation' of 'having an impossible life to live', a life that generates intolerable inner conflict. If, out of this extremity, psychotic breakdown occurs, the resulting therapy follows the same essential principles as with non-psychotic individuals. Shlien draws, in his analysis, on self-theory and conditions theory, with passages from Carl Rogers' own first paper explicitly on psychotherapy with schizophrenics, presented in 1958 (Rogers, 1961c).

The case illustration given by Shlien is from the author's work with a hospitalised Korean war veteran. Three stages in client and therapy progress are carefully described. That the client improved and was discharged is a matter of record. Shlien's account speaks not only to observed effects, but points to rather clear steps and vicissitudes in the unfolding of the client-therapist relationship. There is no suggestion of complete healing, although afterwards the client *was* managing his life at home, and working again. Nor is the therapy itself seen as optimal: after all, it was an early case of its kind for the therapist and the approach. Few would read the case and doubt that it involved pioneering advance and learning (Reprint in Shlien and Sanders, 2003 pp. 30–59).

3. In the late 1950s Carl Rogers moved from Chicago to the University of Wisconsin, as professor jointly in the departments of psychology and psychiatry. A major research programme on psychotherapy with psychotic patients was soon underway. One resulting paper describes how therapy with 'unmotivated patients' was initiated (Gendlin, 1961b). In this experimental treatment approach — to one side of the main research programme — the participating therapists worked with 24 patients in a state mental hospital. Two criteria applied generally to these patients: (i) none showed evidence of brain damage or mental defect; and (ii) there was no expectation by their ward physician of discharge 'in the foreseeable future'.

Therapy interview meetings in this work came about through invitation, and grew out of low-key rapport-building contact *on the ward*. Only two of the 24 persons elected to come immediately to private consultations. For the rest, the therapists first made sensitive effort to become present and known to patients, within the ward milieu, engaging patiently and without imposition, and then *offering* individuals private office therapy meetings. Within a five-month period, 22 of the prospective clients came to the office for at least two consultations. Sixteen of the 22 came six or more times. Three patients opted for over 40 sessions. The described situation at the end was that 'with all but a few patients the project has reached the stage where lack of motivation as the chief problem has given way to lack of time' to accommodate the patient demand for personal therapy (Gendlin, 1961b: p. 5).

4. In a 1962 article concerned with lessons from the work with schizophrenic patients, Rogers outlines a number of learnings. For example:

> We have come to realize that almost none of the individuals with whom we have been working have ever affirmed themselves. They have never, in any meaningful way, said 'I feel', 'I live', 'I have a right to be'. They have instead been passive receivers of life's hurts, blows and events. It takes, in my experience, great patience to wait for the germination and budding of the will to say 'I *am*, I deserve to *be*'. Yet, the phenomenon of growth is in some respects all the more exciting because it has been so long dormant (Rogers, 1962b, p. 9).

Of course, there is no implication that the therapist is literally and only 'waiting'. To be inert would be to leave things as they were. The therapist's quality of listening and presence is like a radiation, some of which passes through whatever wall of embattled, fearful confusion surrounds and grips the client. That which does penetrate not only reaches the suffering and divided self within but begins to soften its desperate and isolating shield. Another conclusion in Rogers' work is as follows:

> The simplest way of stating our present attitude is to say that we have learned how relatively unimportant is psychotic material. This could easily be misunderstood. The hallucination, the delusion, the bizarre language or posture has of course, its significance in the psychological dynamics of the schizophrenic individual. But in the therapeutic relationship it simply forms a more difficult language of communication (Rogers, 1962b, p. 9).

The language posed a special challenge but did not suggest or call for any new and different therapeutic principles. Further, the language itself tended to normalise as client stress diminished through the therapist's way of relating — as vividly seen, for example, in the case of 'Loretta'. Loretta was the code name of a hospitalised patient interviewed in situ and in turn by three prominent therapists quite unknown to her beforehand: Carl Rogers, Albert Ellis and Richard Felder. With Rogers, Loretta soon was rather freely self-disclosing and exploratory; her delusional and other symptoms receded, and her meanings were generally clear. Not so with the other two therapists, each quite different in approach (see Loretta transcript [pp. 33–43] and Raskin's commentary article [pp. 44–56], in Farber, Brink and Raskin, 1996).[2]

---

[2] I still have a large reel audio-tape copy of these interviews (and a typescript of Loretta's recorded session with Albert Ellis), which were conducted during a workshop conference of the American Academy of Psychotherapists, *c.* 1961.

5. The Wisconsin programme of research on psychotherapy with schizophrenic patients finally was reported as a whole (Rogers et al., 1967). Some 14 author-investigators and several distinguished outside commentators, contributed to the weighty volume, reporting the first major project of its kind. The study overall was ambitious and complex, the majority of patients were in 'chronic' stages of schizophrenic disorder, and the findings do not fall into any simple pattern. Various indications suggest that the therapy tended to have beneficial but modest impact, with very wide individual variation.

The volume includes a chapter by Carl Rogers reporting a case in which he was the therapist. His account (Rogers, 1967 pp. 401–16) is aptly titled 'A silent young man'. The transcript of two interviews is given in full: the patient's words in total fill the equivalent of less than two printed pages! (Duration of the long silences is noted.) A striking feature is the unwavering constancy of the therapist's receptivity and attention to the client's experiencing. Gentle, direct expressions of responsive interest, empathic guessing where clues are minimal, and sensitive, accurate unfolding and drawing out of the client's meaning where there is overt expression, all reveal an active reaching-out quality on the therapist's part — quite opposite to the stereotype of purely *re*active and neutral reflection.

Near the end of the two interviews, the dam of the client's restrained agony finally bursts. There still are not many words but his convulsive sobbing and other expression vividly suggest that a corner has been turned, that there has been a shift or 'moment of change' as Rogers puts it, and that the future could not simply be a replication of the past. However, there was still a long recovery path ahead. The therapy continued for more than another year. 'Mr Brown' left the hospital in stages, resumed a course of technical or tertiary studies, found a suitable living situation, made new friends and became re-involved in the community. A quoted letter from him gives a vivid example of his outlook and engagement. 'As of this writing [Rogers concludes his report] he is completely on his own, functioning well, with friends of both sexes, entirely out of touch with the personnel of the hospital or the research group' (Rogers, 1967, p. 416). At the time therapy began, Mr Brown had been hospitalised for 19 months, without visible prospect of recovery.

Before the Wisconsin report was published, Rogers had moved to California and was busy with new applications of the client-centred approach. Gendlin was again at the University of Chicago, on the faculty. Shlien was soon to develop a new doctoral programme, joining clinical-counselling and social dimensions, at Harvard University. Other exponents of the approach were expanding the range of practice and contributing to refinement of theory. The examples given here of work with psychotic patients are pioneering ones, from when this application was a new, closely studied focus. Although such application is now more taken for granted, it is a sphere in which particular exponents continue to break vital new ground (Prouty and Pietrzak, 1988; Prouty, 1994).

Conclusion

This chapter has spanned a range of issues concerned with development, process and applications of the person-centred work, especially in psychotherapy and counselling. Misunderstandings easily arise around new ideas and practice, and I hope that this discussion helps to reduce some stubborn examples — and draws the reader to inquire further into the distinctive nature and potentialities of the approach. Besides the references I have mentioned, including my previous book, there is a generous range of other recent sources and significant new volumes are appearing every year. In a substantial innovation, interest tends to 'wax' or build strongly for a time, then diminish or wane, and finally build again in a fresh 'waxing'. At the point of revising this paper for its present publication, this further waxing is going strong in Britain and Europe. To the reader new to the approach, and intrigued or drawn to what you have found so far, I want to say 'come on in, the water as you see is fine, and there is more of interest to come.' And, there is a great need in the culture for the humanistic values, present knowledge and continued learning associated with this work.

Chapter 4

Unfolding the meaning and processes of empathy

This chapter starts from the question 'What is distinctive about empathic understanding?' I set myself the task of answering this in one (very full) page, and was happy with what I found it possible to convey, for my students and as reproduced here. The next, larger section of this chapter on the 'phases of empathy' is adapted from the latest (1993a) of my published articles on its topic. Different measures of interpersonal empathy, even ones claiming a common theoretical base, were yielding different results. As I pondered over this, I could see that the total process in interpersonal empathy involved several distinct steps or 'phases', beginning with a special kind of receptive attention to the other in their own world of experience and meaning. These phases are not locked in sequence like cogs in a machine; each phase only makes the next phase possible, and the varied measures were tapping different phases. A clearer picture of the empathic process came into view for me and, if the excerpts adapted here carry my meaning well, this picture may be useful in your own understanding.

A few years after this work, I was invited to write a paper for a planned book on empathy in therapy. Not to repeat myself, I decided this time to focus on client empathy rather than on the therapist's responsive empathy. I felt that the capacity for empathy toward others is diminished in a person who is worried and anxious, despondent about themselves or perhaps deeply depressed. This lowered empathy further isolates the person, making them more despondent, in a vicious circle that is very hard to break out of without help. I reasoned that the 'recovery of empathy' often would be a vital potential effect of therapy. It also struck me that the experience of empathic understanding in therapy leads first to a new quality of inner connection and, in close sequence, a shift in receptivity to and awareness of how others feel and experience their world. The process of inner connecting can be viewed as self-empathy. The therapist's empathy nourishes the process and growth of this self-empathy. In order to work all this out I also needed to probe further into the nature of self, which is where I pick up the story from my 'recovery-of-empathy' article (1997), in the middle of this chapter.

➺•➶

Empathic understanding is the most crucial kind of responsive knowing in interpersonal-relational life. It is not just a knowing *about* the other — their life situation and circumstances, their standing, achievement or knowledge, or even their personality dynamics. It is a knowing *of* them through direct experience of their living feeling self. Such understanding, in the helping relationship, entails a caring but disciplined opening of one's own self to the immediate feelings and meanings of the other. It is the other's distinct and separate consciousness that is reached and bridged from the self of the therapist-partner in moments of deep empathy. However, even at points of strongest resonance, one retains a background awareness that the feelings and flow of expressed consciousness so alive to the listener is originating in and belongs to the other person. It is this awareness that helps to make empathy distinct from identification or sympathy.

An act of communication can be approached and treated in (at least) two very different ways. *In one way — of great relevance in some contexts — we respond entirely to the literal content of the other's statement.* Our concern is whether it is logical or makes sense to us, whether it all hangs together, whether it is tested or supported by evidence, and/or whether we can safely act on it. The source of the statement is mainly important in the context of judging and relying on its soundness.

The second way of responding takes the other's words as an expression of their inner experiencing, view and meaning, at the time. It is the immediate living experience of the other person that the listener is focusing on. Their experience usually would include a feeling quality (at the least, some feeling about the process of sharing), a search for the words to carry the inner feeling or meaning, and the personal meaning itself. Clearly this is quite different than the first way of responding to the other's statement, and grows out of a different kind of concern or aim.

Every time we say something that isn't rehearsed or said before, we are *finding the words* to capture and convey whatever it is, which isn't exactly articulated until those words come; and even when the words do form they may be only a first approximation, an approximation often leading on to more exact or complete expression. In the second way of taking a communication we are not primarily interested in the thought but in the thinker and the whole moving ground of subjective experience which the particular statement springs from and partly expresses. Unlike the first way it is very closely connected to the process of empathy.

On an Email network some time ago a colleague posed questions about empathy that he hoped others would respond to. One of the questions was to the effect 'How do you prepare yourself to be empathic?' Replies varied but most implied that they needed to clear their mind from any other prior absorption and assume a highly receptive stance. With me, at least with clients, usually no very conscious effort is involved. In effect, I create conditions for letting myself be absorbed in the other person and their immediate experiencing. Things can distract any of us from being totally attentive to the other; from opening oneself with them and sustaining genuinely high and undivided receptiveness. In the helping relationship, this special receptive stance is a matter of intention that becomes spontaneous in the moment. An absorbed focus on the other's felt inner experiencing and meanings carries the potential for empathic understanding.

I'm indebted to a colleague-friend in Chicago — Dr Barbara Brodley — for the terminology of 'empathic following', referring to a sustained process of tracking the other person's feelings and meaning and repeatedly letting them know what one's sense of their felt experience is. One 'tracks' by keeping one's sights on *their* communication and meaning. Tracking in this sense is a very active process that has an immediate impact on the person one is following. One's expressed empathy aids that person in their expressive-exploratory engagement and process, such that this can unfold and not circle around repetitively. It is as though this response helps an inner door to open in the other person, and what lies beyond that door is now visible or accessible to them. As they examine and share this vista, and experience the listener following and seeing with them what they *now* perceive, another door swings open. Such companioning, step by incremental step, can be powerfully enabling to the person in finding *their* way.

The phases of empathy [1]

As noted, empathic understanding is by no means the only modality of interpersonal response. Rogers (1975) discusses this, with articulate passion, in his paper 'Empathic: An unappreciated way of being'. In my phasic model, the prerequisites for empathy to occur at all, include the condition of being attentive in a special way. In formal language, I call this an 'empathic attentional set', as distinct from other kinds of stance or readiness one may have in particular situations with others.[2]

Given the necessary quality of attentiveness, an empathic awareness of another person's felt experience may happen even without those involved being in each other's physical presence. Expressive sharing recorded in writing, film or any media may carry a quality of psychological-emotional presence to the actively receiving person. Effectively, the other *person* is experienced in their recorded communication, and this establishes the potential for empathy. Aside from recorded experience conveyed between persons who know each other,

---

[1] This section and the next are taken and freely revised from my article 'The phases and focus of empathy', *British Journal of Medical Psychology* (1993), 66, 3–14.

[2] Some people adopt such a set or stance much more often or wholeheartedly than others do. Some move into it only very selectively. My impression is that nearly everyone has the capacity for it within their repertoire, whether rarely or often expressed.

eloquent documentary presentations of people in crisis — or under any striking circumstance or emotion — may evoke an experiencing of them as if present or even reaching out to the receiver/viewer. Thus, a literally empathic inner response is possible.

Even in the case where individuals are physically together, a person expressing him/herself might not be conscious that a companion is in fact highly receptive and in closely tuned contact. This unawareness of empathy can result if a group is present, if the interaction is cut short, if the empathically receiving person does not venture to show his/her response, and in other natural circumstances. Unexpressed or 'silent' empathic inner response can have little or no direct impact on the other. (It may work indirectly in affecting future interchange.) Even when such inner empathy is expressed, its effect depends also on how the message is understood and taken by the person receiving it.

These instances and ideas are all in keeping with thinking of the total process of interpersonal empathy as involving three main phases. The first phase assumes that one person (A) is actively attending with an empathic attitude to another person (B) who in some way is expressive of his/her own experiencing. This empathic stance includes an active openness to knowing the other person in their own present experiencing of their world, including themselves and the immediate engagement. It amounts to a precondition for empathy, and implies that empathic listening has begun.

Sooner or later, as this process continues, A resonates experientially to B in an immediacy of recognition of the felt experience and meaning that B has shared. Features of B's experience, sometimes its whole quality and substance as expressed and implied, are now also alive and in motion in A's consciousness. This inner process and quality of experiential understanding constitutes the essential first phase of empathy. At this Phase 1 the inner recognition and understanding is not yet conveyed and known to B.

The next step (which may follow immediately) is the communicative *expression* of A's inner empathic response. This communication of empathy, purposed or involuntary, verbal or non-verbal, is identified as Phase 2 empathy. If A has merely observed the other's words, and technically mirrors back their substance with *manner* and form only of concern and understanding, this response is not arising from an inner empathic process and is, therefore, not Phase 2 empathy.

The expression of an actual empathic response by A potentiates the culminating stage of Phase 3 empathy, which is B's experience of being personally understood and known, at least in that moment. This is the phase of received or apprehended empathy. Awareness of being heard and understood deeply, in some personally vital sphere, has its own direct impact; whether of relief, of something at last making sense, a feeling both of inner connection and being less alone, and very possibly a sense of something further to express — which *opens in the wake of having been understood.*

Clearly, the three phases of empathy may not occur in a complete sequence. Phases 1 (the listener's inner resonation) and 2 (expression of empathic awareness) each potentiate the next phase but do not govern its occurrence. In practice, the phases are semi-autonomous (Barrett-Lennard, 1981). In fuller, step-by-step description the process is as follows:

When A closely attends to B, in ways that imply an active empathic receptivity, the possibility of an empathic understanding process exists. For this possibility to bear immediate fruit depends, first, on whether person B is self-expressive, especially of feeling or felt meaning, and, second, on A's capacity for empathic attunement to B, around these particular feelings and meanings.

Further, even if A does responsively and accurately tune in to B's felt experience and meaning (Phase 1 empathy) there exists the possibility only of a message back to B which fully expresses and conveys this inner empathic recognition. Various conditions can work against realisation of this possibility, even in therapy situations. A (the therapist) may not consider it important to convey a message of his/her felt understanding right then. B may be very anxious and A may hesitate to 'interrupt' by verbalising the resonance that he/she is feeling, as B presses urgently or fearfully on. Perhaps A is empathising quite strongly but is uncertain, at that delicate moment, how best to convey and check her/his understanding. Or, depending on the therapy orientation, A's resonance to B might suggest counter-transference, or, in another context, just serve as a pointer to the next step in guiding B's exploration. The 'hour' may end, or an interruption occur, which cuts the cycle between Phase 1 and Phase 2. In short, many factors can result in non-expression, or in indirect or aborted expression of actual Phase 1 empathy.

The challenge of conveying (and checking) an empathic quality of understanding has been a major impetus for turning-point developments in psychotherapy and counselling practice. Such a turning-point was the wholly unique concentration on reflection and clarification of client/patient feelings and meaning that has characterised client-centred therapy. Generally, the communication phase or aspect of empathic response has been more developed in client/person-centred work than in other schools — with some risk as well as significant gain. The risk is that portraying 'empathy' could in some quarters become an end in itself to the neglect of the crucial inner process of empathic arousal and recognition (Phase 1 empathy), without which the portrayal is just that; it is not an expression of empathic resonance and understanding (cf. Mearns, 1997, pp. 94–6).

To complete my train of meaning on the relation in practice of one empathy phase to the next, let us suppose that a message *is* sent which adequately expresses A's experienced empathic response to B. However, this message may or may not be received without addition, subtraction or qualitative change. And, if it is not picked up or is significantly misperceived by B, the way it was taken may or may not be conveyed back to A *and* lead to A trying again with more success. In all, several potential 'slippage points' are evident, which work to attenuate the close functional and correlational relation that might at first be expected between adequate measures of empathy in its different phases.

Only if the chain of possibilities referred to were all necessities, as in a type of closed system where the motion of a single element totally controls the next, would it be reasonable to expect close congruence between empathy measured in its different phases. It may be the case, however, that in high-empathy relationships there is relatively less slippage and more congruence of level among the phases than in comparatively low-empathy relationships. And in cases where empathy *is* found to be relatively even in all phases therapy outcome might well be more positive than when client and therapist have quite different views of the therapist's empathy.

I cannot resist returning briefly to the discussion of empathy and reflection. Empathy, in essence, is a special kind of responsive personal knowing. Restatement is a familiar way of showing that we know something, in all sorts of contexts. Hearing from another the essence of our personal feeling and meaning which we have been struggling to articulate and express, and which perhaps is like a chameleon that keeps changing and disappearing as we pursue it, and which may also evoke sickening anxiety in us; to hear in this context a listener who is devoting his/her whole attention to what we are going through speak back to us that which we ourselves are strenuously and barely grasping can have the impact of a skilful midwife assisting in a literal birth. But does the listener in such a case as this release us solely through reflective restatement as such, however inclusive of implied as well as explicit meanings? My own answer is 'no', although it is my view that this quality of restatement is a powerful modality *when it does reflect the listener's genuine empathic resonation.* Put another way, reflections can be an excellent channel for the flow of empathy, which is the active ingredient.

No reason is seen for sensitive restatement to be the only effective channel for communicating empathy, especially in caring relationships or among persons from the same bonded community or linguistic-expressive subculture. Nor is it the only avenue to express empathy in therapy. Responsive use of metaphor and imagery, not as reflection but as imaginative impression and comment, also can be richly communicative of empathy. On occasion, a simple question that pops forward could not be asked, would not occur to the questioner, without an empathic awareness of the other's inner experiencing. Similarly, with images, which may arise quite vividly in the listener's inner eye without conscious effort or cultivation. Sharing such images that form spontaneously can, in my experience, be evocative for the client-person, sometimes strikingly so. They are not restatements but intuitive-associative responses that may express one's sense of something about the person's life stance, or of their present existence or dilemma, or a quality of their feeling and presence in the moment.

Expression of empathic awareness without restatement can also take behavioural forms, as may occur between adults in relationships of affection, or between parent and child. For example, a mother may respond to her young child in a way that is caringly knowing in an empathic sense but which takes the form of gently receiving, meeting and holding the child in an awareness and behavioural acknowledgement (say) of the child's distress. In another example, the parent may show perceptive awareness of their child's excitement over some new-found self-expressive mastery, through responsive play with the child as they act on this mastery. This engagement may include a simple verbal expression of how this accomplishment must feel to the child. All this variety to me is heartening, as well as sometimes bewildering, for it implies that empathy cannot be formularised on an action level. Nor is responsive empathic awareness only elicited by *individual* experience — although generally defined and described as though this is so.

Empathy and relationship systems

There is a predictive level of empathy-like awareness, which is not any one of the primary phases I have described. I (as a therapist, say) may be deeply in touch with your felt experience, which in the special sense of Phase 1 empathy comes alive and resonates in me too. I may even convey this quality of being-with-you in ways that you hear and feel in turn (empathy carried to Phase 3). But what you are struggling with and bring to our meeting comes out of your life apart from me. Our relationship is an avenue for your working through, it is not the main stage of your life. Your self-focus may mean that I receive little direct feedback on how *you see me* responding to you. And, I don't question or prompt you on this level in light of your distress or absorption, my direct sense of contact with you in what you are going through, and the confirming impression that my response actually is reaching you because of the way you go on.

Suppose, after meetings between us, that you are asked to give the information I did not request as we went along, particularly, your detailed view of the ways and extent to which you have felt understood by me. Suppose, too, that I am separately asked what I think your candid view of me in this way will turn out to be, point by point. I would be trying to predict your replies from my sense of your experience and picture of me, at best only partly conveyed in our meetings. This is distinct from Phase 1 empathy, for I am not going by an immediate process of resonation and sense of contact with you in your experiencing. Rather, I am reflectively trying to look *through your eyes at me-with-you,* from knowledge of the pool of experience with me that you have to draw on, and my sense of how you will interpret this experience in replying. In the circumstances, I'm not sure that I will be closely on target, even if our experience together included numerous instances of significant empathy in each of the phases described.[3]

My term for the capacity to predict the other person's view of one's own empathic understanding of them is *meta-empathy*. Limited, direct research evidence suggests that the meta-empathy level of counsellors in significant dyad relations with clients (or other relational 'B' partners) can change through intensive (residential) human relations learning workshops involving the counsellors only. Although the B partners' views tended to be better predicted by the counsellors after the workshop, these partners were not as a group immediately conscious of being better understood. In other words, empathy at Phase 3 evidently had not increased (Barrett-Lennard, 1998, p. 296). Possibly, counsellors were more open and attuned to clients' attitudes *toward them* but clients were not yet picking up a difference in sensitivity to their felt issues of concern.

Meta-empathy is concerned with A's awareness of *how B is taking A's response*. It pivots on how closely A is in touch with B's feeling and point of view in regard to A's understanding. It taps into their dyad system in the sense that it is not about one partner's experience or perceived response but the convergence between their two frames of reference on a vital aspect of their relationship. This relationship is itself an emergent whole which can be apprehended directly, especially, by viewing the relationship as a living system.

The notion of *system* might at first seem a rather lifeless abstraction, but it can be (and is, to me) full of experiential meaning. Couple relationship systems help to illustrate this meaning. Any twosome in which each member is substantially involved with the other contains three distinct entities. From inside the relationship these are 'I', 'you' and 'we'. From the outside, let us say from the standpoint of a child in relation to his or her parents, there's 'Dad', 'Mum' and the Mum-and-Dad twosome, as You or They. A child typically experiences his/ her father and mother directly as a pair unit as well as one by one. Indeed, sometimes a child has more trouble seeing his or her parents as separate and individual than in perceiving them as a unit with a collective intention or attitude. Children tend to have many strong or distinct experiences of their parents' interaction and relation, which combine to make this relation a major feature of their family world. (These and related issues are further explored in Chapter 7.)

Given the child-parent dependency relation and a child's early stage of development, an intense reaction to the parent relation can occur with no great width of perception and understanding of it. Even as life-experienced

---

[3] Taking an opposite possibility, I have encountered people whose accuracy as predictors of the way that others will respond in particular circumstances, seems much greater than their capacity to resonate and sensitively accompany those others in a primary empathic sense.

adult helpers working with a client couple it is a big challenge to tune perceptively to the *inter*active experiential process, the world of shared meanings and mutual/reciprocal feelings, and the motion and experience of the joint *we*. Most of us as helpers are used to responding to the moment-by-moment feelings and meanings of each single person in interactive contexts, and to other noticed elements in the experience or behaviour of each one with the other(s). This broad way of being sensitive is readily associated with empathy. And if, for example, the listener's attention is focused on recurring interactive behaviours and the roles each person takes in their interaction, empathy tends to take a back seat. Inferential analysis and reconstruction of between-person dynamics is one way of being perceptively aware, but it is not a mode in which empathic recognition is prominent.[4]

However, if qualities of feeling, outlook and purpose apply to a twosome and, by the same token, to a family and any closely bonded group, one can imagine responding in broadly empathic mode to the human multi-person whole. In principle, this mainly requires expansion of what is being attended to by the empathising person; a change in scope of attention not in the quality of an empathic attitude. With experience, the same listener can at one moment be attending and responding empathically to a single other, and at another moment to the collective other which contains that single person as an interdependent part of the multi-person whole that is also in being.

Viewed slightly differently, each participant in an active relationship may be considered to have two interwoven streams of consciousness. One of these — the 'I stream' — reflects their individuality and distinctive positions in the relationship. The other, 'we stream', is an expression of their joint being and runs through the experience of all participants. The voice of this 'we/us' consciousness speaks *through* each member but not from them singly. The referent and source of this voice is not *a* self but a twosome, or larger emergent relational whole with its own presence, a presence which exists in intricate relation to the I/me selves of each member.

Empathy on this system level entails seeing *relationships* as having life, and in tuning in to this life; on listening to communication in and from established relationships, listening to it not only as the voice of one person to another but as having its source in the dyad system or larger whole. Such a system in this perspective is not merely an interactive pattern, although it partakes of such patterning when viewed abstractly, but exists as a basic level and feature of human life.

The process of empathy is of the same phasic nature as earlier described

---

[4] This seems especially true if the focus is primarily on role interaction, whole system behaviour patterns and other abstracted or externally viewed features of structure and interplay.

whether the focus is on individual self-experience or on the expressive phenomenal 'we'. In the case of a couple, the twosome will not be felt and perceived identically by the two partners. However, when the focus is very distinctly on the 'we/us' (not 'me in response to you' or 'you toward me') then differences shrink and, at moments, disappear. The empathy of the helper may be triggered by the 'we' consciousness of either participant or, at moments, by the acutely felt presence of their joint being or twosome. Following the helper's inner resonation (Phase 1 empathy), its expression (Phase 2) could lead on to Phase 3 received empathy. Reception would be by the couple, engaged in their 'we/us' consciousness. Where the helper's empathy is evoked by and expressed in reference to the relationship presence, its accuracy can be inferred both from its effect (such as easing of immediate tension or opening of stopped communication) and from concordant feedback from both partners. Thus in principle, empathy toward living relationship systems parallels empathy in response to individual self-experience.

Interpersonal empathy clearly is a many-sided phenomenon but not (necessarily) an elusive one. My account has emphasised therapist-to-client response, which I see as a special case within a much wider sphere. Whenever a person is positioned to be a resource (or a threat) to others, which includes the whole spectrum of human services and most personal relationships, the presence or absence (or level) of empathic awareness is a significant issue. The last part of my discussion has suggested an even broader issue. I see the need for a quantum jump in consciousness such that individuality becomes commonly experienced as *one* main form only of natural human existence. One test of whether we are making this leap lies in being able to think of and experience empathy toward emergent human existences such as relationships, family systems and living communities — almost as we do, at best, toward individuals.

The recovery of empathy — within self and with others[5]

In classical client-centred work much fruitful attention was given to the self-concept: how it forms, what it does, and how it works in psychological health and disability. The underlying self itself was singular; one for each person. Even in a self torn by conflict, this conflict resulted either from contradiction within the self, or incongruence between the conscious self and a more basic given — the person as living organism. In his comprehensive account of client-centred theory, Rogers (1959a, p. 200) wrote: 'We began to see the development

[5] From this heading on, the balance of this chapter is adapted and revised from my article on 'the recovery of empathy' (Barrett-Lennard, 1997), referred to in the introduction.

of self as a criterion by which the organism screened out experiences which could not comfortably be permitted in consciousness'. In other words, self and organism were distinct. The implied notion of *duality* may not go far enough, however. Rogers himself stresses that theory is an abstraction from the phenomena it refers to, and elements in his theory of self might be reconstrued. He goes on to say: 'One of our group is working on a definition of self which would give more emphasis to its process nature. Others have felt that a plural definition, including many specific selves in each of various life contexts, would be more fruitful' (ibid., p. 203). This interesting idea is newly worked out in a chapter of my other current book (2003) but was not pursued by Rogers himself.

The well-functioning person may be more integrated than the self in conflict, not because s/he contains less diversity but because the component self-systems are working in partnership. Complex systems (such as persons) are not homogenous units but have components that do different things. Humans on a biological level have a great array of organs and systems with very distinct functions, yet in the healthy person these work in intricate, cooperative and interdependent harmony. Given this great complexity on the physical level is it plausible to expect experiential-mental life to be vastly simpler, literally one indivisible whole if the person is healthy? Or, is it more credible to look for differentiation of components in this domain also? The questions are rhetorical; the first calls for a 'No' response, and the second invites a 'Yes'.[6]

A person is both one and many. A first-order division involves the duality of articulate consciousness and the I-self, on the one hand and, underlying this, a sentient and complex biological self. To speak of having a relationship with oneself used not to make sense to me, but it does now. A person might say, after therapy or other growth experience, 'I now have a more comfortable relationship with myself'. Outside the context of therapy, one hears remarks starting with 'I am', or 'I feel', and ending 'about myself', or 'with myself'. The words in between might be 'anxious' or 'uneasy', 'depressed', 'pleased' or 'happy', 'relaxed', or any of many others. In each such case, a relation is implied between 'I' and 'myself'. Distinctions between our mental-experiential and physical-organic selves are often made in everyday discourse. The idea of a person being dual is in no way novel. I will describe one careful way of viewing this duality, and implications relating to empathy that flow from it.

A person can be said to have (on the one hand) an articulate, reflective, doing self, a self with values, goals and intentions, a self which speaks for

---

[6] In the presentation of his 'model of positive health', Seeman (1989) provides a searching, integrative analysis of the intricately interdependent working of systems from a biochemical to interpersonal level, in states of wellness.

itself and for the bodymind whole, a self of agency that is implied in saying 'I' and which sees itself as the centre of being as a person. This self is like an executive officer; it 'runs' the whole person-system (or imagines it does) but is not by itself the whole. It is reliant on resources and information from other components and levels of process in the total human organism — although it may reject or block out some of the information. A name for these other levels, inherent in the person's biological being, is the *organic self.*

The organic self is not mere machinery but a living, sentient system of interwoven elements and subsystems dynamically knit in a union of such exquisite complexity that it supports and gives rise to the conscious, symbolising, self-knowing, articulate self. Although the latter self lives in essential, intricately interdependent relation with the organic self, it has its own nature and functions and does not operate in any simple lockstep with the underlying biological systems. It is not just a spokesperson for those systems but actively looks, learns, initiates, chooses, and is a custodian of meaning. The organic self on some of its many levels (including that of sensory nerve 'messages') has a fairly direct route to the conscious self. This 'I' self can be highly attentive and receptive, or, pre-committed to a 'policy direction' at odds with some of the voices and needs of the organic self.[7] In the latter case, the I-self is watchful but a poor or selective inner listener. When attentive and truly receptive inner listening does happen it opens the way to a form and process of empathy turned inward.

Listening within

Interpersonal empathy hinges on a special quality of attention and listening to another feeling self; listening in order to sense, recognise and know the other person in their present felt experiencing and meanings. The corresponding precondition for what I am calling self-empathy is respectful, open *inner* listening, a sensing quality of listening for the flow and signals from one's own organic being. (The signals form into words or other symbols through the act of recognition.) The person, in effect, is deciphering aspects of their own inner state and process. The 'message' they discern may be compelling, but it does not possess or overwhelm them, if the process is self-empathic. The construing 'I-self' is fully present as 'listener', although not obtrusive, and open to being taken by surprise. It is seeking awareness through fuller connection with its underlying life flow.

A person's total organic being is in living motion all the time, with an

---

[7] This state of affairs can be linked to strongly conditional/judgemental attitudes from significant others in childhood. How the process works is discussed more fully in Chapter 9.

intricate flow of message signals among its varied parts and levels. Signals that reach higher integrative centres in the nerve-brain system have the *potential* to be heard in articulate consciousness. The situation is like that of a person who expresses some felt personal meaning and, in this expressive mode, *might be* heard empathically. But, this actually happens only *if* there is another, listening person who responds in an inner human echo of recognition. If there is mostly no such listener in the person's life, s/he may stop expecting to be received, and reach forth self-expressively less and less. Correspondingly, inner signals that are of a nature to reach consciousness but are not in fact received in awareness may grow weaker. If, and when, there is deeply receptive attention by the construing I-self, the signals can flow through strongly and be encoded in consciousness. They add and may correct information, now in dynamic interplay with other elements in awareness.

The primary phase of empathic process in self-empathy requires a distinctive name. I refer to it as *formative recognition*. As in the case of empathic resonance, there is a certain quickening or energy arousal, as new meaning comes to life in a clear sense of recognition. In self-empathy, the forming recognition arises from indwelling attention to signals from the organic self, and there is an energising and satisfying quality to such recognition. Another way of expressing the process is that a sense of something comes to the edge of awareness, and is apprehended in a literal process of formative recognition where form and sense unite as one.

In self-empathy the formulating process itself works as inner communication, thus resembling the communication phase of interpersonal empathy. The (inner recognition) process may catch the exact nuance of what is sensed or move in steps from an initially rough approximation. Full, accurate recognition by the attending self has an easing effect for the organic self, this easing also felt by the attending I-self. It seems that where signals are only half heard, any easing effect is muted. The attending self, especially with previous experience of the fruits of self-empathic attention, may become aware that it is not yet on target, and perhaps is not in fully receptive mode.

When empathic resonance occurs in response to another person, and is effectively communicated and received, the recipient person is aware of being companioned in experiential understanding. In the case of self-empathy, the impact of recognising and accurately articulating the message of signals from a deep (precognitive) level of inner being seems to radiate through the whole person-organism. At that moment, the dual self is one; there is a peak of integration or wholeness. The underlying, organic self effectively has been 'heard' *and is influenced by this opening to articulate consciousness*. The effect of the inner communication is not only a greater unity in the moment; there has been fresh affirmation of a partnership of selves within the total human person.

Awareness arising from very distinct experience has a compelling quality that leads naturally to adjustments in behaviour. In self-empathy, the extended awareness by the articulate self is not that of a separate individual but of an *alter ego* sharing the same life as the self of which it is more deeply aware. This deepening of inner awareness can be assisted by another empathically responsive person. A *self*-empathic process is activated (or enhanced) through the experience of sustained empathic sensitivity and knowing from any caring human source. Self-empathy, in turn, brings the potential for a wider scope of sensitive attunement to others in the person's life.

Interrelation of interpersonal and self-empathy

Multi-level empathic response (from a therapist, say) is tuned both to the articulate self, who experiences being fully heard and received, and to the more implicit voices of the organic self. The closely attuned listener registers what is expressed, staying close to discernable cues. These cues include but are not confined to what is expressed directly, and are not all in the client's clear consciousness. Their existence implies potential for movement in awareness. Carl Rogers, no advocate of interpretation, spoke eloquently about responding to a wider flow than the client's immediate consciousness, concluding (as mentioned in Chapter 1) that 'the client-centered therapist aims to dip from the pool of implicit meanings just at the edge of the client's awareness' (Rogers, 1966, p. 190).

The term 'implicit meanings' refers to what is stirring in the person on a felt level, thus with *potential* to come into conscious discrimination. What Rogers does not go on to explain here (1966) is that movement in therapy is more than achieving gains in self-awareness. It can amount to fundamental change in the way an individual 'works' in relation to felt experience or, as I would now put it, the way the person relates self to self, both inwardly and in relationships. Rogers comes close to this issue in a later paper centred on empathy: 'Being listened to by an understanding person makes it possible for [an individual] to listen more accurately to himself, with greater empathy toward his own visceral experiencing, his own vaguely felt meanings' (Rogers, 1975, p. 8).[8]

An individual may ruminate, introspect and interpret his/her reactions, question self endlessly, anxiously watch over daily bodily functions, or otherwise

---

[8] In his 1960s book on empathy, Katz, too, had already implied the idea of linkage between interpersonal and self-empathy. Whether in the position of therapist or client, he wrote, one requires the capacity 'for being in touch with one's own inner experience and for being in touch with the inner experience of others' (Katz, 1963, p. 103).

be 'self'-attentive, without this having the quality of self-empathy. When the inner responsiveness of self-empathic listening flows readily in a person this implies an openness and sensitivity to felt inner experience that also would be manifest in responding to another person-self communicating from their experience. Put another way, the person who is at home with the subjective stirrings of his/her own inner being tends to be sensitive to the inner felt world of others, and not afraid of responding from this awareness.

Thus it can be said that self-empathy opens the way to interpersonal empathy. Deep empathic engagement with others probably also fosters self-empathy. Therapy training, for example, typically challenges the person in training to be in fuller listening contact with their own underlying or 'precognitive' experiencing. Indeed, it seems that trainees within a context that emphasises development of empathic sensitivity and responsiveness will often choose and decide at some point in this training to enter therapy themselves.

Further views on the therapeutic recovery and value of empathy

Facilitation of self-empathy probably is compatible with most forms of psychotherapy but most clearly so in the case of client-centred and related experiential therapies (Gendlin, 1974; Leijssen, 1990; Raskin, 1985; Rogers, 1964b, 1975). Receptive inner listening is a key element in therapy for exponents generally of person-centred approaches. In my perspective, true listening of this kind is the core condition for self-empathy. I also have been interested to discover related thinking among colleagues of somewhat differing therapeutic orientation. Snyder (1992, p. 320) discusses the effect on client self-listening of the example and impact of the therapist's empathic response. In another example, Quintana and Meara, (1990, p. 130) propose that self-referred clients are seeking 'an interpersonal relationship that they are not providing for themselves'.

Clarke (1991) studied episodes of self-experience involving distinct conflict with beliefs cherished by the individual. She describes the conflicting experiential information as 'emotional experience which was previously out of awareness, or automatically processed' (ibid., p. 396) — thus essentially at the level of the organic self. A fruitful creation of meaning episode, in her terms, entails attending to and feeling the emotion and discovering an adequate symbolisation, this leading on to emotional relief (ibid., Figure 1). A form of self-empathic process clearly is implied.

The capacity for interpersonal empathy is quite often distinguished as an aspect of mental health (e.g., Jahoda, 1958, pp. 52–3; Katz, 1963, pp. 102 ff.; Kohut, 1977, 1984; Snyder, 1994). Katz proposed that low or impaired empathy was an underlying motivation for therapy (1963, pp. 109–12), and suggested that a client's progress 'can often be measured in terms of an increase in the capacity for empathy' (ibid., p. 102). Mente and collaborators viewed the interactive working, facilitation and development of client empathic understanding as core features of group psychotherapy (Mente and Spittler, 1980; Giesekus and Mente, 1986; Mente, 1990).

For Kohut (1977, 1984), empathy and the development of self were cornerstones of his innovative departures from previous psychoanalytic thought. He came to see the defining aim and result of the 'curative process' in therapy as 'the opening of a path of empathy' between self and significant other (Kohut, 1984, p. 66). In other words, the crucial feature was change in the capacity for relationship. Evidently Kohut agreed, however, that empathy is not solely interpersonal but can also be inward focused — as implied, for example, in his mention that 'the patient's empathy with himself' is at times superior to that of the analyst (ibid., p. 72).

Snyder (1994) built on the idea that the capacity for empathy is a central aspect of social intelligence (see Mead, 1934, p. 141). She implies that personal meanings grow from communicative encounter and inward 'observation' interwoven. The primary function of the therapist, she proposes, is to facilitate the capacity 'to enter one's own life . . . on a level that includes keen attention to our embodied emotions, the continual formation of meanings, and the capacity to constitute and interpret experience in a way different than we habitually or reflexively do' (Snyder, 1994, p. 90). Later she goes on to say that 'The ability to deepen one's own awareness is self-empathy' which involves 'an attitude of compassion and curiosity regarding one's own experience that enables one to be simultaneously conscious of feelings and detached from them' (ibid., p. 97). I trip over 'detachment' but the rest is familiar. Snyder also proposes that 'the therapist's ability to facilitate the client's ability to put himself or herself in the places of others' (that is, to become more empathic) is one of the keys to being helpful.

The idea that fear and/or denial by the acknowledged I-self toward reactions and inclinations of the organic self gradually dissolves in successful therapy seems only a small step from the views outlined. These positions also are compatible with thinking that therapist empathy, beyond immediate clarifying and releasing effects, contributes to a different inner receptivity to and processing of experience, a change toward enhanced self-empathy. The furthered quality of *self*-engagement reflects individualised discovery by the client of how to tune in receptively to information available from his/her own organic and intuitive being, and of the difference it makes to draw on this knowledge in a spirit of partnership with self.

Summary-conclusion

Empathy as responsive human recognition of another person's felt experiencing and meanings is fundamental to connection between people. Without activation of empathy, the individual lives in emotional isolation. Society with high incidence of non-empathic modes of interaction is a milieu of separated lives; lives often lived in proximity but outside the frame of directly felt 'I-thou' and 'we' relationships. When empathic engagement does occur, it is largely confined to closest personal relationships. Then, the social collective is a community in name only.

Empathic engagement looked at closely is not a simple or single process. It starts with an active readiness to engage with the inner experiencing self of the other. This readiness gives rise to empathic listening in the presence of the other's expression of self. Empathic recognition may then occur if, and when, the listener resonates with an experience-based recognition of features of the other's inner world of experience and meaning. This distinct responsive awareness (empathy in its crucial first phase) may be communicatively expressed by the listener (empathy in its second phase) and *may* then be experienced by the client or sharing person as a true echo of personal human understanding (the third phase, of received empathy). The first stage, and even the second, of this process can occur without being consummated by the third phase — as closely explored in this chapter.

Empathy or its lack not only has profound bearing on relations with others but also has a crucial role in the person's inner world. It is a twin phenomenon, in the perspective of this chapter. The 'twins' are familial, not identical, but closely interdependent. One twin is interpersonal empathy, in its various phases. The other twin, in counterpoint to the first, pivots on quality of communication within the individual, especially, between the conscious, recognised self and the person's underlying organic being. Isolation and even intense loneliness arises from being 'out of touch on the inside' (Barrett-Lennard, 2003, Chapter 8), as well as from unempathic relations with others.

Surprisingly, client change in empathic functioning has received little attention in therapy research or theory. When this aspect has been discriminated in research, the focus has been on participant relationships in couple or family therapy. Therapist-to-client empathy, studied now for nearly four decades, is largely accepted either as integral to the enabling process or as a foundation for other factors to be effective. The ability of client-persons to engage empathically in relations with others is a dimension potentially of vital concern in therapy, both for its relevance to the life quality of individual clients and in respect to its social importance. The concept and process of self-empathy is seen to be pivotal in theory and offers a new dimension for reflection on practice.

Chapter 5

On *not* seeking to change my client:
Seeming paradox

This short chapter is developed from the prepared part of my remarks in a lively panel discussion at the Second International Conference on Client-Centred and Experiential Psychotherapy, in mid-1991. Our title for the session was 'Changing persons — by intention, or by the way'.[1] Since therapy is about healing and growthful change it would seem paradoxical to argue that as therapist helper I am not trying to bring about change in the client, a person usually coming to me over painful difficulty in themselves and their lives. My consciousness in the immediate human encounter with the Other who happens to be my client is a different consciousness than that which occupies when I am seeking to describe or explain therapy as a phenomenon. I believe that this difference is crucial for being in an authentic (helping) relation, without which we are at best in separated worlds of self-informant and outside interpreter or 'expert' guide.

The concept of 'managed care', now in vogue, calls on the professional to diagnose and efficiently treat circumscribed conditions or symptoms. It posits that recurring behaviours and feeling states, or other separated out and 'decontextualised' aspects of functioning, must be identified and then treated by a specific remedy known (hopefully) to change the problem pattern. This whole approach comes from another universe of thought and assumption than the stance conveyed in these pages — although it is not my intention here to embark on a critique of other visions. Also, so far as managed care itself goes, far more energetic and searching appraisals than I would attempt have already been made, notably including that of Arthur Bohart and colleagues (1998). My following statement is informal in presentation and I would welcome feedback 'conversation' from any engaged reader wishing to respond.

I do not experience myself engaged in trying to change or modify the other person(s) while working as a counsellor-therapist or group facilitator. Sometimes change happens, as seen by a client's family, friends or fellow-workers. Perhaps something moves inside the other: an inner release, a quality of being more

---

[1] The conference took place at the University of Stirling, Scotland. My fellow-panellists in this session were Maria Bowen, Barbara Brodley, David Mearns, Bernie Neville, and Nat Raskin.

alive and at home with self, an infusion of energy. It is the person's outlook and spirits that would be most likely to strike others as having changed, not their basic personality or make-up. I am happy when a shift or change is noticed, whether it is in the other's mood, their ease with themselves, or their responsiveness to others. However, I am not trying to modify the other as a person, not working to change who they are in themselves. Further, each of us has a basic style, intrinsic to our individuality and not something to tamper with. If change on any such broad levels occurs it is a by-product, a spin-off from the nature and immediate meaning of our encounter. Yet, to call my work 'therapy' implies that it is, or should be, making a difference; and I do want this work to have helpful effects for my clients — and perhaps even beyond them for others in their lives.

To the careful reader I may seem to be talking in riddles. Perhaps my point of view will be less puzzling if I talk about what is usually meant by 'change', and compare this with other kinds of effect. I will also say more about the way I wish to be with my client. Change, in therapy investigation and discourse, refers typically to enduring alteration in personality, emotional states or behavioural characteristics. Many believe that the desired alteration must first be clearly targeted. In their kind of model or approach, a problem is identified or a condition diagnosed and then steps are taken (psychotherapeutic or other) intended to overcome the problem or change the identified condition.

It is not surprising that we tend to see problems as implying a need for change. Suppose that a child stays away from school and this forms the apprehended problem. Further inquiry may reveal that the school situation, or a particular element within it, arouses anxiety in the child. Perhaps the child also feels humiliated and is struggling to preserve self-esteem. From this understanding the goal may be to produce change in the child's anxiety in school, and to ensure their opportunity to experience success. Achievement of these aims is expected to lead to behaviour changes, notably, the behaviour of going to school voluntarily. Assuming this all works out as intended, the change has been effected largely though external planning and agency — starting with an analysis of the problem and with the child placed in the position of recipient. The priority of knowing and empowerment *on the helper's part* would have been affirmed.

In another kind of problem, a person is admitted to a psychiatric hospital. Their condition, let us say, is diagnosed as a particular form of psychotic or severely neurotic condition. The desired change is the removal or substantial resolution of the patient's pathology and, thus, a shift in functioning that permits their discharge from the hospital in a relatively symptom-free condition. Here, the patient is in the role of recipient of the therapist's expertise. His/her part is secondary in setting the 'treatment' goals. The therapist-patient relationship is just a means to an end. Cure, symptom reduction, recompensation, or theory-derived terms of like nature, form the language of change.

Change by itself does not of course imply alteration in a particular direction. Deterioration is change. The concept of growth implies a natural unfolding development that is dependent only on essential nutrients and the absence of impediments. In the case of living beings with their own built-in directional tendencies, such unfolding is broadly similar to healing, both in direction and in respect to the crucial enabling conditions. The way I want to be as a therapist-counsellor or facilitator is not pointed directly at curatively healing the persons I am with. I would like to engage with them in ways that release and facilitate open-ended growth and development. In theory, the 'active ingredients' of my response include the nutrient of human empathy — an honest, respectful and caring empathic understanding of the other within *their* world of experience and meaning.

I take it for granted that human beings need and desire, on some basic level, closeness and communion with others. Communion fits better than communication although certain kinds of communication are the vehicle by which communion happens. Buber spoke of the 'I-thou' relationship, Rogers of 'basic encounter', Jourard of transparency, Bugental and others of 'authenticity' in relationship. These ideas all imply things done for their own sake, for their intrinsic meaning or value. Love without desire to possess, caring as an experience of compassionate regard without evaluative personal judgement, active empathic sensitivity to the subjective consciousness and feelings of the other, and trusting, uncalculated expressiveness, are all facets of being with another in the sense I mean.

I do not care for my wife and children in order to change them. I am not empathically sensitive and compassionate to the friend who confides in me about some deeply troubling concern or circumstance in their life in order to 'cure' this friend. I would like to be a facilitative person with my students, but do not consciously strive to mould their thinking or attitudes or instil a particular vision of truth. In each of these as well as in more formal helping contexts, when I really permit myself to feel and respond to the hunger in the other and in myself, in human terms, what happens is a deeply important end in itself, not just a means to some other end.

In the actual counselling/helping process, I am trying to reach the other person in their feelings now, trying to open and bring myself to them so that I can feel their presence and experience and they in turn have the chance to feel me in my response. Thus, the moment between us can become alive in an actual meeting. Out of such meeting the person's 'in-touchness' with themselves can also grow. If they have been stuck, their experience may begin to flow. There is likely to be a shift from a more impersonal to a more personal focus or quality of expression, remoteness can give way to greater immediacy, tightness and anxiety tend to lessen or dissolve. The person may feel freer, easier within themselves, more awake or conscious, affirmed in their own selfhood. Little by little, shifts can take place in the larger patterning of the person's conscious experiencing and behaviour. However, such shifts generally are not in my sights (unless my companion helps to bring them into view), in the presence of the other person and as I attend to them, to myself with them, and to the moment-by-moment emergence, interplay and unfolding of felt meaning between us.

In the I-thou of our encounter I am not moving chess pieces, or doing and saying things step by step with the calculated aim of producing change. Change when it happens is an outgrowth of our engagement, a possible consequence but not a guiding intention of mine during the process of our meeting, a spin-off perhaps from the meanings that are alive in us as we proceed. The way I am with the other is not purposed and played out to cause change in the other's make-up and identity, nor for that matter is it to *show* responsiveness to their suffering and searching, or try to *demonstrate* that I understand them. Growthful personal change may happen, may even be facilitated, but the real thing (like falling in love) is not susceptible to manufacture. An intervention formula applied to the individual may have real effects but not those of organic recovery and growth toward a fruition of being.

Being exposed to the conscious efforts of parents, teachers, bosses, political or religious leaders, salespersons and many others to change, modify, influence or make one over in some way, is one principal cause of stress, emotional conflict, getting mixed-up. In short, exposure to the efforts of others to influence and change us — even 'for our own benefit' — seems to be a major factor in leading people to *seek* personal counselling. I do **not** want to be party to another instance of this pattern, or to help perpetuate it inadvertently. I do want to enter a real relationship, as companion and assistant to the other person as they venture to share and search into their world of feeling, action and meaning.

Should the other person find my lack of guidance and general attitude in respect to goals confusing and unsatisfactory, and perhaps even devote effort to setting rules for me to use with them, I hope I would take them seriously and respond quite honestly. This would mean that I have perceptively heard them, and that we have encountered each other through their candid expression and my open response. If I have sensed felt needs not directly expressed but close to their consciousness, I may share this sense with them. In these and other ways I would also be staying true to myself, to working principles of my own, to values and findings from my own journey. This is not to imply fixity for *this* relationship and other fresh experiences are inherent further parts of my journey. We may find we want to continue together through the experience and challenge of our difference as well as the discovery of commonality. It is also possible that the other's present search and aims are truly in a different direction than the resources and interest I bring to our engagement, that they are now clearer still about the kind of assistance they are seeking, and know better where to look for it.

Presuming, as I do, that our lived world as humans is a world of relation, that even our states of withdrawal are a relational stance, it would be an artificial thing to try to separate most of me as a person from the relation with my client. Human selves are born in relation and prosper or wither not just one by one but in and through their experiences of relation. To try to help troubled selves by standing apart from them, and singling out certain technical procedures to insert or apply with one client, and other selected procedures to apply with another client, would fly in the face of my own consciousness and sense of our nature. It is not that I experience or advocate a literal constancy of response. Each person I meet in any depth, as a client or otherwise, at best engages me fully but distinctively, and no client relation calls forth my whole possibility or repertoire of being in (helping) relation. I discover a bit more of who I am in the relation with each client person. This is not eclecticism; I don't consult an inner manual of alternatives and choose one or another method according to its seeming fit to the problem and style of my particular client. A certain individuality of response and relation emerges naturally and unbidden from our composite uniqueness.

'Empowerment' is very much in vogue in helping circles, and as a broad effect is accepted as a good thing. I would like my clients to come to feel their strength and resourcefulness, to feel unencumbered by strong inner division or conflict, and to experience significant agency in their lives. The language of empowerment is evocative but I think it important to ask the twin questions of how this effect comes about and what exactly we mean by it, especially in a personal helping context. For example, it would be a contradiction of meaning for me to think that I actually give or produce this empowerment in the other. What I leave open and do not do may be as important as the more active features of my response. Our engagement places little 'requirement' on the other but, at best, provides much opportunity for expression and release of what has been constrained in their inner process and relations. Out of such self-freeing there tends to come an enlargement of interest in the generativeness of others and *less* inclination to exercise power over them.

The personal change that I have most interest and confidence in comes through discovery, with a quality of self-appropriation. It broadly includes some growth in consciousness of one's process of being. Crucial aspects of this process are how one engages both internally and in relation. Such discovery-based self-knowing brings a new realm or quality of choice and of felt responsibility for choices. It is a truly developmental process growing out of the person's motivated engagement in a conducive context of relation. The challenge for me as counsellor is to be able to enter into such a relation with the particular other who has come to me. It is not in my capacity to do this with every other person, or in every contact with a particular other. And, when it comes to the point, my would-be client may fear, more than they desire, to expose and search into and around their wounds, feelings of failure or confusion or despair, or other personal crisis. Above all, the question is whether my client and I form a We that 'falls into' not romantic love but a trusting, searching, healing, growthful personal-helping relation — not merely an 'alliance' but a relationship both rewarding in itself and in its fruits beyond itself.

As I reflect on issues around change in therapy, it is clear to me as already mentioned that in the immediate process of engagement with my client I am in a quite different 'place' than when thinking about our work together; and that the distance is greater still when I am conceptualising or investigating the process broadly. What I am up to and what is going on in me in the first context is quite unlike the last-mentioned. But I am also conscious of exceptions. With some clients, or at some moments, these universes merge, with dubious effect. As instance, my focus of attention might shift from what is immediate in the other and between us to reflecting on a broad feature of the client's pattern, or thinking *about* our process in terms of a general quality or what movement is or is not occurring, or what I might do for the sake of its hoped-for effect.

Usually, I am so engrossed with 'taking in' the other through their communicated and implied feelings and meaning, checking out my understandings, keeping track of me with them and letting this show (or not hiding it), that I am not evaluating such issues as 'where is this leading?' or 'how can I produce a shift in this person's feeling or grasp of something' or 'what would help this client move out of the groove or cycle of despondency I can see they are stuck in?' There is nothing wrong with such questions, and they might occur to me in fleeting moments or after the hour, and may have some effect on what I responsively share or discriminate empathically at a later time. However, to the extent that thoughts of this kind occupy me within the process of our encounter, my responsive presence and companioning of the other in *their* sharing and search is diminished. They may even feel, understandably, that I have turned away from *them* and become another observer or judge. Whatever their process with me before this 'turning away' it could not be the same while they felt me outside and apart.

I hope that my comments have gone some way toward resolving a seeming paradox. On the one hand, therapy to be worthwhile has effects. It may make a difference in any one or more of the ways mentioned, depending on the particular client, the therapist, and the qualities of their emergent partnership. Outside the frame of the therapy encounter I am very ready to think and talk, in a textured way, about change. In fact it seems essential to me for some conception of movement, and how it happens, to be part of our theoretical discourse as counsellors or clinicians — as the reader would see from other parts of this book. But something quite different *is and needs to be* going on when my client and I are together. Connecting with them in their moving world of feeling and meaning, truly opening myself to take in and sense empathically what it is like for them moment to moment and in larger zones of their experience (as they try to become further known to me and to themselves), returning clear messages so that it is apparent what I understand and have not (yet) understood, following them so closely that their sharing search flows naturally in its own unfolding direction, all this and further elements of our engagement fill my consciousness. I am not capable of consciously engineering change if and while doing all this, but from the living process of this doing valued effects follow.

Chapter 6

Experiential groups for discovery learning: Deciphering the process

I began to conduct intensive groups back in the early to mid-sixties, via the first residential 'workshops in therapeutic counselling' held in Australia. By the late sixties, my teaching, then in Canada, included formal studies and training workshops in the small group sphere. One of my accounts of the group process was published in Canada's Mental Health *(1973) as Supplement No. 73. This paper reflects my client-centred therapy background and, by then, a decade of engagement in and enthusiasm for the small-group medium. I soon went on to publish a short version in the journal* Psychotherapy: Theory, research and practice, *(encouraged by the then-editor Gene Gendlin) but I still like the longer article and have dusted it off editorially to form the first part of this chapter.*

My article for CMH *was headed 'Experiential learning groups in practice — general process description and guidelines', and the readers I had in mind included people planning or entering an intensive group experience. I also felt that the statement could be of interest to general readers who were uncertain but curious about the human potential/ encounter group phenomenon. I saw the broad aim of this kind of group as being to foster personal developmental learning via 'an open-ended, low structure, experience-based interactive process'. My description assumed that members were present by their own choice, not 'acquiescence to someone else's direction'.*

No single window on the rich and complex phenomenon of intensive groups can reveal its total nature, and I soon was drawn to describe the process on further, complementary levels. The links between group composition, the ensuing process and the resulting outcomes also interested me; and the whole range of ideas came together in an ambitious article (written on leave in 1974) initially titled 'Process, effects and structure in intensive groups: A systematic view'. Later parts of the present chapter freshly outline and update features of this systematic view. The first part, based on my CMH paper, works to bring the group experiential process qualitatively to life.

Experiential groups in practice: Process bearings

My provision of descriptive guidelines for intensive experiential discovery-learning groups reflects a belief that meaningful choice and initiative — in particular, a decision of whether to participate in an experiential learning group — requires some knowledge of what is being chosen, of the kind of experience presenting itself and the nature of its potentialities. This account falls between the possible alternatives (i) of a description that presents the process in such broad or general terms that it could encompass situations differing basically in their actual characteristics and effects, and (ii) of a sharply focused and prescriptive definition that leaves no room for variation in process and goals. In the same sense that 'traditional' educational procedures imply value choices, the following guidelines also reflect a choice among possible kinds of relational and developmental goals in human living. Woven through and as part of this choice is a broad observation, namely, that the force and effectiveness of any personal learning hinges on the extent to which it springs from intensive, strongly involving first-hand experience. Beyond this, a major value principle implied here is that persons should have the opportunity to be contributing architects of their own being and becoming. It is assumed also that this self-becoming occurs largely through experiences in relationship.

Intentions of the intensive group experience include the idea and possibility of becoming more inwardly open and at home with oneself; more genuinely attentive and perceptive in communication and relationships; more aware of one's priorities or values and more confident in applying them. In becoming responsive to a wider range of experiential data, it is as though some inner/outer channels open, or some that are uncomfortably restricted expand. There may be subtle changes in the person's consciousness as new shades of perception and meaning come into view, some 'colours' become more vivid than before, new patterns and textures are perceived, and the person's world moves somewhat in the way it is seen or configured. Importantly, in terms of process, the individual experiences self and other group members (at times, at least) as formative, unbound and 'in-process'; as embarked on a voyage of discovery and development — a voyage that can continue after this expedition.

In terms of practical description, the process-experiential features that stand out to me, and seem basic in a fruitfully working group of the 'genus' in view, are as follows:

1. *Once a group begins, each person belongs because he or she is present.* Each of us in the group has his or her individual history, including the aspects leading to the choice to be there. The group owes its existence and its identity to the prior circumstances and convergent choices that have brought all of us together. As generally the case in a family, the right of each family member/group member to be part of that family/group is not an issue. By taking each other's membership as a given, despite our differences, we learn how to 'make it together'. This has awesome relevance in the larger community and world we live in.

A member's purposes and needs in participating in the group clearly are a

different matter than his/her right to be there. In effect, responsively moving
and engaging with one another with our distinctive intentions is what the
group is for. It can be highly relevant for any of us to express our initial and
developing aims, and our blocked and wanted experiences, in the group.
Different, too, from our right to belong, is an actual, felt experience of inclusion
and belongingness. This experience may develop and grow in the group (usually
with marked ups and downs) but it has no instant variety.

2. *A first purpose is to gain a sense of one another as inwardly active, feeling,
thinking persons.* It is a feeling for the other as a human being like oneself, a
direct sense of 'the other person's living inside himself' (Gendlin and Beebe,
1968). Words may or may not be necessary to gain this contact. Simply looking
openly toward the other, catching their eyes, seeing their expression, posture
and movement may bring them to life for us, and ourselves for the other. Then
when we speak, or carry forward in our expression, we are communicating to
someone, sharing perhaps tentatively but with an immediate sense that the
other is hearing our words and may understand our feeling.

3. *Group members endeavour to be personal, direct and specific in their
communication.* This may be difficult generally, or at certain times, but members
try to avoid general and abstract statements if they blur, or only express in a
roundabout way, their immediate meaning, reaction, intuition or felt concern.
Although it may feel risky, or even scary, generally a participant wishes to use
language to be in touch (to express him/herself in the immediacy of experience
with the other, and to receive the other in kind) rather than to maintain distance
and separation (or keep from personally knowing and being known).

   Quite often, in the group, someone will feel or think something that they
fear to say or show right then, or that they feel might be too hurtful, troubling or
unfair to someone else. Short of doing this, the member may venture to share
their felt uneasiness or fear of expressing their more specific inner feeling or
perception, and find that this sharing frees them in some way, or increases their
sense of safety in the group. It is likely, then, that they will have a clearer feeling
of whether they want to disclose what they feared to express initially — which
may itself have changed a bit as they tested the waters.

4. *Each of us listens to other members*, not always with patience or sensitivity
but generally with a concern to know what they are experiencing. Primarily,
our listening is *not* to grasp the other's meaning simply as an opinion that we
then proceed to examine logically and critically. Rather, we listen to hear and
know the other personally as a fellow human self. The focus is on the level of
personal meaning, observation and feeling rather than on the 'soundness' of
the other's ideas, viewpoint and knowledge. We listen in a way that recognises

differences and uniqueness, as well as commonalities, and in a way that is empathic rather than critically analytic. When such empathic recognition of the other's lived experience or situation is clearly conveyed and received by the person who is being understood, its impact may be deeply moving and releasing to them (as also discussed in Chapters 1 and 4).[1]

5. *We tend to let our inner feelings of relatedness show as these feelings actually arise and develop in us.* Actual feelings of warm concern, closeness or appreciation, of impatience, bafflement or frustration, of responsive sadness or excitement, of sharp anger, hurt or embarrassment, of being at loss, stuck or confused in relation to someone else, of mutual enjoyment, fun or pleasure — and many other feelings-in-relation — can be expressed, shared and fully experienced in the group. There is no rule that anyone *should* feel any particular way but there is an understanding that it is all right, and generally helpful, to show the real feelings that arise toward and in response to others in the group.

This general understanding is not, of course, immediately effective in leading everyone to actually feel comfortable or able to express their feelings openly. Also, relational feelings that are experienced quite strongly may at the same time be mixed, confused or very unclear, especially at first. Sometimes it is hard to discriminate feelings about oneself from feelings toward others, and the 'same' experience may turn out to have both of these sides to it. In moments such as these, our experience of struggle, being stuck or of not grasping, may itself come into focus as the immediate issue. Recognising this, when it is true, amounts to attending to our own immediate process, which we can now explore or simply acknowledge.

The development of an actual climate of trust and openness in the group, in the expression of relational feelings, starts from initially ventured expressions — whether tentative or firm, positive or negative — and the ways in which these are received and responded to. Relational experience and sharing, in the context of other described qualities in the group, grows on itself, deepening, with ups and downs, as the process and life of the group unfolds.

6. *The group is a place for honesty and realism.* Most of us have learned to be

---

[1] I do not mean to imply that the levels of experiencing and interpersonal process that characterise an experiential group are the only important levels for significant knowing and being-in-the-world. Rather, these levels are viewed as comprising a major and fundamental 'band' within a larger spectrum, a spectrum that includes more detached and analytical observation, abstract thinking, and comprehension of how things interrelate and work in our non-personal environment. However, the qualities of self-experiencing and relational process described here are frequently neglected or stopped in our culture, resulting in literal deprivation in the individual's experiencing and development.

more or less on our guard in social situations. We 'know' that certain kinds of things may be expressed but that there is no room for some of our deeper feelings and perceptions. In a close personal friendship our guard drops more than in other relationships. We feel freer, closer, more openly sharing of our feelings, interests, wants and ideas, in short, our inner selves. We are more transparent with a close friend and he or she with us. Although, in ordinary life, such friendships usually take some time to form and blossom this is not inevitably the case. Sometimes, a genuine and lasting friendship springs into being quickly.

In infancy and early childhood, human beings normally are openly expressive, spontaneous, unguarded and transparent. It is partly this quality that endears us to small people. We evidently *learn* to be guarded and concealing but usually maintain a desire or hunger to be ourselves in a fuller, freer, open way, and this appears to be one of the main forces at work in an experiential learning group. Its strength, the forms in which it can be expressed, and the felt risks of disclosing sensitive, 'unfamiliar' or usually protected and guarded aspects of one's inner experiencing will of course vary from person to person in the group. But the presence of this hunger for open connection, the particular sanction that experiential groups provide for its expression, the experience of being really listened to on an empathic level, and one's own experience of and response to the more immediate and self-expressive communications of other group members, are likely to become a powerfully releasing combination for participants. Movement into deeply searching and sharing communication and relationships may occur much more rapidly than in most other life-situations.

The described expectations and climate of a group are conditions which tend to foster honesty and realism, but are not of a kind to *make* this happen. In my view, an intense, direct striving or insistence on being 'ruthlessly honest' or 'totally open' is likely to be ineffective and can even lead into a kind of make-believe. In effect, such intense striving contains elements of self-contradiction — like straining to be spontaneous.

7. *Group members are not seeking to sit in judgement on each other.* Judgemental feelings and perceptions may spontaneously arise and, as in everyday life, tend to evoke counter-judgemental reactions. Usually, in the group, such a cycle is soon broken because other kinds of potent processes and communication are happening. Typically, the group leader or some other member(s) are listening for the inner experiencing of both 'accuser' and 'accused'. As they are able to, they express what they hear — the anger, hurt, mistrust, fear and other more complex feelings and personal meanings of the persons judging and being judged. Others who are not in the immediate firing line may find themselves with feelings similar to those they sense in a person who is responding judgementally. These feelings may come out differently, expressed and owned as felt reactions and meanings rather than as an accusing evaluative judgement.

By themselves, judgemental attitudes and messages inhibit rather than facilitate the kinds of relational learning and self-discovery for which the group experience can be such a potent vehicle. In conjunction with the other kinds of response mentioned, and the general group ethos, spontaneous judgemental reactions can be integral steps or phases in a larger process experienced as bringing members into deeper and more helpful connection.

8. *Each person in the group has responsibility for himself and to others.* Generally, participation in the group implies that the person wishes to become more fully him/herself with others; that in a very significant sense he/she stands in need of others. However, it does not imply a surrender of responsibility for self. To the contrary, the person's presence expresses choice and action on his or her own behalf. If another group member feels or tries to take on responsibility for the person this implies a perception of them as incapable or powerless. Even if the person should feel this way him/herself, the experience of being responded to as incapable would tend to confirm and reinforce such self-perception rather than fostering a sense of agency and resourcefulness.

To relate to another with responsive concern for their well-being, not instead of but as well as one's own, implies a caring readiness also to be an ally in the other's caring for self; and perhaps to perceive the other as an ally when the going gets rough for oneself.

9. *In our communication and relationships, in the group, we often provide each other with personal feedback.* The term feedback inclusively refers to direct messages from another person as to qualities and characteristics that the other sees in us, and that may feed into our own sense or awareness of our identity and potentialities. Helpful feedback may point to some valued aspect of ourselves, or a visibly developing potential within us, and be directly self-confirming in this way. Feedback messages may also serve to draw attention to, or even help us to discover, attributes that we want to change or to bring forth in ourselves.

The giving of personal feedback happens whenever we directly share with another our perception of some particular quality or way of responding that strikes us, together with our own attitude or feeling about this quality or pattern. In feedback communication my observation and feeling is something in me (something I am experiencing) that points more or less accurately and/or helpfully to something I see in you or in your behaviour. If my message makes it clear that I own or share responsibility for what I see, and at the same time clearly or vividly conveys my 'picture' of you in this way, and especially if I feel genuine concern for or caring toward you, there is a chance that you will experience my picture as meaningful and relevant. Thus it carries the possibility of contributing something to your own view of self, as well as telling you something more about me, or about me-with-you.

Besides these aspects of tuning in to each other's feelings and worlds of experience and meaning, particularly including relational feelings in the group, we are conscious of one another as having outside lives and an identity that extends beyond what we directly see in the group. Our feedback communication reflects and takes advantage of the fact that we are truly attentive to one another, experiencing each other's involvement, effort and ways of managing this rather unique experience. Our engagement process is often very expressive of who we are and how we function. We form pictures of each other (etched more clearly through awareness of likeness and differences), based on substantial and salient 'data', and the mutual communication of these pictures may significantly enhance our knowing of ourselves.

10. *What we express from within ourselves may productively call forth varied meanings and different kinds of response from distinctive others in the group.* Fruitful learning and development happens in a group because we serve as catalysts and resources to one another in our active and reactive, expressive/ receptive and personal/relational searching.

The same experiential communication is received by each group member in a distinctive context of past experience and immediate personal process. As connection and trust develop, the individually varying impact on other members of someone's deeply felt and evocative expression can then be freely shared, and lead perhaps to further variation as differing expressed reactions are in turn responded to. In this way, the threads of meaning and discovery can multiply and may weave an experiential/relational texture of great richness.

One person's self-expressive searching may, for example, open an inner doorway for another to some important quality or pattern in their own experience. It may evoke in a third person a concern to check (and possibly help through) his/her personal understanding of the first. It may speak to a fourth of something vividly recognised in self-experience but not previously known in another, and which dissolves some part of that person's feeling of separateness. It may provide the capstone for a clear and illuminating feedback message from a fifth person; and give to a sixth a compelling example of a *process* which they too can try in their own search within the group. Finally, it may communicate to a seventh person an attitude sharply in contrast with previous conscious meanings but now comprehensible and real to them in another human being.

11. *When decisions are made that commit the whole group, everyone in the group takes part and shares in the decision process and outcome.* Once an experiential learning group is ongoing, fresh decisions that commit the group as a whole are based on agreement by all members. They are not determined by majority vote or rule, or by the group leader (or any other member) acting

on his or her own. Decisions which everyone in the group participates in, and accepts, effectively begin before the first group meeting. Each person on the basis of the information available in advance, has chosen (or agreed, in some active sense) to be there. Any arrangements or plans of consequence that were not presented in this advance information fall within the scope of fresh decisions.

Genuine consensus is not compatible with some people agreeing as a result of pressure from others, or making themselves go along with a decision because they don't want to be a nuisance, or because they fear rejection if they disclose their real preferences or needs. Nor does it imply that everyone has arrived at exactly the same point of view or attitude, or experiences the same level of enthusiasm, interest or support for the decision. It does imply that the relevant issues, as perceived and assessed by each person, balance out in the same direction for everyone.

When a matter for joint decision is discussed in the group there is opportunity for every member to say what he or she thinks or feels, but there is not a requirement for each one to put forward their view. If a person stays quiet it usually would be taken to mean that they felt they had nothing to add and that the outcome is all right with them. If an emerging decision does go against the grain for anyone, s/he has a complete right — even an obligation — to say so. If someone else feels quite involved, but very unclear as to their position, the leader or other group members ordinarily would feel concerned to help the person sort out and clarify where they stand. If a particular proposal is made, especially if it is something consequential that most members have not been expecting or thinking about in advance — and especially if no fresh decisions have so far been worked through to a point of clear agreement — it is important to provide lots of opportunity for discussion of what anyone finds difficult or does not like about the proposal. This might result in a working-through process in which feelings and ideas change to a point where everyone supports the suggestion or is at least genuinely willing to see it acted on. Alternatively, there may be a clear decision not to follow the proposal.

Sometimes it is better to put off a decision because one or more persons remain concerned but uncertain, or because the discussion leads to other personal issues or relational feelings that become the immediate, actual focus of attention and concern in the group. On occasion, further information is needed that cannot be obtained while the group is in session. Also, when a group decision is called for, it may seem very unclear at first how, or on what basis, a decision can or should be made. Members may have the distinct impression that they are now confronting an administrative or organisational matter that seems to call for a quite different kind of procedure for its resolution than those which 'normally' apply in the group. At such times, it can be helpful for members to ask themselves anew why they are in the group, what their purposes are — individually and together. Their answers are likely to involve a common theme which clarifies the basis for decision and which might run somewhat as follows: 'This group exists for us. We want to be guided in what we do by our need, what we value and what we expect to be helpful.'

12. *The group leader is a member of the group, with purposes and needs and 'uniquenesses' like everyone else.* Some of the leader's resources and responsibilities typically differ in degree, but not necessarily in kind, from those of other group members. He or she may have some outside objective(s) additional to those of other members, such as — if group members consent — drawing on data from the group for teaching or research. The leader usually is more experienced in groups of the immediate kind than other members are, which affects his/her discernment of process qualities and where they can lead. This implies a perception of *more than average responsibility* within the group for facilitating a fruitful quality of process — fruitful, for example, in terms of qualities outlined here. In the nature of these qualities they can only be realised within and through the interaction of members, and the leader's distinctive part is more evident in the initial stages of the group than its mature development. Structurally, there is more of a service emphasis in the leader's position and role in the group than in the case of other members, although this does not imply basically different qualities of engagement by the leader than by other persons in the group.

Usually the group leader takes it upon him/herself, to a greater degree than other members, to be attentive to all members of the group and to try to ensure that no one gets neglected or 'lost'— especially when feelings are intense and attention is strongly focused on one or a few persons. However, by attending to active participants a facilitator sometimes will miss subtle cues that something very important is building up in a silent group member, and no one else should wait for the leader to notice this before expressing his/her own recognition and concern for the feeling or struggle of the silent member. The official leader's responsibility and attention in this way is not in the least exclusive; it is simply more intentional and may be more consistent.

A familiar and delightful characteristic of young children is the way that they transparently and expressively assume and try out the roles, behaviours, attitudes and imagined qualities of people, creatures and important inanimate objects in their world. This partly imitational but self-expressive experimentation and learning continues, in lesser degree and more subtle forms, in adulthood. Where there is purpose and opportunity for personal/interpersonal exploration and learning and, particularly, in a situation that is novel and ambiguous in its specific demands and possibilities, there is a heightened tendency for individuals to take their cues rather directly from each other. This is true in an experiential learning group, especially in its early stages. Because the leader is usually known to be experienced in such situations and because each of us is used to persons in a leadership position setting or offering the pattern for others, the leader's functioning usually is more strongly suggestive and evocative as an example than is the behaviour of other group members. The differential influence of the leader as a model (and the 'modelling' phenomenon altogether) desirably and usually diminishes over the course of the group's lifetime.

As relationships develop and the process unfolds, in an experiential group, the leader typically becomes increasingly assimilated as a group member and partner in a common enterprise. At the same time, the uniqueness, as well as commonalities, of each person's characteristics and his/her contribution for others in the group, come to be more fully accepted, actively welcomed, and at times cherished.

During the original framing of this statement I was participating and serving as the designated leader in two different experiential learning groups. The currency and freshness of that experience certainly influenced the details and style of my presentation. It portrayed a living, growing development, both for me and in a larger social sense. My experience since then has confirmed most of my former perspective, as in the version just presented. It could be said that the intensive group experience itself has less magic in it than many of us (including Carl Rogers) once thought. Perhaps the perceived universality or magic of any phenomenon diminishes as understanding deepens and the phenomenon itself is embraced within a larger perspective. As the group experience and process has become better and more realistically known its application in varied contexts has grown. What I have just described is not identical, however, with other widely applied forms, and may be distinctive in leadership and attitudinal climate.

One level of understanding the extensive involvement of people from many walks of life, in experiential groups, derives from the social conditions and matrix of our time, particularly in industrially 'advanced' societies. Such societies comprise a civilisation marked by an unprecedented, continually accelerating pace and complexity of technological and social change. Many of us are left with more leisure (less required 'work'), more physical comfort and security in the short run, and more informational knowledge on some levels than ever before. Often we are also left very lonely, 'displaced persons' relationally if not geographically. In many cases we feel like foreigners or strangers in our own community and country. Or, we may be left inwardly unfulfilled, without deep purpose or clear meaning in our lives. While wishing to take charge of our lives and development, we can encounter great difficulty in knowing how, or in finding the resources to do so. Many of us are concerned for our fellows but unable to freely express and give of ourselves, to enrich their lives as well as our own. These are among the reasons why many seek and deeply value exploring, encountering and growing with others, in intensive experiential learning groups.

A more theoretical view of process and motion in groups

The further part of this chapter is a change of pace from the very practical description so far given, which itself is a much fuller view of territory briefly outlined in my previous book (Barrett-Lennard, 1998, pp. 159–60). Next presented is a tighter, more theoretical view, reworked from previous formulations to carry my meaning more readily and to add new features. The main focus is still on the 'group' process itself.

One main angle of view on this process is to look systematically at *the between-person dimension*. Members are continually communicating with one another, with growing mutual awareness and evolving relationships. In the nature of the group communication situation, participants are taking turns — except at moments of talking over each other or letting someone stay over-long at the centre of attention.

Imagine that a group is underway. Members are sharing and responding, involved with themselves and each other. Someone has just said something and a second person follows, perhaps in direct response to the previous speaker. Or, possibly the first speaker has triggered something that speaker 2 now wants to share with the group, or say to a third member. A further participant may have been especially conscious of the interaction or feeling between speakers 1 and 2, and wants to respond to them jointly, from a personal sense of the feeling and/or message in this exchange. What this speaker says contains elements of feedback to the original pair and may of course help to evoke further response from any other listening member.

At another moment, a responding member may focus on a subgroup — the men or the women, those older or younger, or some other breakdown. And, for a given person at certain moments, no one member is in focus in their awareness, and their reaction or reaching out is to the whole group. Underneath any of these messages are the felt and evolving relations with and between other members. The dynamics are complex and I want to unfold a systematic way of coming to grips with some of this complexity, using a form of demonstration. First, a word about dyadic relations in particular.

Twosomes are arguably the most basic unit in interpersonal communication and relationship. Each person in an experiential group tends to become increasingly aware of the presence and qualities of each other person. Thus an important aspect is each one's experience of interchange and relationship with other individual members. Each twosome or dyad offers somewhat distinctive experience, perhaps with elements that are new to the persons involved, or at least that are engaged in a different way than in previous social situations. Part of the overt process in a group consists of what amount to one-to-one interchanges, with everyone else for the moment an involved witness. Any of the participant-observers may then follow-on and become active in another one-to-one exchange — or a one-to-*two* or more widely beamed response as so far discussed.

Following is a demonstration exercise that I like to do, to illustrate the dyadic dimension or structure in a group, and the influence of group size on the mushrooming of dyads. I will stay as close as I can to language suited to the context of actually working with a present group of student colleagues or trainees, and the reader is invited to form a mind's eye picture or on-paper diagram, to follow the series of steps described. The sets of cords (and strings) mentioned would have been prepared beforehand.

• 'Please would any seven people make a fairly even circle.' [I think of seven persons as being about the lower limit in size for an experiential group, if it is to realise the unique potentials of this medium.] 'Let's give each person a number: person 1, person 2, person 3, etc., on to person 7.'

'**Person 1** take six pieces of cord (already tied together at one end). Hold onto the knotted end and hand one of the free ends to each other person, taking up any slack so that each one feels a gentle tug. Make eye contact with each other person and begin to imagine, if you wish, that you are in an immediately active group together.'

'**Person 2** please take a five piece set of cords tied at one end, and hand a free end to each of the remaining five persons (person 1 has already connected you with them).'

'**Person 3** take a four piece set of cords, and hand the free ends to persons 4, 5, 6, and 7 (you are already connected to 1 and 2).'

'**Person 4** take a three cord set, and hand the free ends to persons 5, 6 and 7.'

'**Person 5** please take a two cord set, and hand the free ends to persons 6 and 7.'

'**Person 6** just needs one extra cord to link to person 7.'

'**Person 7** is now also connected, by the action of others, with everyone else.'

'*Let's count how many two-person connections there are altogether:* 6 [by action of person 1] +5 [added by person 2] +4 [person 3] +3 [person 4] +2 [person 5] +1 [person 6]. A quicker way of getting this total of 21, is by the formula $n(n-1)/2$, where 'n' is the number of persons — in this case, $7 \times 6/2$.'

- *'Now let's see what happens when we add three more, making a group of ten.* The first seven all keep holding onto your present cords, but make room in the circle for three others.'

'**Person 8** take a set of nine cords, to link up with each of the original seven plus persons 9 and 10.'

'**Person 9**, already connected to 8, needs eight cords (to link with the original seven plus person 10).'

'**Person 10**, now connected with 8 and 9, needs cords for each of the original seven members.'

We have added 9+8+7 connections. With the original 21, this sums altogether to 45, or *more than twice as many dyads as in the seven-person group.* By formula, the number is n(n-1)/2, in this case, 10×9/2.

- 'Imagine a group of 14, just double the size of the original seven. This would generate 14×13/2 dyads or 91 in all — more than four times as many as in the group of seven! And, for each individual, instead of six there are 13 two-person relations in the group.'

Clearly there is a big, qualitatively variable and complex network of two-person relations and interchange within any sharing group. If an experiential group is too large, or its life too brief, not all of the component dyad relations can develop significantly. I was once in a diverse intensive group of 19 persons. Even though we met daily for nearly two weeks, I believe that there were some dyad combinations in which little direct one-to-one interaction occurred. It wasn't essential for each person to somehow come to terms or reach an understanding with every other person, as tends to happen in smaller groups that meet over a significant period. And it was easy for a member to get lost from view by most others, in some sessions. I think that 14 persons are about the maximum for such a group, of limited life. With 20 or more members, certainly with 30+, there is a very different order of subsystem complexity, and the group/community experience becomes a different phenomenon with differing potentialities. All of this is even more evident if we look further.

The exercise so far, while vividly suggesting the multiplying relational range and complexity of groups, as they increase in size, is concerned with two-person 'diameters' only. Each group member is witness and participant in many further kinds of relational avenue and interplay. A principal further avenue, with many counterparts in everyday life relations, is that of threesome interchanges. A potentially salient example in an experiential group develops from a two-person interchange during which all others for the moment are participant observers. Then, as may happen, a third member responds to this pair in a way that involves both prior participants and refers in some way to their communication or perceived relation. From the position of the new participant, this is a 1-2 triad — a 'me' responding to a dyadic 'you'. Since any group member potentially could respond to any other active pair, great variety and choice is possible. This potential variety can be illustrated through a further exercise as follows:

'Let's start with seven people again, already connected in pairs by 21 cords but with each cord having a tied loop in the middle.'

(Turning to person 1 — P1:) 'You face six other people, and among these six there are 6×5/2 or 15 connected pairs. Here are another 15 pieces of string (of different appearance than the original cords), tied together at one end for you to hold. Let's now connect the free ends, one by one, to the 15 loops in the cords connecting the other pairs.'

(Focusing now on P2:) 'You also face six others and 15 pairs between them. Again, use 15 pieces of string to connect yourself with these pairs.'

'Let's repeat the same process for P3, using another 15 strings; and then imagine also doing this for P4, P5, P6 and P7. Each one of the seven would then be connected to 15 other pairs, adding up to 105 "1-2" connections in all — among only seven persons!'

'For any one member in a group of ten, how many twosomes of others would there be, for possible 1-2 triad interactions? By formula, the number would be 9×8/2, or 36. Thus, among ten members there would be 10×36 or 360 possible triad configurations altogether, of this kind. Among 14 persons the 1-2 triad possibilities sum to 1,092!'

'Clearly, as a group increases moderately in size, the range of possible triads mushrooms exponentially. A formula for all the possibilities of this particular [1-2] triad configuration is $n(n-1)(n-2)/2$ — but you don't have to remember this to work it out, as just shown.'[2]

---

[2] In this method of estimation, each group of three has within it three possibilities of the 1-2 kind — one for each person. If one considers only the numerical extent of different trios, in a group of seven there are 35 (7×6×5/2×3). If one were to count every *sequence* (ABC, ACB, BAC, BCA, CAB and CBA) within each trio, as distinct, the total would be 6×35, or 210.

It is most unlikely that 1-2 threesome interchanges in **all** the *possible* combinations would occur in a group, even an experiential group of only seven persons. No given member would be likely to experience direct involvement with *every* other pair, although at some moment in the life of an extended group of only seven persons members might very well witness some interchange between every pair. Reacting to what is happening *between others* occurs all the time in families, friendship groups, and work settings. Exploring one's own and other people's ways of responding to patterns of interchange and feeling between others (others with whom one also has a one-to-one relation) is an avenue of new experience and learning that for some members could be as important as any other. I believe that in groups where such three-way interchanges and systems are not noticed, or not facilitated or discriminated as part of the life of the group, a vital potential is being missed.

Possible subsystems of more than three could be similarly examined. These include four-person or 'quadral' interchanges, of more than one kind. One variety is a double pair (2-2, 'you-we') configuration especially likely to be visible at times in groups composed of couples but which on occasion can surface and be important in other groups. The interested reader would find close discussion of these and larger potential subsystems in my earlier writing (Barrett-Lennard, 1975/76, pp. 69–70, and 1979a). Also, a related analysis and illustration of relational subsystems *in families* is given in the next chapter of this book.

Another dynamic that is prominent in some groups involves the emergence and working of *factions*. Factioning tends to start with a subset of members feeling significantly identified with each other and distinct from 'others' in the group. Those others, partly in reaction, may then feel a shared identity in contrast to the first subgroup. In an experiential group such factioning is likely to be recognised and explored as to its origins and meanings. Out of such exploration, the factioning may dissolve or change its form. One possibility is that members will come to see that their self-images and esteem are bound up with belonging in a particular 'like-me' reference group and *not* in another perceived category of people. Thus, the factioning dynamic and its working-through is another potential source of learning about one's own make-up and the wider working of relations between people.

One other process dynamic to mention, with application in many life contexts, is that of each individual's felt relationship with the group as a whole. Especially if a person is feeling stressed, worried or 'out on a limb' in some way, it is easy to feel that the surrounding others have a single collective judgement or feeling toward the person in focus. The 'myself-them' or 'me-to-all-of-you' relationship is something for members generally to work out and deal with in their own way. Almost all of us have had experiences of not belonging, and of feeling the need to somehow gain acceptance. We want, perhaps yearn, to be an accepted and valued partner in larger wholes and yet to be ourselves within these group wholes. In an intensive group these issues are 'grist for the mill' of exploration and further personal/interpersonal learning.

Beyond the many-layered between-person dimension so far discussed there is also *the process of the group whole.* From this further angle of view, the 'group' is a single entity or human relations system in motion. Besides being a whole to an outside observer, members themselves often refer to 'the/our group'. What features of the group can usefully be discriminated and how might one build a picture of this whole? A starting point is to think of the group as having its own kind of inherent features, ones that are not just the sum of individual or subsystem properties. But what salient features distinctively apply to a *group* and can be employed in distinguishing one group from another? As I pondered this question, three main dimensions particularly struck me (Barrett-Lennard, 1975/76, pp. 71–4).

First in mention is the *level of cohesion* of a group, how bonded or close-knit its membership is, the quality of 'we' feeling among members. Cohesion probably develops most strongly in full-time residential small-group workshops since contact is relatively continuous and within a shared total environment. In a group whose members are initially strangers to one another, cohesion starts almost from zero but may build rapidly and become stronger than in groups composed of persons who are already acquainted. In the latter case, the separate established relationships influence group qualities. Naturally, groups differ in how quickly cohesion develops, how much it oscillates, and the peak it reaches. Mention of speed of development brings to view a second main aspect:

Groups differ in their flow and visible energy, in the pace of interaction and in tendency to bursts of motion. *Tempo* is a convenient overall term for these elements of overt energy and motion. A group might be deftly on the go, or it may thrash about in nearly continual motion, it may tend to move deliberately in relatively slow and careful steps, or it may be quiet but intermittently very active, perhaps moving in staccato bursts. In a generally fast-paced group, there is little waiting for someone else to take the initiative, stillness is the exception and any silences may be filled with inner activity and preparation. It is possible for a generally more slow-moving group to be developing quite strongly, with occasional metamorphic shifts. Tempo and productivity can be high in the same group, but no simple or consistent correlation is expected. Nor is the further aspect of 'intensity' simply related to tempo.

Group intensity has to do with depth of emotional involvement and immediacy of communication. How freely and openly expressive members are of felt experience in the group bears directly on their group's intensity. There is some research suggesting that the predisposition of members to be personally trusting of others is a key to the intensity likely to be achieved (Wilkinson, 1972). The 'mix' of members and the setting and continuity of the group experience are likely to have bearing too. A group could be cohesive and generally active yet not highly intense.[3] Like tempo, intensity in the same group can vary widely within and between meeting sessions. Whether the highest intensity periods are the most memorable and valued depends on the purposes as well as openness of members, and on the developmental stage of the group.

These three highlighted features are not of course exhaustive of group qualities and differences. In simple form, they are encompassed, along with a range of other aspects, in a 'semantic differential' questionnaire that I invite members to answer periodically, in groups that I conduct. This rating form is included as an Appendix to this chapter (and readers who work professionally with groups are free to utilise it — with acknowledgement of my authorship on the form). Some of the items could in principle be rated in reference to individuals but all are readily applicable to a group.[4] Once the form is used initially, it takes members only two or three minutes to rate a session, and in my experience the data can be valuable for research (Barrett-Lennard, 1998, pp. 296–8) as well for the members' own monitoring of qualities and changes in their group.

I am aware of not having closely worked to delineate the way experiential groups tend to unfold — their 'natural history' of development. Although groups are unpredictable and distinct in detailed sequence, I do think that a broad regularity to this unfolding can be discerned, even where the members know each other beforehand and, most obviously, where they begin the group experience as strangers. Ariadne Beck's creative work on phases of group development is closely presented in my last book (1998, pp. 148 ff.) and Carl Rogers' original (1970) portrayal of 'steps' is outlined. My own corresponding perspective would have elements in common with both of these but not be the same as either.

Conclusion

In this chapter I have concentrated on group process. This process has consequences; effects that are implied in its nature or to be discovered in research.

---

[3] One result of Wilkinson's study (1972) was that groups tended to find their own optimum intensity level. When facilitated toward intensities discrepant from their preference and readiness, less growth seemed to occur than in cases where intensity and predisposition matched.
[4] Sometimes item 17 needs a little explanation, but it *can* have so much meaning that I have chosen to retain it.

This domain also needs approaching on more than one level. I think of intensive experiential groups as one kind or class of possible formative life episode (FLE), in the experience of members. There are a variety of such episodes in anyone's life. One FLE can open the door to another, or be a sequel to an earlier one. This way of thinking, the model of change it leads to, and its application in studying the experience of people who had taken part in residential experiential learning groups (and who later identified a broad range of personally very eventful or formative adult life experiences) are the focus of a chapter in my companion volume (Barrett-Lennard, 2003, Chapter 2). I commend that chapter (or a previous report — Barrett-Lennard, 1996) to the reader interested in a fresh way of thinking about outcomes of group experience, personal therapy, and many other kinds of developmental or life-changing experience.

In the case of experiential groups in particular I see five distinct kinds or levels of *potential* outcome. In a word, these include developments in interpersonal awareness and communication, in self-awareness and process, in enabling ability or skill, in social values and later action, and in effects beyond the worlds of individual members — for example, in their shared organisation or community. These kinds of effect (further spelled out in Barrett-Lennard, 1998, pp. 166–7) would occur in varied degree and balance according to the make-up, context and other particular circumstance of each group.

The process of a group mediates whatever change effects accrue from the group experience. I say 'mediate', not 'produce', because the latter could be taken to imply that the process in the group, itself, literally brings something into being. This, in my view, would be an over-simplification suggesting too much from one cause — and it would not fit the idea of interacting formative life episodes as pivotal influences in the flow of change (Barrett-Lennard, 2003, Chapter 2). I see the process that mediates change in turn, as depending in varied part on how the group is composed (who is in it, how many, the motivation, mix and variety of members), how it is convened, who leads it, where it takes place, its duration and whether 'full-time' or arranged with spaced meetings over a longer period. Again, the interested reader will find fuller exploration of these and related aspects of group context and structure in my previous book (1998, pp. 168–9).

In summing up the picture given here, I will adapt my words from another place: '*Typically, the experiential group has only a short history and life span, comes into being not to fulfil an external function but to meet learning-developmental needs of its members, develops continuously rather than stabilising, centres on process with little concern for structure, and tends to become close-knit and highly valued but without trying to preserve its short life beyond an arbitrary limit.*' Altogether, an unusual species! The next chapter explores another very distinctive and far more long-lived variety of small group, crucial in the relational and developmental life of almost all of us — the family.

Appendix to Chapter 6

Group Atmosphere Form

Your first name or code _____ Date and time _____

Please circle the scale point between each of the following pairs of opposite words that best describes your perception of the atmosphere and process in the **group**, during the session that you have just taken part in. If you wish, also place brackets to show the range of variation.

	Extremely	Quite	A little	Neither or both equally	A little	Quite	Extremely	
1. Active	+++	++	+	•	+	++	+++	Passive
2. Harsh	+++	++	+	•	+	++	+++	Gentle
3. Turbulent	+++	++	+	•	+	++	+++	Calm
4. Guarded	+++	++	+	•	+	++	+++	Trusting
5. Fast	+++	++	+	•	+	++	+++	Slow
6. Safe	+++	++	+	•	+	++	+++	Risky
7. Tense	+++	++	+	•	+	++	+++	Relaxed
8. Sensitive	+++	++	+	•	+	++	+++	Insensitive
9. False	+++	++	+	•	+	++	+++	Genuine
10. Deep	+++	++	+	•	+	++	+++	Shallow
11. Distant	+++	++	+	•	+	++	+++	Close
12. Caring	+++	++	+	•	+	++	+++	Hostile
13. Closed	+++	++	+	•	+	++	+++	Open
14. Stuck	+++	++	+	•	+	++	+++	Free-moving
15. Warm	+++	++	+	•	+	++	+++	Cold
16. Lively	+++	++	+	•	+	++	+++	Lethargic
17. Reactive	+++	++	+	•	+	++	+++	Responsive
18. Flowing	+++	++	+	•	+	++	+++	Static
19. Superficial	+++	++	+	•	+	++	+++	Searching
20. Intense	+++	++	+	•	+	++	+++	Muted/Subdue
....	+++	++	+	•	+	++	+++	....

Add some further dimension, or explain any rating, if you wish to.

Please go back and fill in the top line (name and date), if you have not done so.

Questionnaire form developed by Godfrey T. Barrett-Lennard, Ph.D.

Chapter 7

The family structure-relationship connection and learning world of children

My interest in the topic of this chapter stems partly from being one of seven children in my parents' family, from my wife and I having five children, and from these children and their partners having families of one or two children. Dramatic reduction in family size over the last couple of generations is a marker of our times in the Western world and in some further regions of vast population — notably including China. There are many reasons for this revolution, not least the dangers of world overpopulation. However, its impact on the relational life and interpersonal learning of children has received too little searching attention.

My fascination with small-group processes (reflected in the previous chapter), especially in self-development and therapy groups, evolved and flourished before I first focused on family process. Indeed, my systematic interest in this area rode on the back of a particular way of viewing the dynamics of small groups, centring on the between-person interaction and relationships. My first translation of this thought to the realm of family process dates from colloquium-style talks given in 1979–80, one of these while a visiting professor at Southern Illinois University. A SIU student chose to base his master's thesis on this work, using adapted forms of my Relationship Inventory, and his study was in turn a further stimulus for me.

In 1982, the First International Forum on the Person-Centered Approach was held in Mexico. The paper I contributed there grew out of my talk at SIU, and afterwards I revised it further for the edited volume by Levant and Shlien (1984). Later still, for another presentation, I shifted the balance — preserved here — to give increased attention to larger families, in contrast to small ones. In this chapter I take for granted that qualities of the parent-child relationship play a crucial part in childhood development. My analysis complements this familiar view.

My theme in this chapter, put broadly, is that the membership structure of a family has direct, major bearing on the kinds and variety of relationships that are possible and likely to be experienced by child members. The total make-up of members governs the potential avenues of a child's relationship experience and associated learning opportunities within the family. Especially, the aspect of family size and features linked to this central dimension, are seen to be of great consequence when viewed through a lens that is sensitive jointly to interactive systems and inner experience.

Family relationships increase exponentially in number and in kind with increase in family size. If, for example, a nuclear family with two parents doubles in number from three members to six, the potential range of quite distinct varieties of relationship, from the position of the first-born child, increases at least tenfold! My intention here is to closely trace this mushrooming of avenues, and to draw out some of its implications.

Family composition does not govern the qualities of particular relationship systems but determines the range and types of system that can have life in the experience of family members. Effectively, the approach to be presented blends experiential-phenomenological *and* structural systems ways of thinking. Each potential relationship system can be derived from knowledge of family structure but its reality and meaning needs also to be found in the experiencing of members and exists within a dynamic network of relations. A family member lives not only as an *I* or *Me* connected to other members one by one, but also (especially in larger families) within a diversity of *We's* relating to a spectrum of single and multiple *You's*.

The family relationship systems I will go on to distinguish rest on the model of 'A' in relation with 'B', where A can be one person (an *I* or *me*) or more than one (associated as 'We' and 'Us') and B also can be either one person (*you, him* or *her*) or more than one (plural *you, they* or *them*). All relationships and interactions are viewed as having this A-B form; although, for a given family member, several or many such relationships coexist, and particular interchanges have even greater variety. In the notation adopted, 'A' (written on the left or stated first) always includes the referent person, and is experientially an *I, me, us* or the equivalent. 'B' always represents the *you, him, her, they or them* side of the relationship. The exact scope and spectrum of available relationships will differ according to the position in the family of the member in focus.

The approach developed has not drawn directly on any pre-existing model although, after its initial formulation, I was interested to discover some points of intersection with the work of a handful of other investigators (Lindsay, 1976; Kantor and Lehr, 1975; Toman, 1976). The original stepping stones in my own thought include a theoretical article in the small-group field (Barrett-Lennard, 1979a) which in turn grew out of earlier work (Barrett-Lennard, 1975, pp. 67–71). Helping processes and theory in the group and family spheres are presented in breadth in my previous book (Barrett-Lennard, 1998, Chapters 8 and 9). An earlier passage on couple relationship systems links back to my immediate topic:

> The specific features of a couple's *we* system often include a characteristic style and quality of communication and distinctive landscape of topical content. Typically there is a climate of feeling

and attitude within which particular elements vary more or less predictably, spheres of mis-(or non-) understanding, eggshell regions and paths with firm stepping stones . . . A parental *we* dyad can be an open system or a very closed one . . . Mutual empathy, openness, and non-judgemental caring, stand out in the interplay of some We's and, by contrast, others exist in which the partners implicitly conspire to tear each other down, perhaps jointly feeling that victory or victimisation are the only alternatives (Barrett-Lennard, 1984, pp. 224–5).

Parent twosomes, effectively, are living entities with the dyadic equivalent of character and personality. Although each member contributes in crucial ways, the twosome which emerges is of a different nature than the component individuals, with its own distinct properties; properties that differ from any other dyad containing *one* of the same persons.

Children's perceptions of their parents' relation must differ over a vast range, and their experience of this relation in action is (for most children) an important axis of their lived world. Naturally, each parent is also experienced by the child in a one-to-one relationship. At times, for a child, it must be as though three others are present, each parent as a single and the parent couple as a pair, all speaking or interacting with different voices and attitudes. In the smallest intact family unit, these 'voices' correspond to the full range of You-to-Me relationships in the child's family.

The one-child, three-person family

This whole family is a triad. In our world of widely declining birthrates it is a major family configuration. Of course it is not the smallest intergenerational family unit since single-parent-and-one-child families exist and probably are rising in frequency. The total analysis advanced here is illustrative, not exhaustive, and will focus on two-parent families with one or more children who are still growing up. Also in the interests of comparison and manageability, I will view relationships primarily from the position of the first-born child. Readers with particular interest in another family position (perhaps that of a parent, or youngest child), or a differing constellation of members, would be able to apply the same principles to the composition of interest to them.

In the intact one-child family triad there is, to start with, the relationship with each parent. Formally stated, there is a same-sex (SS) and an opposite-sex (OS) intergenerational dyad, shown schematically within Figure 1-a. There are no other nuclear family twosomes of which the child is a member. In addition, there is one threesome, which from the child's position takes three distinct and likely forms:

1) The form I have already mentioned is the child's relation to the parent's own relationship dyad. Especially, the parents' communication with each other, the feelings between them, and their behaviours toward the child when involved with each other, will all influence the child member's experience of them in *plural You-Me* interactions. Figure 1-a shows the parent couple system as a curved dumbbell bar, and the child's relation with this twosome is represented by a straight line with a double arrowhead or stitch-like connection, at each end. P_m stands for the male parent and P_f the female.

2) A second kind of three-person process is a We-(single)You interaction (as in Figure 1-b). A young child is very likely to have experiences of 'mother-and-me' engaged together in interacting with the father. Afterward, there are likely to be episodes, perhaps growing in frequency, where the child is actively in a 'we space' with the father, interacting with the mother from within the father-child twosome. These relational interactions could vary in quality over a huge range: including protective alliances with one parent in frightening conflict with the other; situations of felt connection with one parent and then the other in which the child is a human bridge between two adults whose dyadic relation is stressed and conflictual; and experiences of a loving, sharing connection with the mother in a joyful reunion with the father, or a drawing together of one parent and the child in a goodbye parting from the other parent.

3) The third form of triadic relation I see emerges at moments of distinct experience of the family as one We or Us (Figure 1-c). The child would in some way be feeling the bondedness of all members, joined as one whole; 'my family'. Such strongly felt between-member bondedness and 'we' sense (leaving no one out) may arise with or without outsiders present. If they are present, the 'we' feeling could be partly an alliance against this presence, or it may flow positively from the larger relational ambiance.

In summary, the child member of the three-person family engages in a one-on-one relation with each parent and a different *I-you* relation with the parent twosome. The child also, and only, experiences *we-you* interchanges in which the *We* is cross-generational and the other parent is the *You*. Finally, some experiencing of a We composed of the whole family would occur at special positive moments where the 'I-self' fades into an inclusive sense of oneness. Alternatively, the emergent family-We could arise in facing alien outsiders or a common danger.

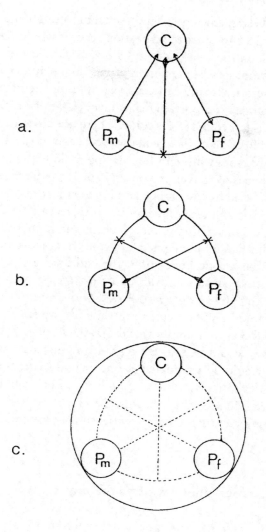

Figure 1: Schematic outline of relationships in the one-child family

Altogether, there are several distinct avenues of relational experience in the family with only one child, each varying greatly in quality from family to family. However, the advent of a second child magnifies and alters the first child's family world of relationship out of all proportion, as previously portrayed (Barrett-Lennard, 1984, pp. 228–34). This chapter complements that earlier analysis through a detailed exploration of the explosion in avenues of relationship and interpersonal learning when a family expands from three people to six, including two parents and four children. Only a limited part of the quantum leap involved applies in the four-person/two-child family.

In contemporary Western society, a family of four young children and their parents rates as large; two or three generations ago, it would have been considered modest, even on the small side. In China, at least in urban areas, indications are that enormous social pressure is placed on parents to have one child only. In Western settings, many couples *choose* to limit their families to two children, and a significant proportion delay having a family until a stage in life where one child is a favourable outcome. There are obvious, perhaps crucial, reasons for this direction of change in our world as a whole. But there is also another side, insufficiently brought out, having to do with the costs in human developmental terms of converging on very small-size families.

The nuclear family, often highly mobile and independent of one or both parents' families of origin, is still seen as the most critical setting for the social experience and learning of young children. It can be instructive to think about implications of one-child families, imagined as the norm and extended over several generations. In the second generation, the child (whose parents are only children) has no first cousins and no aunts or uncles in its parents' generation. As a *parent,* this child would mostly start with no prior experience of infants (as occurs in multi-child and communal family systems), and with memories of their childhood in a family world of adults only. By the third generation, near relatives would be limited to grandparents, and even those relationships probably would be attenuated as one or both parents followed work/career opportunities to new locations. Family bonding would be with adults only. This picture is in total contrast with the range and web of family relationships and learning-developmental potentialities for the child in a six-person family.

The four-child, six-person family

A change from one to four children brings a literal explosion in interpersonal avenues and systems. In portraying them, a convenient order is to start with twosomes and work up to the six-person relational systems.

Relationship twosomes

There is a *huge expansion of dyad relations* in the family of six, up from three (in a family of three) to 15. These twosomes now include three cases where the first child (C_1) pairs off with one or other sibling (C_2, C_3, or C_4), each a distinctive relationship experience. The age difference between C_1 and C_2 may be small enough (even zero) that the two children are experiencing much the same world together, and it may be large enough between the oldest and younger siblings that C_1 is an important secondary caregiver, protector or hero to C_3 or

C_4, and a bridge to the world of older children. Among four children the odds are quite high (about 87%) that both sexes will be represented, thus giving C_1 the experience of opposite-sex (or OS) sibling relations. There is a similar chance of a same-sex (SS) relationship experience.[1] It is *likely*, therefore, that C_1 will have the complementary potential advantages for developmental learning of relationships with both brother and sister siblings.

Triad relationships

Threesomes of *two* siblings and one parent constitute an important configuration unavailable in the one-child family. These occur in more than one form and a variety of possible cases. In one familiar form, C_1 and another sibling are relating as a pair to the mother *or* the father. A likely variant of this We-You (2-1) triad is a partnership of common cause in assertive or 'defending' response to the parent. Another variant of the same form would be an enjoyed play-partner experience between the two siblings, which the father or mother enters into without displacing either child or their ongoing interaction.

In a second possible kind of 2-1 form, C_1's We-partner is a parent and the You is a younger sibling. C_1 might, for example, be experiencing the parent as an ally in coping with a small brother or sister, or as a companion enjoying the behaviour of the small person. In a very possible I-You (1-2) situation, the 'you' engaging C_1 would be the youngest child-with-mother pair. Gender also could play a role in such engagements as in the case, for instance, of a girl reaching out and 'wanting in' but feeling rather excluded by a twosome of males representing both generations in her family. In another context and moment she might turn the tables in relation to either of these males via a We coalition that she is part of but they are not.

A further class of triad relationship now possible involves siblings only. This also has 2-1 and 1-2 alternatives, the former illustrated in Figure 2-a. The figure shows C_1 paired with each of the other siblings in a potential We linked to the third or fourth sibling. It is very likely that the 2-1 form of relational interaction will occur, and recur, in at least one of these combinations. If, for example, C_1 and C_2 are often or strongly involved together as *we* and *us*, the age-removed youngest child is likely to be the *you* member in one variant of

---

[1] Since each of C1 through C4 could be a boy or a girl there are 2^4 or 16 possible order configurations of gender. These include an all boy sequence and an all girl sequence, and 14 mixed gender sequences, any of the latter ensuring at least one OS relationship for C1. Similarly, given that C1 is a boy (or a girl), eight configurations of the remaining siblings are possible, only one of the eight being a run of three of the opposite sex. Thus there is also an 87% chance of one or more same-sex (SS) dyads being open to C1, in the four-child family.

this triad. Alternatively, C_1 and C_4 may be far enough apart in age and role in the family for there to be little competition and positive grounds for them to slip easily into a complementary twosome — engaging with a third child who is reacting to their interplay with each other.

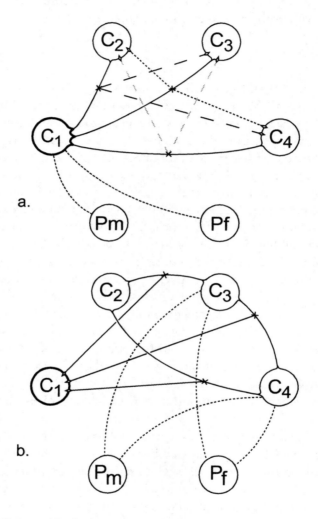

a.

b.

Figure 2: Triad relationships with siblings, in a six-person family.
We-You relations (a) and I-You relations (b)

In a 1-2 form of triad relation among the siblings the paired 'other' could well be C_3C_4 (the two youngest); although two other combinations are possible (see Figure 2-b). Possibly, the dual other would be same-sex and opposite in sex to C_1, and age differences and other factors would combine in helping to determine whether the system was an occasional occurrence or a readily triggered and consequential one for C_1. Or, the dual 'you' could simply be the two most visibly bonded others who are inclined to react jointly to C_1, who feels on the outer when they are engaged with one another.

Thus, C_1 in the six-person family is very likely to engage in a number of types of triad relation different from any in the three-person family. Each form of triad, within a particular family context, has its own distinct potentiality in regard to experience and learning. Significant experience in threesomes of varied composition and kind can itself help to prepare the child for their wider social world.

Foursome relationships

The experience of four-person interaction and relationship cannot, of course, occur at all within a one-child nuclear family. In *two-child* families it may assume importance, although its forms (such as kids versus parents) have to involve the whole family (see Barrett-Lennard, 1984, pp. 230–3: figure and text). I see three basic kinds of four-person relation or 'quadral': double-pair (2-2) configurations, I-You (1-3) interactions, and We-You (3-1) forms. I will focus especially on the double-pair combinations, interesting in their own right and a means to further illustrate how to map out and visualise all the possibilities.

Being always alone (within the one-child family) in relating to the adult parent twosome, as against having a sibling to be in off-and-on alliance with when engaging with this powerful pair, clearly are very different situations. Complementing this allies-in-opposition mode, is the situation of parents delighting *together* in seeing a twosome of their children jointly absorbed in play or exploration of their world. If C_1, while absorbed with C_2, senses the parents' shared response then a 2-2 dynamic is present experientially. As further example, a gender-based pattern could take the form (where the children are of both sexes) of a mother-daughter versus son-father We-You experience.

Altogether the four-child family has a wealth of options for 2-2 interactions and relationship systems. As seen in Figure 3-a, if the We/Us pair is C_1C_2 there are six other *possible* twosomes (including P_mP_f) to form a You engaging with Us. The same scope applies if the We consists of C_1P_m or C_1P_f. If C_1C_3 comprise the We (Figure 3-b), again there are six possible You pairs to combine in a distinctive foursome. The same applies if C_1C_4 form the We (perhaps in an easy oldest-youngest connection). While there is no magic to the numbers alone, they reflect manifold potentialities that do not exist or occur only in limited range in smaller families.

There is an equally large number (30!) of different *possible* combinations of members through which 3-1, We-You experiences could now occur. These include an all-sibling alternative, a three-sibling We engaging with a parent, a

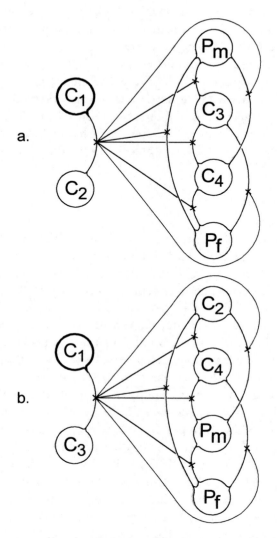

Figure 3: Illustration of We-You, double pair configurations
in the six-person family.

two-sibling-plus-parent We in joint engagement with the other parent, and a We of the two parents and a sibling (perhaps the oldest, C_1) in shared involvement with another child member (possibly C_4). The 'We' trio in any such interaction is complex itself, and there may at any moment be an element of We-You feeling within the threesome, as well as an overriding sense of the conjoint 'we' when the fourth person is being most distinctly experienced as the 'other'/You. A crisis of conflict with this other might produce a strong sense of 'we', which dissolves again when the conflict ends. Equally, the experienced We could arise in a positive feeling instance, such as sharing in expectant preparation and response to the member in focus as You during a birthday celebration for them.[2]

A You threesome could involve two other siblings and a parent, and additional combinations are possible in keeping with the picture already given. Although, for C_1, there is a single case only of the all-sibling form (C_1-$C_2C_3C_4$), episodes of this 1-3 pattern, and even a continuing sense of it for C_1 as the oldest child, appear likely. This situation may be amplified by age and/or sex combinations that set C_1 apart, or by C_1 being in the position of alternative caregiver to his/her younger siblings. It is not essential for the younger children to be feeling a strong 'we' sense themselves for C_1 to experience and interact with them as a joint 'you'.

Quintet and (whole family) sextet relationship systems

In terms of potential I/We-You relations, the basic configurations involving five and six persons are 1-4, 2-3, 3-2 and 4-1, and 1-5, 2-4, 3-3, 4-2, and 5-1. Are these unwieldy-looking variants just abstract possibilities, or are they likely to be represented in C_1's experience? Let us look at some of them more closely, starting with patterns that involve a one-many or many-one relation.

There is one case only of the 1-5 alternative, in which C_1 experiences his/her relation with the rest of the family, felt as a whole but rather undifferentiated 'you' or 'they', reacting to 'me'. The potential quality of this dynamic, of course, would be extremely diverse. Apropos of one example, exclusion is a form of interaction that is likely to fall at some point within the family experience of most children. Feeling the odd person out in a large family would tend to be a painful or demoralising experience, but has more positive learning potential if felt re-inclusion happens through some clear process. The mirror image 5-1 subform, where one sibling or one parent is experienced as a single You, involved with a complex Us felt to include everyone else in the family, may tend to be a fleeting pattern. For it to be a recurring system, a single member probably needs to be seen as very different or deviant in an active and powerful sense.

---

[2] In a related instance in my own family, four of our adult children and a daughter-in-law hatched a plot to give my wife and me a special wedding anniversary surprise. Came the day, one daughter took us out to a riverside haunt while the others 'got the house ready'. On returning we had a leisurely meal, viewed family slides and then wandered out into the back garden near our ailing swimming pool — where finally the surprise dawned: a big new pool filter miraculously installed in our absence. An impromptu photo shows the fivesome girdled with a big ribbon from the gift, together enjoying the 'miracle' they had wrought and our astonished pleasure. The five-person We was itself emergent from a diversity of relationships, visible at other moments.

The most obvious case of a 1-4, I-You experience has a parent, rather than C_1 in the 'I' position, since the parent is likely to have distinct experiences of felt engagement with all the children as a collective. In a 4-1 subform, there is an all-sibling We that has coalesced, say, in a situation of sharp conflict with a parent — where numbers could be a vital factor in feeling safety or control. In an example of positive ambiance, such as a celebration centred on one parent, C_1 might well experience 'all of us kids' as a single 'we' jointly initiating, giving, receiving, delighting in or otherwise feeling together, in relation to 'Mum' or 'Dad'. In another possibility, a pair-pair interchange (maybe a game, with two siblings on each side) shifts into a single sense of 'we' when a parent enters the scene and becomes a focal You responsive to the children's engagement with each other.

In other potential subforms, one parent is on each side of the We-You relation. Recognisable instances include those of a We joined in anxious concern for the other parent, or even a We that is huddled in fear of the second parent. In a further variant, both parents are included within the 'We', and the child 'You' is actively experienced in some distinctive way. In one kind of 2-4 alternative, C_1 has such a strong bond with a particular other member that it tends to hold the rest of the family in a collective 'you', 'they', etc., position.

In the hurly-burly of family life, interaction patterns may be constantly shifting. Those I have been discussing would tend to have lines of cleavage, both forming from and reducing to smaller systems. These smaller relational systems tend to be significant and even complex in their own right, as already discussed. Specifically, from the position and experience of C_1, any of the multi-person We clusters could be at other moments an A-B relationship by itself. It is evident from considering the larger systems that the same subsets of members would relate and interact in varied contexts.[3]

The family of six is also one whole. Distinctly experiencing this inclusive whole, almost as an enlargement of self and with a sense of individuality receding into the background, rests on a temporary subjective fusing of the variety and difference among family members and relationships that are keenly experienced at other times. For C_1 in a given family, such experiences of a oneness with all may be rare and precious *or* more taken-for-granted. In another family, the

---

[3] The remaining (3-3) subform would involve the complex situation of interaction between a pair of threesomes. As example, the We group could be the three older siblings (perhaps all of the same sex, all in school and/or more similar to one another than to C_4 in age and interests) and the You group consist of the parents and youngest child (for whom they have protective affection). In an opposite form of pairing, C_1's We would contain both parents, leaving the three other siblings in the 'you/they' camp. In the remaining variant, a parent would be in each of the numerically balanced 'we-you' groups, possibly each group of the same sex.

experience may be wished-for but happen only in fantasy, or it might scarcely be imagined. In any case, experience on this level could have significant bearing on C_1's sense of communal belonging in other life contexts — how strong it tends to be, its particular quality, and what triggers or prevents it.

Relationships in the six-person family: Summing-up

This outline of relationship avenues in six-person families, viewed here from the oldest child's position, could be adapted to focus on any family member or extended beyond the nuclear family. At the level of dyad relationships, the distinctively striking feature is the range and diversity of sibling engagements, typically including both OS and SS relationships. Triad relations can include 1-2 (I-You) and 2-1 (We-You) combinations in which all members are siblings, as well as varied parent-child combinations. Foursome relations are in the picture, with a great range of possibilities. These include double-pair and other I/We-You forms composed of siblings. With inclusion of one or both parents in the quartet, a wide range of distinct subforms, most with a variety of possible 'cases', are encompassed. Quintet systems can now appear, including 1-4, 2-3, 3-2 and 4-1 I(We)-You forms and a host of specific 'choices' of member composition. Relationship systems made up of the entire family include at least five basic configurations and a variety of subforms and cases.

Among the very numerous possible member combinations and configurations of relation, some would be infrequent or transient interactions. Many others would be established in pattern and quality as relationship systems. Context can be of great importance to the interior process of relationship. The same two or three members that form a distinct We in a whole family interaction (say) may on their own be a complex I-You relationship system. The qualities of twosomes and triads are influenced by wider dynamics in the family and feed into those dynamics. For a given person in his/her family, no relationship system merely duplicates another, in its experiential-process features. Each has unique values (or liabilities), and is a distinctive avenue for aspects of interpersonal learning and development of meaning.

Clearly, in larger families generally, relationships are of great range in kind and formidable complexity in total mosaic; their working entails a broad and subtle diversity of transitions from active engagement in one relationship to another and then a third, often overlapping in membership; and the same compositional patterns come in a great variety of qualities. In particular, the six-person family potentially contains enormous riches for children (and adults), and the possibility also of torturous relational systems and dysfunctional learnings. The *territory* of its potency is on an altogether different scale from that of the smaller families.

Concluding discussion and implications

A concept of favourable parenting is not a focus of this analysis but is part of its background (Barrett-Lennard, 1998, pp. 192–8). In particular, the ability of parents to connect with their child with an openness and sensitivity to the child's feelings and world of meaning, while also giving genuine expression to experience of their own, is assumed to be of vital importance in the parent-child relation. Parents also need to be able to express their own stance (with caring perceptiveness) regarding behaviours dangerous to the child him/herself or deemed destructive to others. Clear response of this kind, desirably, would not entail any censure of the child's *feelings* or belittling of their awareness. The view advanced in this chapter vitally complements an emphasis on parent attitudes. It implies that, even with parental disposition and attitude held largely constant, children in families that differ in size and linked features of composition live in vastly different interpersonal-relational worlds. In a word, numbers matter in families, especially in the variety of relational experience that can happen and the learnings that result.

For the potential advantages of larger families to be realised, I would expect personal qualities of the parents and their relationship to be of greatest importance during the earlier life of the family. However, from the position that learning and development continues through the life cycle, and that having children is a very formative experience *for parents*, effects of their own experiential learning can flow forward into their children's *adult* lives and relations with grandchildren.

I do not mean to imply that nuclear families are self-contained. The context of a larger kinship system, and any other communities of belonging in which the family had its being, may affect the very structure of the family, the qualities of relation within it, and the patterns of linkage beyond itself. How long a family remains intact, whether there is loss or 'addition' of a parent (or of a child member), the experience of the children outside the family, and whether outside engagements work to 'expand' and connect the family or to isolate it, are among many factors with bearing on the specific unfolding and quality of relationship patterns within the avenues indicated. As children mature and relationships evolve within a family, cause and consequence are hard to distinguish, and the same events often can be seen in either light. Indeed, linear views of causation obscure more than they illuminate as the interpersonal systems within a family evolve, multiply and develop their own dynamisms and character.

A family has properties as a whole, as a network of interwoven subsystems in motion and, finally, as a group of conscious active persons who are not merely recipients of influence but architects of meaning and choice. Choices, however, occur generally within some given context. For children, the composition of their families is seen to be a hugely important 'given'. The engagement systems that emerge from this composition are formative for children through a powerful mix of opportunity (for relationship) and necessity (for engagement).

This approach to analysis of family relations and their likely effects remains to be further tested in practice and research contexts. Although influenced by my therapy experience it has not grown step by step from practice observation but more from an unfolding direction of thought — with some leaps along the way. I would be glad to hear from readers who find that the approach helps to inform their thinking, whether about their own families or in their professional work. The perspective also has implications for social policy development and education as it relates to families and their functions in society. Varied lines of research could flow from or connect with this system of thought. The examples that occur to me include the following:

- My Relationship Inventory (Chapter 8) and perhaps other existing measures of experienced relation and communication, could be adapted for the study of relationship configurations and profiles in families of varied composition and background. A beginning to such work, studying 1-1, 1-2, and whole-family relations in intact one- and two-child families, has been made (Gomes, 1981; Barrett-Lennard, 1984, pp. 238–9).

- A related focus would be to discover and test ways to systematically identify the particular relationship systems (especially the more complex systems, in four-person and larger families) that family members can and do discriminate as recurring and eventful.

- Empirical research exploration of ways in which variety of relational experience in families beneficially prepares children for other life relations would further anchor and help to refine my present theoretical-descriptive analysis.

- Comparison of larger families (1) in which there is much repetition and recycling of a limited band of interactive processes, with those (2) in which a far wider range of the potential relational systems is manifestly active, is suggested as another potentially illuminating focus of investigation.

- In the sphere of therapy research, the thought advanced here could open a new window to discovery-oriented investigation of the interior relational life of families before and after family therapy. The results of such work could simultaneously throw further light on the theory and on therapy outcomes.

I would be pleased to see an interested reader take up any of these lines of research, or to develop another focus of inquiry that is in some way stimulated by the perspective advanced here. This is a point of closure for me, on this chapter, except for a broader final remark. The family has been the basic social microcosm in which new human life generally begins and most formatively develops. Population pressures, altering lifestyles and the explosion of knowledge in biological and medical sciences, are already having a very big impact on the forms and role of families. In fact, the family in any forms we are used to may well be on trial for its existence. At the least, continuing change and new variations are sure to occur. If the 'window' offered here contributes to understanding the interior process and discriminating the functions of families, large and small, then it may also assist in preserving what well-functioning families achieve. The functions at issue involve primary processes of human bonding and developmental learning with the potential to position children for lives of active and fulfilling connection.

Chapter 8

Measuring experienced relationship:

An odyssey (1957–2003)

Sometimes, when I look back, it amazes me that the longest-continued and one of the best-known strands in my professional journey pivots on a questionnaire instrument designed to measure qualities of interpersonal presence and response in a relationship. It does not estimate trust *directly but hones in on equally subtle qualities, which the person answering the questionnaire may not discriminate even though his or her own perceptions provide the entire data for the resulting measures. Each of four scales rests on a theoretical definition, a definition that is a best attempt to capture the essential nature and process of the phenomenon it refers to. Its complex essence is tapped through answers to a range of brief statements. The result of putting these answers together yields an estimate of the defined quality. The* measure *is not the phenomenon itself, and needs to be viewed warily, in light of all the steps and assumptions entailed. Ultimately, credibility lies in the fruits of such measurement.*

This chapter is the story of how this Relationship Inventory (RI) *questionnaire began, the form it took, its linkage to the core of person-centred thought, its role in my own professional journey in touch with a wide diversity of other users, what has been accomplished and how the Inventory itself has evolved with new forms and potentials. This story, however, looks forward as well as back and, through this tracing works to illuminate a path of ideas and unfolding possibilities and meaning. My aim is to give a personalised but substantive account that I hope can interest readers not engaged in research as well as those who are.*

Rogers' conditions of therapy theory (1957) was both a starting point and a culmination. It was the first systematic, full-fledged and testable theory of therapeutic change, a theory that burst on the psychotherapy scene with almost transformative impact. The ideas he articulated were not new to Rogers himself. The shape of the answer he had been searching for was stated over ten years earlier, when he first spoke carefully of certain conditions needing to be met in order to initiate and carry forward a therapeutic process with predictable outcomes (Rogers, 1946). The ideas continued to work in his thought (Rogers, 1953, 1954) in ways that moved ever more closely toward his 1957 formulation. Thus, for Rogers himself this statement was not a beginning but a consummation in expressing a perspective in which he felt, by then, a great deal of personal confidence. The theory boldly posits the essential change-producing factors in psychotherapy generally, not only in the author's own client-centred approach.

Underlying concepts and broad approach

The factors or 'conditions' Rogers advanced pivot on qualities of the therapist-client relationship. One condition refers to an attribute of the client, namely, that he or she needs to enter therapy 'in a state of incongruence, being vulnerable or anxious' (Rogers, 1957, p. 96). Moving from incongruence to relative congruence was viewed by Rogers as being at the core of healing change in therapy.[1] However, the casting of client incongruence and its expressions *as a prerequisite condition of therapy* did not become a focus of research — in contrast to the main relationship conditions. Another of the posited requirements is the very general one that the client and therapist need to be 'in psychological contact', implying that they are aware of one another and that their association is the vehicle of change. Since further relationship features require and imply this general condition, it too was not singled out for research.[2]

Rogers' other four conditions are qualities of therapist response and client perception. The therapist needs (i) to be essentially congruent (authentic, genuine, integrated) in the relationship with the client; (ii) to be 'experiencing unconditional positive regard for the client', and (iii) to be 'experiencing an empathic understanding of the client's internal frame of reference'. The final condition is that aspects (ii) and (iii) need to be communicated and *perceived by* the client (Rogers, 1959a). Rogers said 'communicated' in 1957 but soon thereafter stressed that the client's perception was the crucial factor. He also acknowledged that although he described the conditions as if present or absent, they can be seen to exist in varying degree over a wide range. By that time, the first studies to test the theory were in progress — by Halkides (1958) (using judge ratings) and myself. I came to be involved in this ground-breaking work mid-way through an extremely formative several-year period studying with Rogers and others at the University of Chicago.

In fact, Rogers unveiled his exciting theory (pre-publication, in 1956) at precisely the point that I was seriously on the lookout for a topic for my doctoral

---

[1] This is implied in the 1957 paper and spelled out explicitly in Rogers' broader statement of theory (1959), already available pre-publication when the 1957 paper came out.

[2] Prouty's work, much later (e.g., 1994), brought this aspect into strong focus. Finding and implementing ways to *make contact* with regressed schizophrenic clients is treated as a major phase of the helping endeavour, and a precondition for other relationship conditions to develop.

thesis. I at once wanted to test the theory, with actual clients in therapy. But how might this be done, in practice, and (in particular) how could I measure the therapist-to-client relationship qualities? There were no established scales, and it would be necessary to invent them, along with some further sharpening of the theory to bring it into testable form. My approach rested on the core idea that it is not what a helper does, as viewed from the outside by an impartial observer, but how *the client* experiences the helper's response that has direct effect and, thus, would be most strongly linked to the outcome of therapy. The quality of the therapist's inner and expressed empathic recognition and other responsive experience would contribute to the way s/he was perceived and, thus, would be related to outcome indirectly.[3] I decided to focus on the pivotal perspective of the client, supplemented by the therapist's own inside view of his/her response.

My aim, in short, was to tap each partner's perspective to yield perception-based measures of the relationship conditions, and I included the client's (and therapist's) experience of the therapist's congruence as a relationship condition. Rogers' complex concept of unconditional positive regard (UPR) defied careful treatment as a unitary dimension. In the end, I separated it into two distinct variables named 'level of regard' and 'unconditionality'. A further relationship variable called 'willingness to be known' was initially included, but my results for this aspect were ambiguous and it was dropped as a separate scale.[4]

The initial plan called for collection of relationship and outcome/change data for my study, from a sizable sample of clients and their therapists. The collection of these data would take considerable time and resources, and the supply of clients available for research was far from inexhaustible. The research committee responsible for determining practicalities and priorities decided that the plan was not feasible, and that its promise was uncertain to boot, and I still have on file a letter right afterward from Rogers expressing his regret and concern for my predicament. It seemed that my whole research dream would founder. However, I'm fairly stubborn (as reflected in getting to Chicago), consulted various colleagues and cast around for some way of moving ahead with the essentials of the project — and a way was found. Another large and ambitious study, informally named the Change Project (Barrett-Lennard, 1998, pp. 248–50), was just starting. The planned sample was considerably bigger than I needed, it would include highly experienced and relatively inexperienced therapists (as needed also for my study) and I could select from a pool of outcome test data. Gathering the RI

---

[3] Imagine two clients with identical characteristics and situations. In this hypothetical case, differences in the inner/outer response of their therapists would be wholly responsible for the different client perceptions and, thus, for differences in outcome (Barrett-Lennard, 1962a, p. 3).

[4] Some elements from the 'willingness to be known' concept and scale (item) content were absorbed into and enriched the congruence dimension.

data from clients and their therapists would be the main addition to what was already planned. This was agreed to, and probably worked out as well or better than my original plan.

After electing to call on the client and therapist partners to provide the measurement data, the question remained of what was the best feasible form of instrument. I was already amassing groups of item statements, each group bearing on one of the conditions variables. In the course of this exercise, the concepts themselves sharpened further in my own mind. The process of deciding how to structure the Relationship Inventory (RI), and the main steps in its development are on record (especially, in Barrett-Lennard, 1962a and 1986). Suffice it to say that I finally opted for a fairly straightforward multiple-choice questionnaire format, in which half of the items were worded positively (for example, 'He/she respects me'), and half negatively ('His/her response to me is usually so fixed and automatic that I don't really get through'). Each item is answered 'Yes' (but with three choices, from a strong Yes to 'probably true') or 'No' (also with a choice of three levels). Every statement, however answered, adds to or subtracts from the score on one of the four component scales. I worked from the start to refine and carefully define the four variables tapped by the RI, since such clarity was part of validating the measures. These definitions bear repeating concisely:

1. *Empathic understanding* was conceived from the start to be an active process, not just a reflective mirroring. It was taken to involve a *desire* to closely engage with and know the other's experience and to *reach out* to receive their feeling communication and meaning. Empathy is viewed as a basic form of knowing which entails a disciplined opening of self to the living feelings and meanings of the other. Even at points of strongest resonation, however, the empathising partner retains background awareness that the feelings and flow of consciousness expressed are originating in and belong to the separate other person. My later view of empathic interaction as a multi-step process was closely described in Chapter 4. The initial phase of empathic resonation and awareness occurs in the *listener's* consciousness, and the corresponding RI is the 'myself-to-the-other' (MO) form, originally developed for the therapists to answer. An illustrative item is 'I usually sense or realise how he/she is feeling'. In the ('other-to-self', or OS) form, which the *listened-to person* answers, this item reads 'He/she usually senses or realises what I am feeling'. In this form the empathy scale taps the experience of being understood, or Phase 3 empathy.

2. Many qualities and strengths of one person's feelings and attitudes in relation to another weigh in to constitute overall *level of regard*. Positive feelings include respect, caring, appreciation, affection, and others. Negative feelings include dislike, disapproval, expressed indifference, impatience, contempt, and the

like. Thus, level of regard combines all of the direct feeling reactions of one person toward another, positive and negative, into one abstract dimension. However, the scale does not reach into the *most* negative zone of possible feelings (hatred, loathing, or extreme fear and aversion) that can arise between persons. Nor, at the positive extreme, does it directly tap strong romantic, filial, or spiritual love experience. For practical purposes, scores right at the 'bottom' end of the theoretical range do not occur, and very rarely (even in closest personal relationships) is the most positive rating given to every scale item.

3. The aspect of *unconditionality* in its positive expression implies that A's personal attitude or feeling toward B holds steady regardless of what B shows of his/her inner self and its experiencing. A's attitude does not swing around according to the particular self-revelations, feeling reactions or other self-expressions of B. Conversely, conditionality implies that A's regard does vary according to the light that B shows him/herself in, or to differing qualities that s/he spontaneously expresses (Barrett-Lennard, 1978, 1986). Acquired 'conditions of worth' (also see next chapter) imply a *self*-judgemental attitude and rejection of some aspects of self. If a client finds their therapist empathic and unjudging, even in the most conflictual areas of inner felt experience, then 'self-conditional' attitudes gradually can soften and open to allow a fuller self into consciousness.

4. *Congruence* refers broadly to wholeness, integration, inner consistency. More exactly, it implies consistency between the three levels of (1) a person's primary, preverbal or 'gut' experience, (2) their inner known or symbolic consciousness, and (3) their outward behaviour and communication. Consistency between the first two of these levels is pivotal but cannot be tapped very directly. This level of consistency enables congruence between levels 2 and 3 — inner awareness and outward communication. Outer congruency does not mean *total* communication of awareness. The crucial feature is that the person is not dissembling; what they say is not in conflict with their inner consciousness. As I put it originally, 'the highly congruent individual is completely honest, direct, and sincere in what he conveys, but he does not feel any compulsion to communicate his perceptions, or any need to withhold them for emotionally self-protective reasons' (Barrett-Lennard, 1962a, p. 4). In therapy, qualities such as the therapist's perceived genuineness, transparency, and honesty with her/himself and the client, are of vital relevance.

The instrument evolving: Form and content

The Relationship Inventory has held to the same essential structure through the evolution of its specific forms and revisions. No sooner had the original research begun to yield clearly positive results than the instrument came into demand for further studies, including the Wisconsin study of psychotherapy with schizophrenic clients (finally published in book form, by Rogers et al., 1967). While I continued to try out longer versions (including one with a scale of 'availability' replacing 'willingness to be known') the first main revision included 18 interspersed items in each of the four present scales. It came in variants worded for a male other (e.g., 'He respects me') and female other ('She respects me'), and was used in most studies over the next few years. From first development of the RI, I had the idea of extending its use to the study of relationships other than those between client and therapist (the *items* never had therapist-specific wording) and this broadened application began almost at once and developed strongly in the 1960s (Barrett-Lennard, 1986, pp. 463–5 and 468; 1998, pp. 307–9; 2002b, pp. 37–8). A moderately simplified version for pre-adult respondents was also prepared, and used by Emmerling (1961), van der Veen and Novak (1971) and others. On finishing my doctorate in Chicago, I moved to the contrasting world (in 1959) of Auburn, Alabama and some of the early RI studies were by graduate students there (including Emmerling, as mentioned; Rosen, 1961; and Thornton, 1960).

My doctoral thesis did not report on the therapist RI data or go into all other features of the whole ambitious study. As expressed elsewhere, 'I feel singularly fortunate that the conditions of my doctoral work helped me to *want* to continue my research afterwards, that an NIMH (US National Institute of Mental Health) 'small grant' was forthcoming, and that there was real encouragement from colleagues in Chicago, Wisconsin, Auburn, and then Australia' (1986, p. 467). I formally wrote up the whole project in Australia and submitted the long report in one piece (against advice from experienced colleagues) to *Psychological Monographs*. The Editor accepted the full article without revision and it was dated the same year (1962) as submitted.

The initial RI revision (72 items) inherited several awkwardly phrased items and some imbalance of positively and negatively worded statements, and in its length and wording was still not ideally suited to its growing use in the study of life relationships. A new 64-item revision, completed in 1964, was the version sent from then on, in response to the flow of requests from other investigators. A periodically updated 'technical note' accompanied the revised Inventory, supplementing my 1962 monograph. A complete report on the revision, detailing among other things an unorthodox but serviceable study of how each item behaved in several data samples, was published much later (1978).

In the 64-item RI, eight positively worded items and eight that are negatively worded represent each of the four scales. As in earlier versions, respondents select from three grades of 'yes' of different strength, and three grades of 'no' in answer to each item. A 'yes' to a negatively worded item has the opposite direction and meaning to the same answer in a positively worded item (and this is true also for a 'no'). All answers, of either positive or negative valence, count toward one or other scale score. (The whole scoring rationale and method are most fully detailed in my mentioned 1986 report.) Illustrative items from the 64-item OS RI form, one positively worded and one framed negatively for each RI scale, are listed below. Letters added in the margin stand for Level of Regard (R+ and R-), Empathic Understanding (E+ and E-), Unconditionality (U+ and U-), and Congruence (C+ and C-). Respondents are asked to mentally insert the name of the other person in the underline space in each item.

R+   37.   _____ is friendly and warm toward me.

R–   33.   _____ just tolerates me.

E+   30.   _____ realises what I mean even when I have difficulty in saying it.

E–   58.   _____'s response to me is usually so fixed and automatic that I don't get through to him/her.

U+   51.   Whether thoughts and feelings I express are 'good' or 'bad' makes no difference to _____'s feeling toward me.

U–   11.   Depending on the way I am, _____ has a better (or worse) opinion of me sometimes than at other times.

C+   12.   I feel that _____ is real and genuine with me.

C–   52.   There are times when I feel that _____'s outward response to me is quite different from the way he/she feels underneath.

The MO form of the RI — originally the 'therapist' form — preserves the substance of each item, reworded for self-reference. For example, the second to last item, above, becomes 'I feel that I am genuinely myself with _____'. In general, each member of a twosome can describe their relationship from at least three angles: their own response to the other, the other person's response to them, and their view of the relationship as a whole. (Also, either could try to predict the other's perception, as I will later mention.) In therapy studies, attention has centred on the therapist's response as perceived by the client. The therapist's own sense of his/her response has received minimal (and insufficient) attention. In couple relationships, the views of self and other by *both* partners, and the multiple comparisons these generate — such as her response to him as *he* sees it and as *she* sees it herself; or, his view of her response compared with her view of his — are all pertinent features to study.

A reliable measure should yield a very similar result each time, if what is being measured has not changed. The way a relationship is experienced, even if long-established, it is not likely to hold completely steady. However, there is extensive evidence of more than adequate stability of measurement, in the case of the RI scales — based on test and retest data and other estimations of reliability. Gurman (1977, Table 1) compiled test-retest reliability correlations from ten samples from which the coefficients, when averaged for each scale, are .80 and above. Internal reliabilities, also calculated from the further span of results Gurman reports, yield an average coefficient across all four scales of .84. The results imply that the RI scale measures are stable and cohesive.

The careful theoretical grounding and various steps in preparation and revision of the RI, together with the high reliabilities obtained, augur well for validity of measurement. A range of more direct evidence has accumulated and been documented in previous reports (most fully in Barrett-Lennard, 1986). Besides reliability data concerning the instrument itself (Gurman, 1977, p. 513), a variety of significant predictive studies have yielded results in keeping with theoretical expectation — especially in the case of the client/OS forms. Other kinds of evidence also bear on the issue of validity (1986, pp. 458–62). One kind involves studies outside the context of therapy in which an independent criterion of relationship quality was available. (As instance, experienced relationships have been compared for couples seeking help versus couples not showing distress (Wampler and Powell, 1982)). However, the considerable evidence of working validity of the RI does not imply to me that it is a perfect instrument, that it should not be tested in new ways, or that it should not be altered in any circumstance.

Desire by some investigators for a shorter version of the RI, especially for use in survey-type studies, led me eventually to produce a 40-item form with ten items in each scale. (The domain of each variable is not tapped in as many different ways with ten items as it is with 16, and reliabilities may be a little lower. I prefer the longer version but the indications are this one is also satisfactory.) As my own thinking about relationships has evolved, so has the RI in terms of more distinctive adaptations. The regular forms focus on one person at a time in a relationship, but each partner can also look at their twosome as a whole (for example, 'We respect one another as persons', and 'We understand each other'). Also, an acquainted third person could provide their 'observer' view of A's response to B (e.g., 'He respects her') or of the twosome ('They respect each other'). Another possibility is to ask A to predict how *B will see* A's response, and to compare this with B's actual perception of A's response.

RI research on the therapy process

My original study, the Wisconsin research, and a spread of other investigations have used the RI in actual therapy contexts. Over 50 such studies are listed in an accumulating bibliography of research using the RI (Barrett-Lennard, 2001a). Interested readers will find concise accounts of the original research in my last book (1998, pp. 264–7) and an even later report (Barrett-Lennard, 2002b, pp.

34–5). Suffice it to mention here that the total sample consisted of 42 clients and their 21 therapists, and that the mean duration of therapy was 33 interviews. The principal RI data were gathered after five interviews and, generally, the client-derived RI scores significantly predicted the therapy outcome indices used; and were higher in relationships with more expert therapists than with a less expert group working with a matched group of clients. Clients of the more expert therapists also changed more. The trend of results using therapist-derived RI scores was in the same direction but not as strong, in keeping with the theory that client perceptions are more directly related to outcome.

The Wisconsin investigators were not able to gather all of the needed RI and change data from their schizophrenic clients, which hampered predictive features of the study. These difficulties, and the results that were obtained, are also discussed in the sources mentioned above. Another of the more visible, large-scale and carefully planned investigations was the long-running comparative study of therapies with depressed clients, conducted through the US National Institute of Mental Health (Elkin, 1994). In a principal report drawing on the RI data gathered in this study, Blatt et al. (1996) concluded that the quality of the therapist-client relationship was a more relevant and better predictor of outcome than the formal type of therapy — although each type had been conducted consistently by experts trained to do so.

The practical and ethical complexities of conducting research with troubled clients who have come for help, together with the preference by many investigators for more controlled investigation, has led to a proliferation of 'therapy analogue' studies — over 80 of which appear in my present bibliography. In these studies, the respondents (often students) are recruited specifically for the research and the interviews (often short) are arranged and structured for the same purpose. In some cases, recorded interviews have been rated by observers rather than (or as well as) participants.

Fretz et al. (1979) report an analogue study, with an unusual twist. RI scores were generated in two ways from brief interviews in which therapist non-verbal behaviours were deliberately varied. In one case, students rated the response of an interviewer in *acted mini-sessions,* the task being to answer as if they were the client. In the other case, ratings followed direct participation as 'client' in helping-style interviews with counsellors who were trained for high and low levels of the same kinds of non-verbal expression. In the former, more fabricated situation, increase in the non-verbal behaviours was linked to higher RI scores; in the more realistic situation, the non-verbal behaviour differences did not drive client RI ratings. In confronting this discrepancy, the authors acknowledged the contrived settings. An issue they did not mention is that the RI is concerned with experience in relationship and the items do not refer to features of brief interaction.

A number of other studies have focused on features of therapist personality thought likely to effect 'client' perception of the therapist partners in counselling-style interactions. In particular, several investigators looked at the influence of assessed counsellor dogmatism. Their studies support the plausible idea that helping relationship quality diminishes with increase in counsellor dogmatism. The evidence, however, was largely obtained in brief-contact experimental situations (see Barrett-Lennard, 2002b, pp. 36–7). Even after a full initial interview in therapy, the expectations with which clients come to their sessions must still play a part in their perceptions of the therapists' attitudes. As mentioned, the RI is not designed to sample perceived behaviour in limited interaction but to tap into and measure *qualities of relationship found in experience*. In a minority of the actual therapy studies the relationship data were in fact gathered after three, four or more hours with the therapist. In many of the analogue studies the instrument is used in a more 'projective' way, which might be to check how characteristics *of the rater* were affecting their interpersonal perceptions.

This last-mentioned interest is quite different from the interests that lead to development of the RI. I am pleased that the instrument has found wide use but, at the same time, am concerned by the application and logic involved in a good many studies. Although other users should and usually do seek my permission this does not position me to pass judgement on their plans and, for that matter, it would not be practical to for me do so consistently. When prospective users outline their plans and invite my comment I do try to give feedback. A broader worry concerns the potential effects of extrinsic contextual factors in research settings, such as the promise of a doctoral degree or career advancement, which feed into investigator motivation and contribute to driving research.

Besides the original English versions, numerous translations of the Inventory have been prepared, for example, by investigators working in Arabic, Dutch, French, German, Greek, Italian, Japanese, Korean, Polish, Portuguese, Slovak, Spanish and Swedish languages.[5] For the most part, these have been direct translations of the 64-item RI. Lietaer's work (1976) is an exception. He added items, largely relating to 'directivity', in his Dutch-language translation. He then revised the scale structure (via factor-analysis), and used the modified RI to compare relationships in psychoanalytic (p-a) and client-centred (c-c) therapy. On most scales there was no great difference in perception of the therapists (see also the mentioned results by Blatt et al., 1996). The p-a group, however, were seen by their clients as distinctly more directive and the c-c therapists as generally more transparent (a factor scale largely derived from congruence).

New uses of the RI in counselling and psychotherapy process research are infrequent now although not, it would seem, through any exhaustion of useful,

---

[5] Colleagues have also used the 64-item RI in American Sign Language and, probably, in Afrikaans, Croatian and Turkish languages.

potentially illuminating lines of inquiry. I have acknowledged the practical demands of mounting such studies, especially in the context of thesis research. More important is the fact that therapist variables measured from client experience have seldom (with occasional exceptions as noted in my bibliography) been seen as relevant enough to study by exponents of the currently dominant cognitive-behavioural approaches. A more positive development that could also curtail use of the RI is that of gradual expansion of non-metric qualitative research, especially by humanistically inclined investigators.

Another effectively limiting factor is that alternative measures were very energetically advanced and in vogue, beginning not long after development of the RI. The most striking case was the extremely vigorous promotion of the methodology of judge rating of the 'core conditions', as advanced by Truax, Carkhuff and collaborators, and initially used in the Wisconsin research (Rogers et al., 1967, Appendix B). Theoretical and practical difficulties with the approach worried me but I did not find energy for public debate of the issues. A rather brief comment in print does appear in my 1986 RI report (p. 469). Evidence from the Wisconsin research, distilled for my 1998 book (pp. 268–70), casts strong doubt on the rating scales,[6] and a number of significant critiques were published (see Mitchell, Bozarth and Krauft, 1977). However, the momentum of advocacy and claims for objectivity of the method continued strongly from the mid-sixties into the nineteen-eighties. Even in a recent review, research evidence from this methodology tends to be lumped in with evidence from RI studies as though they were just alternative ways of getting at the same things (Bozarth et al., 2002). Such generalisation has always bothered me, since research evidence (e.g., Kurtz and Grummon, 1972) does not support it, and close conceptual analysis certainly implies otherwise (Barrett-Lennard, 1981).

Investigating familial, group and friendship relationships

Level of regard, empathy, unconditionality and congruence are, on the face of it, of just as much interest in personal life relationships as in formal helping contexts. The pivotal sphere of marriage/couple and parent-child relations was

---

[6] Wisconsin investigators had themselves concluded that ratings on the Truax (judge-rating) scales for congruence and unconditional positive regard 'raise serious interpretive problems', and that 'it was impossible to have confidence in them' (Rogers et al., 1967, p. 167). The rating scale for 'accurate empathy' was accepted as adequate, although validation evidence suggested that it 'tapped a more global conditions quality of the therapist', particularly including therapist congruence, rather than empathy specifically (ibid., p. 184).

an obvious one for research application of the RI, almost from the beginning. The first uses were in thesis studies by students working with me. As instance, Thornton's work (1960) on marriage relationships, and Rosen's (1961) on parent-child relations are outlined in my 1998 book (pp. 307–8). Rosen surmised that (beyond the one-to-one relations) a total 'child-mother-father' interactive effect was operating, and he also suggested exploring how the *child* sees each parent responding to the other. A related possibility would be to assess the way each member experiences their family as a whole, as done in a later study by Gomes (1981), with Brazilian families. Adapted forms of the RI were used in translation to tap member perceptions of their whole family, and also of the response of pairs of others — parents jointly, and parent-child combinations.[7] There is much scope for further RI research on family process; for example, drawing on the conception of multiple levels of relation advanced in Chapter 7. Other RI studies have focused on empathy in couple relations, relationship effects of marital enrichment programmes, relationships in families that include a disturbed child, and on relationship change through marital therapy (see Barrett-Lennard, 1998, pp. 307–13).

Group relations change and communication development through intensive group experience is another region that drew applications of the RI at an early stage, sometimes in adapted group/plural form (e.g., 'They respect me'). The evolving two-person relationships in a small group (discussed in Chapter 6) particularly interested Clark and colleagues, in mid-1960s work with the RI (reviewed in Barrett-Lennard, 1998, p. 299; and 2002b, p. 37). The unique idea of this work was that the *combination of giving and receiving* substantial empathy and the other measured conditions was especially propitious for beneficial personal change. Research results gave uneven support to this hypothesis, probably because other factors were contributing as well. New, sophisticated and creative work encompassing this idea would have fruitful potential.

Research features of my own work in the small-group field were presented in my last book (1998, pp. 294–9). A particular aspect to touch on again entailed use of the RI to gather data on members' *outside relationships* before and after intensive residential group experiences. The results suggested that participants tended to become more open to awareness of the attitudes of the other person (1998, pp. 295–6). In the same source (1998, p. 305–6) I discussed small-group studies by Cooper, who singled out perceived facilitator congruence as having an important bearing on the qualitative nature of group outcomes, especially toward greater self-congruence (Cooper, 1969, p. 528). A Portuguese study involving members of five different kinds of small group used the *group* response-to-me form of the 64-item RI (in translation). The authors concluded

---

[7] Further information on Gomes' study is given in my last book (1998, pp. 309–11) and an earlier report (1984, pp. 238–9).

that the facilitator's role was crucial in contributing to empathic communication and group integration (Marques-Teixeira et al., 1996). Most other of the 30+ studies in my bibliography that report use of the RI in group research have focused on personal development and therapy groups. Investigating relations in other kinds of groups — ubiquitous in childhood and adult life — would be a promising further zone of study.

One-to-one personal friendship relations are understudied — generally, and in respect to research that has made use of the RI. An exception is found in the work of Duncan Cramer, focusing on the link between self-esteem and the facilitative quality of friendships. Having established such a link in initial RI studies (1985, 1989 and 1990), Cramer sought to pin down the causal influence of relationship quality on self-esteem. The most recent report I have seen (Cramer, 1994) used relationship and self-esteem data gathered twice, with a 15-week interval. In this and a previous study, unconditionality stood out in predictively effecting self-esteem (ibid., p. 332, Table 2).

The realm of complementary relationships

Most of us will have spent a large part of our waking lives in active and often formative association with teachers. Yet, qualities of the teacher-to-student relationship are not often carefully investigated. A number of exceptions to this dearth of close study, reported as early as 1961 (Emmerling), have used teacher-pupil/student adaptations of the RI. The work has been interesting but uneven in quality, and the field remains wide open for further careful and inventive inquiry (Barrett-Lennard, 1998, p. 313–14). To this end, there are up-to-date 40-item versions of 'student' and 'teacher' forms of the Inventory, designed for high school age and slightly younger children. A simpler OS 'child' form is also poised for further use in this and other relationship contexts.

Anyone who is an employee or in training has a supervisor or person they report to, and some quite interesting studies on supervisory relationships have used the RI. One of these focused on the principal-teacher relationship across a range of schools. Teachers described their principal's response and principals answered for the way they *expected* their staff to perceive them. The better-functioning principals (as separately assessed) were generally more accurate in their predictions of teacher perceptions and were seen as more *unconditional* and affirming in their relational attitude (Cline, 1970–71, pp. 32–3). In a later example, investigation focused on the organisational climate of schools as well as on the way teachers perceived the response of their principals, and found a positive association between school climate and the relationship qualities (Jaeger, 1989). Other studies are outlined in my previous book (1998, pp. 317–19), including one in which reciprocal peer supervision in therapy training was the focus of interest (Byrne, 1983). This study yielded results suggesting that peer supervision and feedback can be a valuable complement to the supervision of experienced professionals.

It has intrigued and impressed me that RI-based investigation of nurse-patient relationships, especially nurse empathy as experienced by patients, has long been and remains a focus of fairly active interest. Appreciable direct contact and opportunity for communication is necessary for the RI data from *any* *context* to be convincingly regarded as rooted in experience in the particular relationship. Brief, transitory contact may well give rise to impressions, even strong ones, but experience in and expectations from other contexts can be expected to play a big part in these early impressions. This does not preclude use of the RI in short-association contexts but moderates the meaning of results. Such applications invite both inventive design and critical interpretation.

Studying experienced interpersonal life environments and milieus

The RI has so far been used mainly to tap relationships between individuals or, at most, between a person and their family or a small membership group. Whether the particular relationship in focus is one of a kind for the person in focus, or an instance of a broader pattern, usually has remained unknown. A few studies have looked at the responsive qualities of a human relations milieu, or of a broad grouping within this milieu. Gross et al. (1970) called on patients who were near discharge after 60+ days in their hospital ward to answer the RI worded for reference to the treatment staff generally (for example, 'How much staff members like or dislike me is not affected by anything that I think or feel').[8] Another study in the same time frame (Wargo and Meek, 1970/1971) examined the way clients perceived the climate of response in the *total milieu* of a residential rehabilitation programme. The OS RI used was worded even more broadly (item 1: 'People here respect me as a person'). Meaningful results were affirming to the authors in their choice of method. Despite their advocacy of similar further research I am not aware of direct follow-up. However, in the same time frame, an even broader level of inquiry was incubating in my thought.

---

[8] Staff members saw their response (to the patients as a group) as more positive than the patients perceived it to be, especially on the U scale; and analysis of patient returns showed the unconditionality dimension as quite distinct from the other variables (Gross et al., 1970, pp. 543–4). In her unrelated study, Gilmour-Barrett (1973) found a link between self-perceived unconditionality of response by child careworkers to the children in their care in residential treatment centres, and qualities of management and programme organisation.

My notion was to develop a new form of the RI to tap multiple relationships across the whole spectrum of the respondent's experienced interpersonal world. This world broadly encompasses family, friendship and vocational life relationships. The new form (then 42 items, now 40) initially was tested in a validity study by Holland (1976). His sample included a group of participants who, judged by separate data, lived in a much more supportive family/friendship environment than another subgroup did. Average RI scores were all higher for the upper support group (ibid., Table 7). Overall RI scores were also found to be generally higher, as expected, in family and friendship relations than in vocational/work life relationships. Another investigator in touch with me ahead of Holland's study constructed his own working adaptation of the RI along similar lines. His student sample rated the response of individual family members, friends, teachers, and additional significant others, for a total of up to 20 relationships. It was found, as predicted, that the general quality of relationships correlated with *change* in adjustment (separately assessed), in a test-retest design (Sundaram, 1976, pp. 34–9). Careful statistical analysis supported a model of reciprocal causal interaction between relationship and adjustment (ibid., pp. 49–52).

I was not in a position myself to follow these studies up but my new form received occasional use by other investigators, notably including Townsend (1988). She used total score means *across all relationships* as an index of experienced facilitative environment, and found this correlated strongly with measures of loneliness and of interpersonal self-efficacy (ibid., Table 4). Further results suggested that actual self-disclosure with partners was not a function of that relationship only but of facilitative relationships more broadly. Much more recently, after revision of the instrument and a further student-run validity study, added refinements were made. The resulting form (OS-S-40) — available now for fresh uses — provides for distinctive rating of as many as 11 identified relationships (including up to five in the family sphere).

Beckoning new paths for further study

Very recent or new usage of the Relationship Inventory in *psychotherapy research* appears thin on the ground, despite the fact that the underlying theory richly deserves continued investigation and refinement. A promising focus I have previously spoken of would directly compare (i) the interpersonal *worlds* clients report experiencing (using RI Form OS-S-40) with (ii) their experience of their therapists' response to them (regular OS form). If, for example, empathic understanding has a central role in enabling change, this quality must be experienced on a different level or concentration in the therapy relation than it is in other current relationships in the client's life. This gap, if verified, is likely to narrow over successful therapy and it seems plausible also that such narrowing would be a factor in client readiness to leave the therapy relationship.

Anxiety, depression, and emotional stress generally, can play havoc with a person's availability for empathic contact with others. Lack of such contact may increase their pain and withdrawal, this further reducing their effective empathy — in a process building on itself. As discussed in Chapter 4, responsive empathy toward others and self-empathic response are interconnected. A therapist's empathy plausibly facilitates self-empathy in their client, and assists the client's recovery of empathy toward others. In a potential use of the RI in this context, clients would be asked to nominate significant others who may be willing to contribute to the research. These associated persons then would be invited to describe the client's response to them in empathy-relevant ways before therapy and again afterwards, to test for change. And, if the client's self-view of his/her understanding of these persons was also obtained, client empathy seen from the outside and inside vantage points should in theory be more congruent after effective therapy than before it.

A mentioned experimental form of the Inventory, available for some time but used rarely, is designed to study relationships *viewed as a whole* by the participants (for example, 'We feel at ease together', 'I feel that we put on a role or act with one another', 'We like and enjoy one another', and 'We each want the other to be a particular kind of person'). I call this version Form DW-64 (Dyad-We, 64 items). One obvious usage is in the study of couple relationships. The quality of the experienced *We* reported by the pairs of participants might be similar or different. This similarity/difference, in conjunction with the score levels, would have implication for the health and fruition of the relationship, and could be useful in counselling as well as in opening a distinctive path of research.

Another potential usage of the RI is to call forth the respondent's view of an *ideal or desired relationship* — in therapy, say, or with a partner, a child (by a parent, or parent by a child), a teacher, or a close-knit community or group (by a member). In theory, the more positive an experienced relationship is on the RI dimensions the more facilitating and growthful it should be. However, it seems unlikely that people generally, or therapists of diverse orientation, would all place a premium on high unconditionality of regard. Therapist congruence, too, especially in respect to the transparency aspect, is not likely to be equally valued in all therapies. The RI would be applicable in comparative studies of therapy systems, not only to assess experienced therapist-to-client relationships but to throw further light on ways that therapists in differing approaches vary in how they aspire or *wish to be* in relation to their clients. In like vein, what is the perceived ideal relationship of teacher to student, and how does this vary among teachers and contexts? In contemporary multi-cultural societies, ideals in parent-child relationships may vary markedly, and RI data also could help to illuminate this sphere.

These suggested further avenues of study merely illustrate the bounty of possibilities for fresh research with the RI. I would be very happy for investigator-colleagues to take any of them up, and I am sure that there will be colleagues who continue to add to the avenues that occur to me. As mentioned, I have for a long time been receiving and welcoming inquiries and requests for the Inventory and related information, and wish to assist and not constrain careful work by others along the lines of their interest.

Are the 'conditions' as measured still all relevant?

I shared my later thought concerning the nature and processes of empathy in Chapter 4,[9] thought that extends and further refines the meaning of the empathy measure. The elements and facets of an empathic understanding process on which the various scale items are most directly based remain pertinent and have been closely described in my previous reports, for example, in 1993 (p. 7) and 2002 (pp. 28–9 and 44). The principal refinement in meaning of this scale rests on the 'phases of empathy' conception (Chapter 4). The MO form of the RI (as earlier mentioned) taps the listener's sense of his/her empathic contact and understanding. This arousal of an inner empathic response is the crucial first phase of interpersonal empathy. The expression or visible manifestation of this inner process is the second or mediating phase, which an attuned observer possibly could pick up and rate, for example, using an observer form of the RI. The most-used OS RI form taps the culminating third phase of empathy: the extent to which the receiving person actually experiences him/herself as being personally understood. With these refinements of meaning, and in careful usage, the RI E scale remains the best available measure of participant-experienced interpersonal empathy, itself an axial dimension both in helping and life relationships.

The Level of Regard and Unconditionality scales are only lightly correlated in virtually every RI study reporting their association. This evidence, added to the issues that led to their separation, strongly supports the breakdown of UPR into its component variables. Positive unconditionality implies that the responding person's attitude is even-handed, *not* selectively judgemental, not dependent on the 'voice' or aspect of self expressed by the other person. The experiencing self of the other is neither variably condemned nor highly praised for its feeling or attitude or consciousness. The opposite of these things applies

---

[9] The excellent first and last chapters, by the editors, in the volume *Empathy reconsidered* (Bohart and Greenberg, 1997) constitute one of the other valuable resources. The book on empathy edited by Haugh and Merry (2001) is another mine of related new thought.

in the markedly negative, conditional zone. By itself, unconditionality does not imply either a high or a low level of *positive regard* — hence the low correlation of measures. High unconditionality with low positive regard could be perceived as indifference or even aversion, but not as an attitude that promises and rejects according to what is revealed.[10] High ratings on positive regard in conjunction with low perceived unconditionality is a not uncommon pattern in parent-child or even partner relationships. This conjunction implies a sense of the other as caring, even loving, but *not* as being regardful of the perceiver's whole self.

In making the sharp distinction between level and unconditionality of regard I have sometimes felt like a voice in the wilderness, except with fellow RI users. Lietaer, with a background of use and analysis of the RI (1976, 1979), has sustained a focus on unconditionality as distinct from positive regard, and worked to clarify and deepen the concept (Lietaer, 1984, 2002). However, even he focuses mainly on unconditionality in its positive aspects and meaning. To treat it as a continuum extending over a great range I think one needs to hold the negative pole of *conditionality* in mind, even while considering the positive direction.

Contributors to the volume edited by Bozarth and Wilkins (2001) examine UPR in differentiated ways but mostly without pursuing the idea of two (or more) distinct variables being involved. They broadly agree that experienced unconditional regard is fundamental to movement and change in 'self-conditionality', and that the process is active, not passively non-judgemental. This active reaching-out beams primary attention to *felt* experience and *personal* meaning and, thus, does have a certain directional influence. Within this broad zone there need be no selective reinforcement (Lietaer, 2001, pp. 95–6). The total span and encounter of ideas, including Bozarth's vigorously expressed position (1998, pp. 84–8) and Purton's (1998) searching exploration, imply that issues relating to unconditionality of regard remain a very live focus of debate and refinement.

All this is quite at odds with omitting the U scale of the RI as somehow being of less relevance or importance than the others, which some investigators did for a time. One factor in this omission is that the instrument has attracted interest and usage well beyond the orbit of those who would consider themselves to be person-centred. Although the variable of widest interest has been that of empathic understanding, the meaning of congruence, and its function and relation to the other conditions, also have remained issues of absorbing interest. Recent expressions of this interest include the collection of papers edited by Gill Wyatt (2001). If therapist congruence is simply equated with being genuinely oneself, and unconditional acceptance as being impartially and

---

[10] To be positively facilitative or freeing to the other an unconditional attitude needs, in theory and in my own observation, to be coupled with some warmth of positive regard.

neutrally receptive, a certain tension among principles follows. At best, this tension has been a fruitful stimulus to deeper understanding of the concepts, as Wyatt's book illustrates. The discrimination in client-centred theory of therapist congruence as a crucial factor in therapy arose from an observational base that was at once a source of strength and of limitation to the emergent idea itself. The strength is evident in the durability of the concept and its continuing examination. Limitation is evident if one places the idea within a larger context of thought.

The human organism is inherently an enormously complex total system. Taking this as a starting point, the idea follows that more adaptive and less preprogrammed any species is, the greater the diversity of pattern and thus, the potential for incongruence. Learned patterns can be at odds with each other and with tendencies that are more physiologically based. Becoming 'out of sync' with ourselves is part of the price we humans pay for the complex diversity of our make-up, for our intricate and highly differentiated perceiving, feeling, wanting, thinking consciousness. The potential for incongruence is truly part of being human. In this sense it is worthy of respect and invites our best understanding. Part of this understanding would be to distinguish the natural diversity of self in positive expression from a 'chambered' diversity that restricts inner dialogue or self-empathic process (Barrett-Lennard, 1997; 2003, Chapter 1). Why a high level of *therapist* congruence is deemed beneficial in therapy seems at once apparent and an issue for further reflection (Barrett-Lennard, 2002b, p. 46).[11]

Conclusion

My reply to the question asked in my previous heading is 'Yes', but this answer opens the way to another question: Does the RI tap and measure *all* of the important dimensions of helper response in therapy and related enabling contexts? Lietaer considered it relevant to add and measure the aspect of 'directivity', with low directivity being the positive pole on the scale. However, I believe it is not his view that person-centred (or any) therapy should or can be totally non-directive, partly because being helpful implies influence and also because he supports an active experiential thrust in person-centred work

---

[11] I have never viewed congruence as a constant personality disposition that a person 'has' or 'is', and my view now is even more contextual. It seems clear to me that a person's level of congruence varies in different relational contexts. Research is only just beginning to bear on this issue but what evidence there is from RI studies accords with the expectation that both other-perceived and self-experienced congruence does differ from one relation to another. The emotional safety felt in each relation could be a major factor in this variation.

(2002). Other colleagues passionately believe that a non-directive attitude, positively defined, is the sine qua non of the client/person-centred approach and that any guiding interventions (including those involved in focusing) actually bypass rather than release the client's own actualising tendency (Bozarth, 1998; Brodley, 1990). Gendlin's advocacy and close practical illustration of the philosophy and method of his focusing approach (1996) is laced with features of therapist engagement process that Rogers emphasised but is not couched in the same terms or fully contained by the theory.

Person-centred therapists do not follow and implement a formula, and conditions theory cannot represent the *total* foundation and orbit of any given therapist's response to his/her client. Each brings their individual background of experience and structure of meaning and assumption to the helping engagement. A theory of human nature or personality is a big part of the larger context of meaning. It includes a working understanding of how persons live their lives, and of how their own processes of living form and change. Beliefs about what are more healthful or optimal processes as against limiting or 'unhealthy' ones are part of this understanding. Rogers energetically addressed such issues, and distilled the thought represented in conditions theory from the much larger total orbit of his experience, values stance, and theoretical understanding (Rogers, 1959a). I worked over and recomposed, in more operational terms, axial features of this theory in developing the RI.

Viewing this origin and the steps in context, I see no basis to assert that the RI taps *all* components of the client-therapist relationship and interaction that contribute to healing and growthful change. Assuming, as I now do, that we live interactively, largely in and through relations with others, and that the quality of these relations on many levels is intricately involved in our well-being, I have to conclude that both conditions theory and the RI probably are incomplete. To become *more* comprehensive, theory and instrument need to address, as a primary issue, the quality and range of the therapist's *active* responsiveness to clients' lived relational worlds — as further discussed in Chapter 10. I am still feeling my way on exactly how best to encapsulate and possibly build in this vital further feature.

Another issue very much on my mind is the conviction that helping practice needs to reach beyond the individual therapy and person-to-person context from which conditions theory was formulated. Chapter 10 introduces a widened theory of change and vision of practice. In this perspective, helping relationships broadly in the Rogerian tradition are seen as depending in turn on supporting conditions in the societal and institutional frameworks that make such therapy possible and valued. This issue goes beyond the scope of the RI, even if extended. As it stands, this instrument, in light of its track record and span of forms, remains a significant resource in the varied tried and new contexts sketched in this chapter and in further applications of careful invention.

Chapter 9

Human nature and the becoming self

My last book devotes a whole chapter to presenting the heart of client-centred theory (1998, pp. 71–87). The first half of this chapter covers similar ground but in less detail, and does so in a way that connects more easily with recent extensions of my thought. I resonate to George Kelly's assertion that 'A theory provides a basis for an active approach to life'. Such a theory, in his words, 'is a tentative expression of what man has seen as a regular pattern in the surging events of life' (Kelly, 1955). It is in this spirit that I offer the perspective and propositions advanced here.

This chapter moves in the second half to focus on the self engaged in its own development, drawing on and modestly updating my previous work on the pathway of therapy. The wider movement in my thought is away from a literally individualist mindset and toward the view that persons are not by nature separate and freestanding but develop and live through relations with one another. I see the difference in some contexts as one of emphasis, and in other moments as a basic qualitative shift.

Classical person-centred thought is closely represented in this chapter, but throughout there also are nuances and extensions of meaning that connect it with the still-wider perspective introduced in the chapter that follows. My account employs careful prose but, if you as reader would like to start with a poem, the verse titled 'Point of view' (in Appendix 2) touches evocatively on some of the issues that follow.

Client/person-centred thinking stresses that human beings act on and respond to reality as they experience and perceive it to be; and that a person's concept or view of self is a core feature of their experiential field. One's field of perception is influenced by various factors: needs at the time, values, relationships, the groups and community of which one is part, and the still broader context of culture and environment. Whatever goes into the mix from which a person's view of reality emerges it is this view by which he or she largely acts. Thus, how persons arrive at their understandings is a crucial issue, and the approach I am presenting emphasises the importance of first-hand experiential knowledge as against simply knowing *about* something, or possessing an intellectual awareness of the end-products of the learning, discovery and meanings of others.

The potential of humans to experience agency and opportunity in their lives, to *feel* responsible for self, to have both capacity and courage to look openly within and beyond themselves, and to act purposefully, are stressed in this approach. Also emphasised — in varied balance at different times — are the unique individuality or 'oneness' of each person *and* his/her social nature and life-long dance of engagement with others. Person-centred writers have stressed, with argument and at times with passion, both the obstacles to and the potential for personal psychological freedom and self-determination. They also have assumed that human experience and conduct have causes, that they are naturally determined. In fact, the application of this principle to the experiential realm was very strongly furthered by the determined, highly resourceful efforts of Rogers and his collaborators to bring psychotherapy into empirical, scientific daylight.

In his 1955 article 'Persons or science: a philosophical question' Rogers first publicly shared the two-sided commitment and tension he felt between, on the one hand, his deep involvement in and respect for human subjective experience including the experience of choice and freedom and, on the other side, his search for verified scientific knowledge with its underpinning of deterministic assumption and objectivist method. Both sides are forcefully presented and the author proceeds via searching inner debate to a partial integration, followed up in subsequent papers (including Rogers, 1964a).

There is potential for resolution beyond Rogers' own analysis. When persons are seen as inherently active, directional, curious and self-generating it follows that their *built-in* freedom is of a different order than if they are viewed as basically moulded, patterned and 'determined' by their environmental history (Barrett-Lennard, 1965). In practice, a person's effective freedom varies, depending partly on the process quality of their functioning. A major effect of successful therapy, from a person-centred standpoint, is that of achieving a new level of inner freedom. A later part of this chapter envisions a spectrum of greatly varied ways that persons function and relate from their experience. In this conception, the 'low-process' person, encased in fixed, self-perpetuating patterns, is relatively unfree, compared with more fully functioning or 'high-process' persons. Expanded awareness, fluid discrimination and experiential knowledge work together to increase an individual's autonomy, mastery and freedom. In other language, the well-functioning person fulfils a potential of our nature to flow all of one piece in a continually becoming process of being.

Our species nature: Axiomatic principles

In the discussion so far, several very basic characteristics of the human species are implied. There may be little controversy about these, in my summary that follows. Some points might even seem to the reader to state the obvious. However, the selection and carefully explicit expression of these principles reveals broad emphases of the thought system presented, and provides a foundation for further, more specific theory.

First in mention, *a person is an experiencing (feeling, thinking, inquiring, willing, self-aware) being with a highly differentiated consciousness linked closely to his/her history of communication and relationships with other persons.* While much of the total person-system normally has a self-regulating quality, consciousness is its highest integrating and controlling centre or subsystem. For humans, to be alive means to be conscious, if not at the moment then potentially or at other moments. Having desired experiences and achieving certain qualities of consciousness are ultimate values.

In keeping with a highly developed consciousness, *reality is variously perceived and understood by different persons and groups*; and each acts according to their view of the nature and significant features of this reality. Individuals and groups are better understood from their inner pictures than from some impartial or external mapping of the terrain they face. Further, *people are inherently active rather than merely reactive.* Individual consciousness is not a passive receptacle that acquires its character simply by association with patterns of reward and/or punishment. To the contrary, humans are active, curious, purposive and directional in their inherent nature, and are prone to organise and reflect on their primary experience, expand their capacities, and actively change their worlds — or endeavour to — according to their own goals.

Another aspect, self-evident but deserving mention, is that *a person grows into being.* Life implies and depends on growth and developmental processes which themselves evolve. Human beings do not act primarily to restore internal equilibrium. While they can be said to have survival-type needs, such motivation is not the driving force under most conditions. An underlying growth principle is central in person-centred thinking about human motivation, learning and change. A related feature is shared with other life forms. *For a living thing to grow, certain basic supporting conditions and nutrients are necessary.* Given the nourishing conditions, the human organism will develop according to its nature as a species and individual member. Even a plant actively spreads its roots and leaves to expose itself to the life- and growth-giving elements it requires. Higher animals have vastly greater versatility in acting to find or partially create conditions necessary for their growth and well-being. Humans have unique *potential* for conscious knowledge of their own nature and needs.

The whole human organism

More specific characteristics of the human organism can be identified and expressed as follows. Some features flow rather directly from the broad principles already stated while others are a distinct further step:

- For Rogers, *the human species 'has one basic tendency and striving — to actualize, maintain, and enhance the experiencing organism'* (1951, p. 487). The *actualizing tendency* principle is closely defined by Rogers in later writing (1959a, p. 196; 1963a). In my own broader framing, it takes only a tolerant environment and essential nutrients for each organism to hasten on its developmental path, pushed by imperatives of its species, guided by its individual code, drawn by its own unique experience and, in the case of humans, moving also by the intentionality of evolving consciousness and meaning.

- *The individual human organism* lives *in interdependent relation with others of its kind.* The actualising principle extends to a tendency to preserve, enhance and develop offspring and partner organisms and bonded groups.

- *Humans interact with perceived 'outer' and 'inner' reality in general accord with their actualising tendency.* Implied is a directional energy system, organised to promote life-preserving, developmental and enhancing processes. This unified principle effectively replaces the idea of humans being activated by a diversity of specific needs. As in the working of gravity in a complex river system, there are many channels and kinds of motion that reflect the underlying actualising principle.

- *The human organism, in functioning as an organised whole, responds to its perceptual field.* This perceptual field is its reality, and includes the immediate, fresh incoming data of experience as well as the map of reality charted and built up over time by the organism in its life context (cf. Rogers, 1951, 1959a).

- In infancy, and *through healthy child- and adulthood, human beings engage in an organismic valuing process,* in which experiences that are actualising to the engaged organism are valued positively, and the converse negatively (Rogers, 1959a, 1963b). This quality of process, however, is a strong potential not an imperative. In conditions to be mentioned shortly, the organism develops inhibitory barriers that block the flow of some kinds of experiential data and restrict the organismic valuing process. Personal integration is reduced but social integration may be preserved. There is a potential tension in the complex human organism's life between maintaining individual wholeness while joining and living in relation with others.

- *Differentiation is an important effect of the actualising tendency,* and part of the young organism's experience becomes differentiated and symbolised in an 'awareness of being', of having its own individual life and identity. This awareness may be termed self-experience, and it 'becomes elaborated, through interaction with the environment, particularly the environment composed of significant others, into a *concept of self*' (Rogers, 1959a, p. 223). The self-concept is one pivotal region of the organism's perceptual field, and a major influence in guiding behaviour.

- *The organism is always in motion.* This motion includes the stream of felt processes to which the term *experiencing* is given. In an important mode of experiencing the conscious organism focuses on inner felt meanings and bodily sensed qualities (Gendlin, 1961a, 1969). Effectively, the conscious self 'listens to' and interacts with the organism's underlying body life. This interaction includes finding words or other symbols for organically felt experience beneath the surface of articulate consciousness. As this occurs, shifts on both levels take place. Such interactive flow within the organism sustains its wholeness and integration, and can be supported or inhibited through the nature of its engagements and collective life.

The self

'Self' variously refers to the whole person, the self as actor, the self of personal being and consciousness, or the person's concept of self. The self-concept became a focus of interest and then of theory within a few years after the new 'non-directive' client-centred school began. It was first highlighted by Rogers in his featured address as retiring president of the American Psychological Association (Rogers, 1947). With the appearance of *Client-Centered Therapy* (Rogers, 1951) and, particularly, the system of theoretical propositions advanced in the last chapter of that work, Rogerian 'self-theory' came of age.

The best account of the evolution of the concept of self to a pivotal position in this approach is to be found in Rogers' most systematic general statement of theory (Rogers, 1959a). There, he emphasises the configurational (I would say, 'system') nature of the self-concept, in which change in one element could alter the balance of the whole. As interest in the working of self unfolded, qualitative variation in self-functioning was more and more closely described (Rogers, 1961a, pp. 163–96; Rogers, 1958, 1961b). I will return to this topic after outlining the heart of self-theory in its most systematic form:

1. As the individual's awareness of self emerges, even before it evolves into an organised self-concept, a need for the *positive regard* of others becomes apparent in experience and behaviour. This need is potent and pervasive in the young individual's social behaviour, and it can override the organismic valuing process and affect the working of the actualising tendency.

2. As the individual continues to develop, a need for *self-regard* evolves. Personal behaviours that were associated with regardful and rejecting responses from others now have similar force in satisfying or frustrating the individual's need for self-regard. As Rogers put it, the person 'experiences positive regard or loss of positive regard independently of transactions with any social other. He becomes in a sense his own significant social other' (Rogers, 1959a, p. 224).

3. Thus, self-regard now depends partly on internalised standards. When any expression of self is avoided (or sought) solely because of its effect on a person's self-regard he or she is said to have acquired *a condition of worth*.

4. An effect of conditions of worth is that the individual filters his/her experience. Perception becomes selective in that experience consistent with a person's conditions of worth is accurately represented in that person's awareness while experiential data contrary to these conditions tends to be denied or distorted in awareness.

5. Denial to awareness implies that certain behaviours or inner states of the person are not recognised as *self*-experiences and, in this sense, are not owned by the individual and not organised into his or her operating self-picture. The resulting *incongruence* between self and experience implies 'vulnerability' and potential for dysfunction, although in the short term conscious inner conflict and anxiety are reduced.

6. In the vulnerable person, some behaviours are in keeping with the active self-concept and are accurately perceived and actualising to the self. Other, contrary behaviours can only satisfy and support features of the individual's experiential being that are not admissible to the self-structure. The inadmissible (thus, 'not-self') features do not affect conscious self-regard, or they have little effect (ibid., p. 227).

7. However, in the process described, there is said to be 'subceived' threat leading to protective defence of self. This 'protective reaction' allows the individual to maintain an acceptable view of self, while the implied conditions of worth remain out of sight and unaffected. There are costs to screening out elements of self-experience, including the mentioned aspect of vulnerability, a tightness or rigidity of perception, and the potential for intense arousal or over-reactivity (ibid., pp. 222–8).

8. The propositions, to this point, suggest that a person has essentially one idea or concept of self. In contemporary thought (Barrett-Lennard, 2003,

Chapter 1), the self is viewed as diverse or 'plural'.[1] The complexity of the human organism and variety of individual experience leads to distinctive self-constellations (or subselves) that are activated in differing life contexts. Previous points are framed to accord with Rogers' thought but can be adapted as necessary to fit the complexity of subself concepts.

Just how does 'self-defence' break down or dissolve and forward change happen? The costs of keeping guard over experience and meanings that can be admitted to self are one crucial factor in the potential for change. Individuals can run into experiences which presents them with such intense or starkly obvious evidence of contradiction between their self-picture and their actual behaviour that the defence/denial process fails, and acute inner conflict and anxiety occur. Perhaps also there can be cumulative effects from gradual development of self in areas not constrained by defensive organisation. This development may finally trigger awareness of anomalies in the self; especially, anomalies stemming from acquired conditions of worth.

Conditions for self-change

Conscious inner conflict or anxiety does not alone undo conditions of worth and lead to integrated and healthy functioning of the self. If a disturbing personal desire, attitude or behaviour pattern is to be owned as an expression of self, its subjective meaning and impact on self-regard have to change. It is posited that the change process comes about through the genuinely positive and unconditional responsive regard of an empathically understanding significant other.

It is held that the individual must actually and substantially experience these mentioned qualities in the significant other's response if her/his own conditions of worth and self-regard are to change. Assuming this happens, the customarily threatening experiences can be openly perceived, explored and integratively accepted as expressions of the individual's acknowledged self (or subself). Further, the person is now less vulnerable, more congruent, the internal balance has shifted to more positive regard for self and others, and the individual's functioning is more often reflective of an organismic valuing process. In the classical client-centred view of therapy, and healing/helping relationships more generally, this process and cycle repeated many times, around the 'same' and different conditions of worth and conflict areas, is the nucleus of therapy.

In Rogers' original formulation of the conditions of therapeutic personality

---

[1]The issue of self-plurality is further discussed in Chapter 10 (pp. 136–8), this in turn foreshadowing the full exploration in Barrett-Lennard, 2003.

change (Rogers, 1957), six components were distinguished. As mentioned in the last chapter, the basic condition of 'psychological contact' between client and therapist amounts to a precondition implicit in the other factors and only became a focus of attention much later. The condition of client incongruence is implicitly linked to 'conditions of worth' (or self-conditional attitudes), viewed as leaving the person vulnerable to psychological threat and inner conflict. Recognised *self*-behaviours that violate the rules of entrenched conditions of worth produce an inner tension state of anxiety. This 'syndrome' in some form plausibly helps to propel clients into therapy and even to keep them there at least through the early stages. However, it is not part of the enabling process and has not been treated as a 'core condition' and studied in the way that the other variables have.

The remaining conditions, all highlighted in subsequent work, focus on the therapist and his/her response in relation to the client. In positing a requirement that the helper be 'congruent or integrated in the [therapy] relationship', Rogers clearly does not mean that he/she needs to be a paragon of self-actualizing virtue exhibiting this quality of integration and wholeness in every area of life, or even continuously in therapy (1957, pp. 96–7). Given the great complexity of human consciousness and the self, complete and unified consistency of self is not a credible condition.

The further conditions are also, at base, expressions of the therapist-helper's self. This is implied by Rogers but becomes clearer if one thinks of the self (as I now do) as a naturally dynamic entity with alternate configurations or subselves. One potential configuration is an evolved 'helping self' in open connection with other contextual subselves but somewhat distinct from them. This subself is not just a role or mantle the therapist assumes but an authentic expression of his or her being in a therapy or similar helping context. In this view, the selves we express grow out of experience in relation and are lived in further relations, present to our inner eye and to the meanings of what we do (Barrett-Lennard, 2003, Chapter 1).

The notion of engagement is more encompassing than relationship in its usual connotations. Life is manifested in engagement. The human (multiple) self does not exist in isolation or as a separate and literally autonomous entity. Selves live in and through engagement, particularly including engagement with other selves on many levels. The engagement of therapy is a complementary relation. Client and therapist have overlapping but also differing reasons for their association. The client is mainly focusing on and sharing from his or her own life, including at times the aspect of living in relation to the therapist. The therapist is engaged responsively, in enabling mode, with her/his helping self alert and in action. It is this active manifestation of the therapist's being that is opening itself to the client and, at moments, attaining a close empathic connection that works like a fresh window for the client to his/her own world.

The complementary self-to-self engagement is not of a kind where one is making evaluative judgements of the other. The total receptivity necessary for substantial empathic connection to occur is not compatible with an evaluative stance toward the inner person of the other. This stance would convey selective, conditional acceptance that would easily confound the other's exploration rather than help to release them from the confusion of conditions of worth involuntarily embedded and half-hidden within the self.

The human self requires nourishment to prosper and continue to unfold. Central to this nourishment are qualities of self-to-self engagement. For a given self, especially one that is suffering in its own functioning and inner process, the touch of shared, unjudging recognition and depth understanding by another self or selves appears to be the most crucial healing nutrient. The human self of its nature is aware of itself, but may not be 'well-aware'. Clearly, human consciousness, in reference to the self (and the selves of others), varies greatly. Variety in the working of self is effectively my next focus.

Diverse and changing selves: From fixity to flow

A new way of thinking about variation in self-functioning was brought into view by Rogers in his description of a continuum of self-process, ranging from a tightly constricted, static and repeating pattern to an open, free-flowing expressive self-in-motion. This new thought followed on the heels of his conditions of therapy theory and depicted the direction of movement expected to happen in and through a 'high conditions' relationship. Before-to-after-therapy shift in the client's outlook and functioning had been the main way of looking at outcome effects of therapy (Rogers and Dymond, 1954; cf. Rogers, 1959b and 1961b). The new thought added the possibility of tracking client movement from the discourse of therapy itself. It also was another window through which to view diversity in personal functioning outside the specific context of therapy.

Rogers' 'process conception' distinguishes qualities of functioning across a very wide multi-layered spectrum, each main component and stage anchored in close description and illustration. Strictly speaking, patterns that vary among individuals are directly comparable only when they are occurring under relatively constant conditions (for example, when in the company of the same deeply empathic therapist). In everyday life, widely varying conditions plausibly evoke differing qualities of self-functioning. The range or balance of these qualities may distinguish one person from another.

A central idea of the process continuum itself is that significant change in therapy, or in any personally growthful context, is not a movement from one kind of fixed but faulty structure to another kind of set but adequate structure, not a change from one constantly repeating pattern to a different one. The essential direction is from a relatively fixed or closed, self-perpetuating quality to an open, moving, self-transcending quality. As Rogers saw it, the change is from repetitive fixity to a formative changingness; briefly, from a condition of stasis to one of process (Rogers, 1959b and 1961b).

The continuum, however, is not conceived as one highly specific dimension but as a multi-layered whole with a variety of 'strands' (Rogers, 1959b). One strand is concerned with the degree of congruence between underlying experience and clear awareness. In the perspective of this chapter (and implicit in Rogers' process thought), such congruence is at most a tendency not a constant. It is greater in contextual self-modes where the person is at ease with Self and Other, feels safe rather than apprehensive, and can be more spontaneous and expressive. Another one of the family of strands was concerned with how the individual deals with feelings and feeling life, from an extreme of being largely unaware of feelings and impersonal in expression through intermediate stages to direct, open expression and living ownership of feelings.

Four of the strands distinguished were studied in research. Best known, through Gendlin's work, is that of *manner* (later 'level') *of experiencing*, ranging from a quality of externalisation and remoteness of expression to one of immediacy and easy reference to the person's inner flow of felt experience, articulated in the moment of its expression. Another strand is concerned with the way the person *constructs meaning* and uses these (belief or attitude) constructs: for example, as fixed templates *or* as flexible and evolving hypotheses. Two further strands centre on the person's *treatment of problems* (especially the aspect of owning problem issues as against seeing them as quite external to the self), and on their *manner of relating* to others (e.g., through expression of immediately felt experience and meaning versus no such openly expressive self-to-self engagement). The actual rating scales used for these strands are laid out in detail in the Wisconsin research volume by Rogers et al. (1967, pp. 589–611).

Rogers saw the strands as being much more separate and distinct from each other at the lower end of the continuum than in the integratively functioning 'process' person, where they melded into a unified whole. In his summary:

> At one end of this . . . continuum we find the individual living his life
> in terms of rigid personal constructs . . . He has little or no recognition
> of the ebb and flow of feeling life within him . . . His communication,
> even in a receptive and acceptant climate, tends to be almost entirely
> about externals and almost never about self. The form tends to be:
> 'The situation is . . .', 'They are . . .', 'They say . . .' [or, possibly] 'My
> characteristics are . . .', but he would almost never say 'I feel . . .', 'I

believe . . . '. He does not recognize himself as having problems. He does not perceive himself as a responsible agent in his world. He exhibits no desire to change and . . . shows many signs of wishing to keep himself and his environment as unchanged and stereotyped as possible (Rogers, 1959b, pp. 96–7).

At the other end of this continuum we find the individual living *in* his feelings, knowingly, and with a basic trust in and acceptance of his feelings as a guide for living. His experiencing is immediate, rich and changing . . . The ways in which he construes his experience are continually changing in the light of further experiencing. He communicates himself freely as a feeling, changing person. He lives responsibly and comfortably in a fluid relationship to others and to his environment. He is aware of himself, but not as an object. Rather it is a reflexive awareness, a subjective living in himself in motion (ibid., p. 97).

Rogers also described seven stages in the overall continuum and its various strands (1959b; 1961a, pp. 132–55). It seems that some of the schizophrenic clients in the Wisconsin research he spear-headed were functioning in ways resembling stage 1, at the low end of this continuum, making therapy an exceptionally uphill process. Rogers notes that even among clients coming voluntarily for help some are functioning at stage 2, and 'we have a very modest degree of success in working with them' (1961a, p. 134). At stage 3, a more frequent entry level, persons still largely describe or point to the self almost as an observer, tend to narrate problems and situations as opposed to speaking from inside immediately felt experience, and treat personal constructs as givens. By stage 4, feelings are being reported from the past or in not-now-present ways ('It felt', 'It hit me down deep'), in the client's life generally ('My feeling has always been . . .'), as desirable possibilities ('It would mean a lot to me if . . . '), and in other arm's length ways. Then, in stage 5, 'we find many feelings freely expressed in the moment of their occurrence' (Rogers, 1959b, p. 99). Hesitantly at first, but increasingly through stages 4 and 5, clients *ascribe meaning* to and from their own experience, recognising that the constructs they use are not absolute givens but can be modified and experimented with. By stage 6 there is typically a flowing quality to the person's inner processing, experience and expression.

Except for the experiencing scale, the process conception did not generate continuing research in the way that conditions theory did. Many component elements and ideas, however, continued to resonate in later work, and certainly have played a continuing part in my own thought. The focus I will turn to now flows especially from my work on the pathway of therapy. This pathway is substantially about the engaged human self in the process of healing and further becoming.

The engaged becoming self in therapy

Previous publications (Barrett-Lennard, 1990, and 1998, Chapter 7) provide a detailed picture of my perspective on the course of client/person-centred therapy. The fresh account here selectively distils this view, links it to other ideas in this chapter, and increases the visibility of points of connection with my current thought about the centrality and scope of relationship in human life. The therapy journey, as I describe it, encompasses five qualitative phases, each distinct in principle but shading into the next in practice. To complete this journey through all of the phases places considerable demands on the resources, time and commitment of the travellers. The whole route is a potential journey, which in practice ends at various points, as I acknowledge in describing it.

I think it instructive to ask again '*Why* does a person seek counselling/ therapy assistance?' What combinations of circumstance and personal make-up, what kinds of experienced distress or trauma, what qualities of discontent or other unhappiness, can be decisive in leading a person to enter therapy? Is it the person's 'inner' state, a crisis in a personal or family relationship, or a pattern of behaviour felt to be inadequate or self-defeating, that propels the individual to seek help? Is it the *pain* of anxiety or other emotional stress, is it more an unclear hunger or elusive lack of something, or a disillusionment and loss of meaning, or self or interpersonal dissatisfaction, or a positive but compelling wish for further personal discovery, growth or fulfilment? Is it desire to become a more confident, active agent in one's own world, or to be inside rather than outside the mainstream of life? These questions contain within them pointers to the very varied needs, circumstance, motives and even values that can propel persons into therapy.

This wide spectrum of purpose in its manifold expressions would seem unlikely to reach fruition through any *one* kind of journey. However, it is the process that largely defines therapy of any distinctive orientation, and a consistency of process would suggest coherence in outcomes. A distinctively person-centred therapy is a many-sided living whole in which a certain diversity arises naturally from the uniqueness of each client and of each emergent relationship between therapy partners. The diversity, however, can seem greater than it is, as a result of comparing features that reflect varied aims and entry points and which also may belong to *different stages in a broadly common journey.*

A now familiar face of therapy is the therapist-client relationship, especially the basic aspects of therapist response and client perception distinguished in the therapy conditions model. Looking at the whole phenomenon of therapy in its developmental dimension yields another principal face. Immediate distress may ease fairly quickly in therapy, but pattern change takes more time and literal work, work that hinges on the therapy alliance. A healing and growthful engagement, in whatever balance, does not spring full-blown into being. Much of the 'work' of therapy occurs within this evolving relationship and contributes to it. Client issues also evolve as progress is made, and the unfolding of issues and relationship combine to trace a pathway which constitutes the journey or course of therapy, a dimension as fundamental as the relationship conditions.

A. Beginning: the entry phase

This account of the entry phase of therapy assumes that the client is present voluntarily, even if pushed by inner desperation and pain or if approaching therapy tentatively as a possible recourse, and that client and therapist are meeting together in these capacities for the first time. Whether the client has made an informed choice of therapist and approach *or* has come with little knowledge either of the therapist or the philosophy of helping with which this therapist is identified, can have considerable bearing on just how the entry phase unfolds and thus also on its duration.

Few sessions are as critical as the first full interview of therapy, although later interviews may include more dramatic or 'breakthrough' developments. In an extended excerpt cited verbatim in my previous book (1998, pp. 108–9), the client notes at the start that she has been in therapy before, with some temporarily helpful effect, but 'as soon as anything out of the ordinary happens I go back to stage one'. She feels that 'there hasn't been any — enough change, I find, in my vision or whatever that makes me feel safe enough for the future'. The therapist (T) immediately acknowledges her message: 'You came into this situation, *this* therapy — this prospective therapy experience — with a background of having been in therapy before . . .' Just as quickly, the client (C) responds 'Does that invalidate it in any way?' and T explains 'I am making sure I'm catching your meaning — and what I'm hearing is that you have tried therapy; you haven't given up on it or you wouldn't be here, *but it hasn't been of any long-range help so far.*' The client then describes experience and events leading up to her seeking therapy this time.

As part of going into this 'background' C explains her problem and how she tries to cope by 'repressing' some of her feelings, although this is not working. She goes on, 'And I'm conscious — all of a sudden I started seeing patterns that I haven't seen before. I always saw every situation apart, and I was sort of wondering how much I did to get myself into these things . . .' By now her eyes are moist and her voice is breaking. T responds, there is a further exchange and C resumes her story: 'When I get to the point that I'm functioning well I *add* things. I add too much, and uhm . . . until everything just topples from the load of it.' Shortly, she says 'I'd always been *trying* to explain why I got myself in hot water before. And every time I had a different explanation. And I was wondering if I couldn't find one that would fit everything . . .' T's forceful acknowledgement of her message removes any need for her to repeat it — at the slight risk of overstatement:

'. . . you *really* wish you could understand; that you were on top of whatever the hell it is that's going on underneath in you, somehow, that's behind the things that's driving you or propelling you in the ways that you go.'

Naturally, the client strives to cope with her troubling feelings. The strategy she mentions so far is to discern her pattern and be able to explain her difficulties. Now she goes beyond this issue and moves further into her feelings of how tightly and painfully she is 'holding everything up' in her life. She has been smoking as she speaks, using one cigarette to light the next and, toward the end of this sequence (1998, pp. 93–6), mentions that she had run out of matches. T did not smoke and this problem created opportunity for an episode that undoubtedly brought the therapy partners more distinctly into view to each other. T suggested they look outside the door of the interview room shortly, where he believed they would find a box of matches. Momentarily puzzled, the client grasped the tacit message to unseen observers that she knew were behind a one-way vision mirror. Sure enough the matches were there! T was glad she knew *how* they had appeared, saying that he did not want her to think he was a magician. The spontaneous 'lesson' was fun; and the client was alive in her visible feeling of contact with T. There was increase in her confidence in the therapy situation, linked to a rise in the immediacy of her communication. At the end of the session she planned a series of appointments, envisaged as continuing for a number of months — seven months, in the event.

Several elements help to signify that the beginning phase of therapy is accomplished, paving the way for the working phase to follow. The signs I see are briefly as follows:

- *The client is present by choice.* Even if referred, he/she is taking charge of the decision to be in therapy. This quality of choice and attitude may only become quite clear when arrangements are being made for another interview or series of meetings.

- *The client owns to difficulty.* He/she has acknowledged difficulty or distress with self, with relationships, or with disturbing life circumstances or events. There is a message to the effect that 'All is not well with me, in my life, and that's why I'm here'.

- *Feelings are an issue.* There has been a direct expression of feeling by the client or, at minimum, an acknowledgement that feelings exist and need to be reckoned with.

- *Going beyond rehearsed content.* The client has not only reported experiences but, at moments, has expressed what is coming now in his or her feelings and thoughts.

- *Monologue to duologue.* There is a perceptible shift in the client's attention to the therapist, who is no longer (for example) just a vaguely apprehended professional listener. The therapist is now felt or coming into view as a distinctive other presence.

- *Awareness of being heard.* There are indications that the client has begun to feel heard by the therapist and to anticipate further personal understanding.

- *Being here matters.* What is happening in *this* forming relationship has begun to matter to both participants. Neither one could walk away from their association without significant afterthought or feeling; and in balance both wish to go further.

Within this interview, the client plainly indicated that she was troubled, came to therapy by her own choice and wanted to go on with it; that she experienced distressing feelings which she wanted to change or gain relief from; that although she started out by describing difficulties and reporting on her experience she soon began to pick up on the therapist's responses to her and go into what she was feeling as she spoke; and that the therapist came into view to her as another person closely listening, seeking to understand her and responding actively — mostly in serious vein but, at one point, almost in playful mode. An engagement of consequence to the participants had begun. Thus, each of the mentioned criteria for entry into a therapy engagement was met. What kinds of challenge would tend naturally to follow? The ensuing process, unique in its specifics for each client but with a discernible commonality, is the first major working phase of therapy.

B. Forging a personal-working alliance and the passage from woundedness to hope

Twin streams flowing through the course of therapy can be distinguished. *One stream is the development of the client-therapist relationship.* This encompasses each one's evolving perception of the other, and the view each has of the nature and quality of their partnership in the therapy enterprise. The other stream centres on client issues and process, as these unfold and change over the course of therapy. Since the client is in some way struggling or stuck in his/her own process and circumstance, and has enlisted T's help to gain relief and find a way out of this quicksand, the helping association is a form of alliance. And, as the relationship between client and therapist is employed as a means, the term 'personal-working alliance' seems usefully appropriate.

In this phase the helping relationship moves strongly into being, and the therapist comes to be experienced as a uniquely contributing ally. (If this does not develop, therapy is likely to be aborted.) The client, looking for help, leads the alliance on content issues but is not dominant in regard to the process. No *one* is literally in charge of the process but the therapist is particularly active in a highly receptive mode of attention and in relating from an enabling self open both to the uniqueness of *this* relationship and informed by the preparation of his/her related helping and life experience.

Experiential recognition of immediate feeling and meanings *as these emerge* in the client's expressions is a pivotal feature of the enabling process in person-centred therapies. This understanding includes but also progresses beyond step-by-step experiential recognition so that the client becomes an increasingly known and configured whole person to the therapist — yet still surprising to both partners as new ground is broken and there are shifts in consciousness and action. The alliance evolves unevenly, as any significant relationship does, but generally toward a deeper eventfulness and growing sense of movement both within and through the engagement of therapy. Sometimes, this development begins but then falters or stalls. In the latter case, therapy may stop without the alliance aspect reaching fruition. One might refer to this as a Phase B termination.

Part of the unique 'demand' of therapy is that clients cannot for long coast through a well-practised repertoire without the process becoming visibly pointless. Add further the feature of a therapist-partner who usually begins as a stranger and whose way of responding is unfamiliar in its total pattern. Then, it is indeed the case that the alliance is not simply present or given but something produced through strenuous application in a mode of searching dialogue; at once with self and with the other. However, in a fruitful alliance so forged the engagement becomes self-propelling for both partners. As 'person-centred' implies, the therapist as person is present too, in such a way that experience and skill do not diminish the challenge or lessen the freshness for the helper.

The second main stream and aspect of therapy pivots on the issues that are paramount for the client and the way that these unfold. Although there is wide variation in where and why clients begin person-oriented therapy, I see a common factor embedded in this variety. It struck me that some shift or change happened (and generally needed to happen) in the client's 'feeling space' that affirmed their choice of *this* therapy avenue and their wish to continue. As I pondered on this, I could see that the transition in common was from some kind of woundedness to an increase or awakening of hope.

I think that nearly all of us are wounded at times, in a psycho-social sense, and that old wounds may, under relevant conditions of stress, flare up again. The stresses may be cumulative or come from some fresh hurt or disturbing life difficulty. Felt inner conflict or anxiety or depressed mood or deep uncertainty and loss of meaning, and a diminution of self-esteem, are frequent manifestations of the woundedness I speak of. There is an erosion of individuals' sense of potency or capacity, confidence in their viewpoint, and/or belief that their own efforts can bear fruit. The result, in short, is a loss of hope. Persons choosing to enter therapy have not lost all hope, and the fact of taking this initiative itself typically brings some increment.

Wounds happen *to* us, at least as subjectively felt. We 'suffer' psycho-social wounds, and some of us easily feel that they are a demonstration of our inadequacy — which deepens the woundedness. By contrast, hope arises within us as we take promising action on our own behalf, and have experience that affirms this action; and this hope is energising. In passing from woundedness to hope there tends to be movement from a painful passivity *or* reactiveness to a wide-awake, more purposeful and active mode.

As client and therapist navigate the passage through this early phase, the exploration begins to loosen areas of client pain, anger, sorrow or other woundedness, and the helping partnership that meets this test evolves in the process. One outcome is that the client ventures now to believe and feel that there is a way ahead that is better than the track behind. Therapy has begun to ease their burden, it is giving safety to communication and search from the heart and the edge of awareness, and there is felt promise of further respite and discovery. There is a way forward, change is in the air, hope has reawakened.

This transition, opening into the next phase, is of its nature a matter of estimation and not of literal discontinuity in the therapy process. Phase B might have taken only two or three eventful meetings, or a much longer period of hard-working therapy sessions. The therapy travellers may now feel, if they pause to think of it, 'We are really on the way, and able to count on each other — so let's get on!' 'Getting on' is not a matter of consciously changing gears but of finding and creating the way through a new balance of issues in the alliance and in the client's quest.

C. Trust development, and the quest for self — 'Who am I?' 'How do I want to be?'

The twin streams of relationship development and of client issues and process, continue their flow through Phase C. There is a new intensity or scope of self-exploration, a more literal quest for the heart of the individual's identity and, often, for a reconciliation of disparate elements within the self. I do not equate 'self' with an encapsulated intra-psychic entity but with the person's distinctive consciousness and way of being in their world, especially their world of relation. It is this world which helped to fashion such aspects as the owned accepted-me, the me-I-fear, the wanted-me and the not-me.

To deeply open the self of inner consciousness and outer relation to view and review, therapy must be a safe haven and unusual in the depth of therapist empathy and other crucial relationship qualities. For any of us to searchingly disclose and investigate who this inner/outer person is, this I and Me-with-others who is now struggling, a rare quality of experienced safety and positive trust of T is necessary. This trust, building in Phase B, is in its fuller development and significance advanced as the central feature of the therapeutic relationship and alliance in Phase C.

Trust in my meaning here implies that the client is not only 'received' (Rogers, 1961a, pp. 130–1) but actively companioned in the risky enterprise of open-ended exploration of his/her sensitively feeling engaged self. Basic to the development of this strong trust in the therapist companion is the repeated experience of being heard in depth, of T seeming to know at moments 'what it is like to be me'. It is not necessary or realistic for this quality of empathy to be experienced continuously. The important element is that genuine close personal understanding has happened and has led to confidence that it will recur, especially when the client's feelings flow into unexplored aspects of their living.

Such trust also depends on the client having experienced T's caring interest coupled with absence of personal evaluative judgement. Most crucial are contexts where the client tends to be chronically self-evaluative. Also vital for this quality of trust is the client's experience of T as expressing and owning his/her actual experience in response to the client. Personal realness and transparency work to *disarm* and evoke trust within the other — legitimately so since it is showing what is actually present. Motivation to keep up an accustomed guard melts away in the ambience of this trust, which allows secrets which burden the client to come into open view. Effectively, the client who is at home in the context of a person-centred therapy seeks to attain a self that lives at ease with its own complexity, a self which reaches out resourcefully and without censure from its own core, that senses where it is going and knows how to proceed with the journey, and which feels alive and part of lives beyond itself.

Phase C tends to be the heartland of personal therapy. Within the client, not only are rigid, unchosen older moorings left behind, but any *fixed* anchorages are used in diminishing degree by an increasingly buoyant and mobile, becoming self. A proportion of clients would proceed from this phase directly to termination, or to a termination phase that included foreshortened elements from Phase D. There is no clear-cut boundary between Phases C and D, but a qualitative transition (most evident after its occurrence) in the working process of the therapist-client relationship and the ways in which C is proceeding in his or her quest. These two streams now tend, more than in earlier stages, to move and flow together almost as one.

D. Harmonic engagement; and the becoming self in action

In Phase D, client feelings during dialogue with the therapist are increasingly recognised as influenced by their relationship and its meaning rather than just being brought ready-made to this context. The therapy engagement is 'harmonic' on several levels. First, what is happening from moment to moment in the experiencing of the client and its outward expression to T are of one piece. Second, there is a close match between what each partner is experiencing and meaning in their expression and what they are taken to be feeling and meaning by the other. Expressions of this more 'simpatico' mutual awareness include instances of either partner accurately finishing the other's words, or 'reading' non-verbal signs without distortion of the other's feeling or thought.

The in-phase quality applies in further related ways. At this stage, the client's communication is giving verbal expression to the flow of feeling and experiential meaning *as the latter is occurring*. (In older terms, this implies immediacy.) Very little is said that is planned ahead. While self-exploration may still involve struggle, and almost certainly some trial and error, these features tend to be acknowledged as they occur. Generally, there is a relatively small and diminishing gap between what is immediately beneath the surface of expression and what is put into words or conveyed in a non-verbal way. A cogent feature of the process is the quality of interplay between the client's organically felt or sensed experience and his/her symbolic meaning-giving level of consciousness (Gendlin, 1969, 1981). I refer to this core inner process as *self-empathy*. Initially inarticulate feeling from the client's underlying organic being is recognised and given form in their receptive articulate consciousness (Barrett-Lennard, 1997). This began to happen earlier but is a more spontaneous and fluent feature, inherent in the harmonic or 'synchronous' expression characterising Phase D.

Clients also now experience or notice new levels of personal change. Often, they are conscious that their *values have been shifting* and that there are clarifications and alterations in balance among the life involvements that are important to them. Their personal priorities, what they most cherish, aspects of the ways they wish to live, have moved somewhat or are in sharper focus. *One's body*, visible and internal, *tends to become a more integral aspect of self*, in this phase; and clients may have a new sense of their own whole presence, of the space they occupy when in motion or still, of their mass and momentum and of their life energy radiating and receiving from the energy of others.

The use of metaphor and the sharing of literal subjective images, by the client as well as therapist, generally is more prominent and more telling in its expressive-communicative power in Phase D than in previous phases. Feelings may be portrayed using space-time metaphor, or as geometric forms, or as though they could be touched and had physical texture, or as being like solid objects or living organisms, and in other ways associated with corporeality. In seeming paradox, such language can help to intensify and give more accurately fitting and communicative expression to highly personal felt meaning than more literal and less muscular formulation can achieve.

Effectively, there is in Phase D more poetry both in the therapy interaction and in the way the client tends to construe and express felt experience. Partly because most of us live in a 'left-brain' world, stressing rationality, analytical thought and measured description, in the course of achieving greater wholeness in therapy the more artistic/poetic/intuitive-expressive side comes forward. 'Man', Rogers has argued, 'is wiser than his intellect', and the spontaneous use of metaphor and images reflects this wisdom. Person-centred therapy sustained at Phase D tends to liberate the creative artist within the client, at least in the sense of being a more active architect of self and a more creative builder in relations with others.

Usually, the importance of existing close relationships is affirmed, with a sense of furthered discovery of what is actual and desired in these relationships. As well, where it has been deeply at issue, a desired-feared separation is by now largely drained of internal conflict (and is a matter in and of itself rather than a symbol of something broader), and clients in open dialogue with self can now weigh and choose their course on an organismic basis. They are both more open to the perceptions of others, and less concerned about their image in public contexts or casual encounters. Major decisions are not necessarily made in the vocational sphere, but active reappraisal typically occurs, the client feels less imprisoned where this has been an issue, and the increased vitality and assurance of the becoming self is evident in his/her working life as in other spheres.

With such changes in the quality of his/her own process and needs, the client naturally begins to look beyond therapy. Transition to the concluding Phase E often is influenced by practical considerations as well. These may include the costs of therapy, shifting priorities and new choices — perhaps including travel or relocation — and the development of altered situations and more supportive relationships in the client's life. In these and similar circumstances, it is likely that the client will come to the topic of ending therapy. S/he may explore issues and meanings around this contemplated step via the same kind of in-phase, inward/outward and forward-moving process as other felt issues. Such exploration would mark the transition to Phase E.

E. Termination process: ending and entry

The termination process in person-centred therapies, if following on from phasic mode D (or, Phase C),[2] may resemble the entry phase in brevity —

---

[2] If termination occurs before phasic mode D is evident, but after a period of Phase C interaction and process, the termination phase is likely to resemble the pattern described here. If it occurs at a still earlier point, before fruition of therapy, the ending naturally would differ.

perhaps only occupying one meeting, especially if foreshadowed in a previous session. Where the total course of therapy is lengthy, or where external circumstances known in advance govern the time of ending, the termination phase may directly include a number of meetings.

The ending of person-oriented therapy contains elements of paradox. It occurs at the point where C and T know each other best as persons, value their relationship as a special kind of friendship and, apart from any anxiety around separation, when they are generally most relaxed with one another. Precisely the same features would make it most difficult for the client to continue to 'buy' T's time or for them to proceed on the basis of any contract for service. There is no rule in person-centred therapy against continuing actual friendship or collegial associations but, usually, the personal and life situations of (former) client and therapist work against this. Thus, the ending of their own relationship is naturally a consequential issue; an issue revolving around ways that the therapy partners feel with and toward each other, their special quality of communication, and their pool of experiences together. Each is managing a very real separation which in some ways is a prototype of other life partings.

The process of leaving therapy naturally tends to include some sharing of its import and meaning to the participants. Certain appreciated events and qualities together, and outcomes beyond their relationship, are likely to be singled out. Typically there is reference to current outside projects or forward-reaching plans in the client's life, ones that may sharpen further in their mention, and which express the refreshed and engaged becoming self. As this phase unfolds, termination of the therapy journey may impress itself as a beginning more than an ending, a transition in the client's way of being in life. This way is likely to include increased openness to feelings as they are happening, greater in-touchness and fluency in speaking from differing levels of one's experiencing, a more regardful and resonant engagement with others, and a quality less of effortful or anxious striving and more of confident purpose.

There may be moments of sadness in the parting of client and therapist, but termination when the time is ripe is such an affirming step that there is little or no continuing sense of loss. As with any significant human association, to a degree the relationship lives on within the participants; but the memories bring no regret, in the case of optimal termination. Further, in person-centred therapy, the door is rarely closed permanently. Unless changes in location would make any further contact impractical, the therapist is potentially available in case of future need. Even without this, if the partners' paths should later cross, each is likely to welcome this contact and easily move to sharing communication.

Summation

Over the period in which I was working out the perspective just given, plotting the course of therapy became less an end in itself and more another useful vehicle in the search to further envision the process nature of a psychotherapy in which the many-sided recuperation and unfolding of self is central. It would be contrary to my meaning to interpret the 'phases' deciphered here as uniform steps. My account seeks to catch the essence of an unusual quality of association and quest, one which in its specifics is as individual as are the participants in the enterprise. This enterprise and process tends to build on itself until it could be seen that another phase or level has been reached. No main level can be entirely skipped for each is a crucial part of the foundation for the next. Thus, also, no phase mode in its full expression can simply be switched into at will, or as an instant product of specific technique, for its emergence hinges on relationship development and the journeying of self.

Therapy of course can come to an end almost anywhere along the broad continuum. Moreover, the journey is not always as distinctly unidirectional as my picture might suggest. In or out of therapy, we are subject to mood swings, biochemical rhythms, ups and downs in relationships and achievement, uneven life stresses. Clients can move ahead strongly in therapy and then seem to slip back, with the process being more like an earlier phase. Oscillating motion, or a spiral-like return to familiar issues tackled on a somewhat different level, complicate identification of where the travellers are on their journey. Nevertheless, if therapy is to come to strong fruition, the journey is a progressive one and the underlying direction in general accord with the sequence discussed. Beyond this, client issues or therapist style may work to favour processes in one phase more than in another, especially as between phasic modes C and D.

In introducing this perspective, the issue of therapy as recovery and healing, as re-education or growth, or self and interpersonal learning, or social reconnection, etc., was acknowledged. More than difference in language is implied by these alternative and complementary designations. They connote axes and levels of change which appear in differing balance in the phases distinguished. Literal healing and recovery processes are most obvious in Phases B and C. Growthful change to new levels of functioning is discernible earlier but most evident in Phase D. Clients may largely heal and recover, with important elements of growth, without proceeding through a Phase D-type process. Becoming more expressively at home with all the complexity of a self that is naturally active in varying modes or configurations has roots in Phase B process but comes to most visible fruition in Phase D.

Coda

What is our basic nature, how does the human organism work, what is a self and how do selves form and change? This chapter has inquired into these questions and advanced a range of proposition-answers; a perspective that amounts to a theory. The later part of the chapter has a more directly practical focus in its exploration of the unfolding path of self-healing and becoming in therapy. That thought also had its germination some time ago, although this new presentation is both briefer and in some ways further advanced than previous versions. The next chapter leaps ahead in time to the newest and freshest development of ideas in my own journey of thought. Human experience and actions always occur within a context. Broadly expressed, I have come to see life as lived in and through relationship on many levels. My ideas about the working of context and relationship in human life are most fully developed in the other new volume already mentioned (Barrett-Lennard, 2003). The following chapter extends and links this book to the further volume by anticipating its thrust.

Chapter 10

An expanded view of relationship and healing

My projected further book, with the working title The primacy of relationship: Healing revisited in an altered world, *is already written in draft as I begin this chapter. Both books are up-to-date expressions within their own compass, but the topical scope of the other volume came later in the overall evolution of my thought. The challenge in writing this chapter is to introduce and foreshadow major themes in that further thought, but not as a mere summary and without losing connection with what already has been presented.*

For me, the two books, which I once thought to encompass in a single volume, directly complement each other. This one centres on the experiencing person and on the conditions and process of becoming in therapy, families and small groups. The topics and my approach to them are very recognisable person-centred expressions. However, I always want to see further, and am more excited by fresh awareness than by settled understanding. My other book continues the concern with enabling and recovery processes but differs in that its primary focus is on relationship, relations within and among persons, groups and larger human systems. It reflects another phase in my 'mindful journey'. I will begin this bridging chapter by again focusing on the self, this time in respect to its diverse context-sensitive nature.

My poem, *'A Person'* — placed first in the Appendix of poems — begins with the line 'One alone and many in one'. How do we become 'many in one', how is this plurality manifest, and does it imply both versatility of self *and* the possibility of a sundered self? I am deeply interested in these questions and have searched into them. One starting point is to consider the immensely complex make-up of the human organism and person which, when examined across all of its constituent systems and myriad processes, makes the idea of a highly unified quality of being implausible. The working of any hugely complex, dynamic and, in our case, elaborately conscious system cannot fail to manifest diversity of pattern. But does this variability imply an organised diversity of self? Given that human awareness of self evolves through interchange with other varied selves, especially others on whom a developing person depends for regard and affirmation, the answer I see is 'Yes'.

The diverse selves of significant others not only engage us in different ways, but carry different meanings about what are acceptable or effective ways of being. Who we are to ourselves comes to differ from one pivotal context of relation to another, and alternate patterns or configurations of self naturally evolve. This is in keeping with a contemporary view of self as inherently diverse or 'plural' rather than indivisible or unitary. Clearly there can be more than one specific way of thinking about this plurality.[1] In my perspective, the inherent complexity of the human organism, in the context of formative experience in relationships with significant others of diverse attitude and make-up, leads to variety in self-organisation, an organisation that is context-sensitive. The selves brought into play with a parent, with a sibling or other family member, with a partner or lover, with an own child, a close friend, classmates or workmates, or an antagonist or enemy, are distinctive one to another. I call these organised self-systems 'contextual subselves' — and they are tangible phenomena open to empirical study.[2]

If persons have a family of subselves, the question arises of how this 'family' lives together; what the quality of relation is among member subselves. In addressing this question another appears: how is it best to think about a well or poorly functioning plural self-system and what is saliently different in these two cases? In broad answer, at the negative extreme, the self may be literally sundered. Component subselves may not recognise each other as belonging; the person engaged in one self-configuration regards another as 'not the real me', or denies its very existence. In the opposite, well-functioning case, the subselves openly recognise and are known to each other. Effectively, they are in easy relation and open dialogue. In a broader sense, the person is aware of their diversity and not troubled by it. Each of their (repertoire of) action selves is well-adapted to the contexts in which it comes spontaneously into play. The subselves have overlapping qualities but each is distinct in its total configuration, and the individual's manysidedness equips them for the widely varied contexts of relation through which their lives are lived.

The idea of 'true self' takes on a new, more complex and grounded meaning in this perspective. There is potentially an inner and outer congruency in the case of each subself, and the wholeness of the person lies in the fullness of their engagement during the activation of each component self *and* in the openness of their consciousness in one theatre of life to their engagement qualities and awareness in other theatres. No subself configuration is necessarily 'truer' than another, for the person truly is many in one, with varied constituent truths

---

[1] See, for example, Mearns and Thorne, 2000, pp. 113–19 and 172–95; and Cooper's main chapter (pp. 51–70) in Rowan and Cooper's book *The plural self* (1999).
[2] A Contextual Selves Inventory, developed by the author, has been applied in exploratory research and is available for further investigative use (Barrett-Lennard, 2003, Chapter 1).

and a collective identity reflected in the way this community of congruent subselves works together. In the case that a person's component selves live, as it were, in different and separated chambers, the chambers comprise an aggregate whole not a knit dynamic union powered by its versatile diversity. My poem 'Deception' (see Appendix 2) speaks in more dramatic voice of 'part selves haunted and in fear of other parts, connected by a consciousness without identity — no hand within, no lit communing self, the heartbeat lost though limbs still live'.

The language of 'contextual subselves' ties in with another feature of perspective. I no longer think of persons as sovereign beings, each one finally navigating his or her own way with a separate and unique compass, intention and world of meaning. Although each of us is distinctively aware through a resident consciousness inherent in our make-up as humans, this consciousness is not a self-contained structure but a dynamic process in interaction with the consciousness of others. More still than 'interaction' may imply, it can be said that we *partake* of each other's consciousness and form collectivities of awareness. Notwithstanding, some of us try to live single lives, merely *trading* with each other as needed to satisfy our separate wants but without the conjunction and interflow of living relationship; without our selves merging with selves of others in twosome and larger We's that develop their own life and influence. Such effort runs counter to the interdependent and connective qualities of our nature, and its pursuit can make one's world — like that of Scrooge in Charles Dickens' tale — small, misshapen and incomplete.

Western culture and thoughtways place high value on personal autonomy, and tend to carry the illusion of separateness. I say 'illusion' advisedly because relationship is not just a matter of overt engagement or intention. Even persons who try to cut themselves off, and work hard at avoiding any opening of self to others, are involved in a reactive-avoidant mode of relation. It is also true that feared or despised others live in one's head as much, or more, than in the flesh, and are party to stressful inner conversation. Internal conversations are commonplace, and seem often to include confrontational dialogue with self and/or Other, with no clear line between. The lack of a clear line plausibly comes from the fact that we have 'relationships' among our own plural selves not unlike (and partly stemming from) the relationships we have with the selves of others.

Ideas of the self as sovereign and separate from the selves of others, each running with its own autonomous governor in the well-functioning person, tend to support a view of helping in which therapies of the individual are the ultimate healing mode. One of my respected person-centred colleagues (in another time and place) expressed the belief that if only we could bring about a certain critical mass or, better still, *epidemic* of therapeutic and facilitative relationships the whole culture would change and social problems would dissolve. Others have argued that mental health is the crucial window and route to community and societal health. If only matters were this simple! Observation of the complex real-life diversity of human relations and circumstance suggests a different view. In situations of great personal stress and need, psychotherapy, more often than not, is not a feasible recourse. And, even where it is, and is individually helpful, from a societal standpoint it is a fire-fighting endeavour with little impact on the underlying conditions driving people to seek help.

There are hosts of personally very needy people who do not seek therapy. The reasons vary: for some, personal therapy is so outside their ken it does not arise as anything real; for others, cost and duration, or the unavailability of therapists, rules it out; and for still others it is irrelevant to their self-perceived problem and need. In short, such help is out of reach or 'out of relevance' for many people suffering undue or disabling stress. To put it in more experiential terms, 'why *should* a person take this step if they have the idea that therapy will focus on their own personality and inner self but they are in agony over their relational or communal life systems? For a person caught and in torment in these systems, or deeply alienated by them, where would confidence in their individual capacity to transform their lives, through therapy and self-change, come from?' (Barrett-Lennard, 1998, p. 341).

Personal therapies are at their best only a part-solution to 'psychological' and interpersonal problems that reflect conditions rooted in the working of social, political and economic systems driven by forces beyond individual control. Given that we are so embraced and caught up in a world of interacting, self-propelling systems of engagement, it is 'compelling to think that the damaging misery of individuals is in substantial part symptomatic of communal and societal disorders'. I further argue, in the same place, that 'to place one's whole confidence on an individual healing level of intervention would be to leave the greater part of present human misery and need unattended, also to leave human systems at various levels of organisation and complexity collapsing or very seriously at risk, and to give very inadequate attention to prevention'.[3]

Personal consciousness and well-being can be ultimate reference points even when social and collective life is a major focus. Human system-oriented *and* person-centred emphases are potentially two faces of one whole. One expression of this inclusive perspective is to envision the overall spectrum of human and life systems in our world, in which the *experiencing person* is positioned at the apex of a comprehensive schema that includes nine levels of system common to virtually all of us (Barrett-Lennard, 1993c; 1998, pp. 365–7; 2003, Chapter 4). The individual person is a complex system, as already implied, whose self-diversity

---

[3] These passages from my other book (2003, Chapter 3) stem from my first serious exploration of 'healing on a system level', presented in a visiting seminar to social work colleagues in the 1970s.

feeds into and reflects human relationships differing in kind and level.

A person's *main dyadic systems* (or twosome relationships) are a primary context and level, involving the closest meshing of selves. However, in an important sense the dyad is less inclusive than the individual since no twosome embraces the totality of the persons from whose interplay the dyad derives. *Family relational systems* include dyads, whole family units, and other relationships in the many combinations explored in Chapter 7. *Face-to-face groups* (Chapter 6) become important in a child's world from the time of day care or preschool entrance. Besides developmental and learning contexts, groups are organised around task and team or work functions and social, recreational and special interests of their members. There is of course enormous variation in the qualitative nature and dynamics of group life.

Linkage of individuals and groups though large *organisations* of many kinds also is an ubiquitous feature of contemporary life. Career and work settings in organisations are a major subcategory, with frequent bearing on a person's sense of personal identity and worth — so often bound up with their membership and role in a work organisation. The connective tissue of human life pivots also on varied *communities of association and belonging* that stem, for example, from ethnic affiliation, shared neighbourhood residence, a unifying local culture, and/or shared religious or other belief. A person's emotional bonds with significant communities of experienced belonging may be less visible than in the case of a career work organisation but more central to their life meaning. However, such significant belonging is far from universally experienced; an issue I will come back to.

Membership of *nation states* or other big political, ideological or economic groupings influences life engagements on other levels and thus has indirect as well as direct effects on relationships and identity. Much of the influence and connection with our wider society is mediated through the component smaller systems of most immediate membership. Mediated effects flow also from our membership in the total *human family and race system*. Consciousness of this ultimate whole as a single fabric of interwoven, interdependent lives, communities and states seems vital for our collective well-being, and bears on the health of our *planetary life system* as a whole. Thus, our total spectrum of significant relations extends to the life system beyond the human world, even including 'relations' with parts of the natural environment not regarded as living (the atmosphere and oceans) but which provide the habitat for life.

Earlier chapters have devoted close attention to the helping relationship, and to therapist empathy and other conditions conceived as so crucial to a fruitful process. The therapy relation, seen in context, is a microcosm nestled within a very much larger orbit of relations. 'Standing back' from this valued micro-system allows another level of embracing conditions to come into view, ones that support values implicit in the personal therapy principles. The wide sweep of relations outlined here was part-foundation for an expanded vision of helping/enabling processes first introduced at the end of my last book (1998, pp. 368–71) and more fully worked out later (Barrett-Lennard, 2002a).

When the (Rogerian conditions-based) helping micro-system is viewed in *its* wider context a few features stand out as evident preconditions for its substantial presence in helping relations and therapy contexts. One pre-condition is that the societal and relevant subcultural or institutional contexts need to be essentially democratic and egalitarian in nature. Also, the valuing of emotional, interpersonal and cognitive growth and well-being needs to be significantly present 'in the culture'. And, since a pluralist society will include contrary mindsets, institutional or other systems that work to buffer opposing visions and support diversity may be crucial as well.

Client/person-centred therapy originated in an individualist culture and discipline and did not at the time discriminate human life processes and consciousness as relational in their essence. However, in present view, 'our engagements are *not* just settings that we move into and out of, carrying identical characteristics though each context. *We do not "visit" our pivotal engagements but are distinctively embodied in them.* When they change, we "our-selves" are different' (Barrett-Lennard, 2002a, p. 147). This emphasis has very practical implications, even within therapy and, more especially, beyond it. In 'individual' therapy, as well as in counselling couples and families, clients need to be able to confront issues in their life relations with counsellors who are receptive, experientially knowing and effectively enabling of such exploration. Capacity to *know* the other in their worlds of relational engagement depends on the richness of the therapist's own relevant experience-in-relation, and on his or her sensitivity to the client's subculture and particular life setting. A fusion is called for of empathic sensitivity, personal knowledge of relational contexts, and a searching consciousness toward relational processes.

Children are born into relationship, mostly in families, which are a unique window into the forms and working of close relationship and its impact, expecially in childhood. Families often are under enormous stress, in a perilous larger world, and their welfare and health is hugely consequential. Personal relationship counselling (see O'Leary, 1999) is sometimes helpful but cannot remedy system distortions on other levels. Further kinds of relational healing, however, could be assisted by psycho-social professionals working from an *extended* person-centred or similar base. Each kind is distinct, with its own challenges and specifics of process, as briefly outlined next but more closely explored elsewhere (Barrett-Lennard, 2002a; 2003, Chapter 5).

Internal group relations issues are in focus when a group seeks assistance with its own collectivity and working. The focus and process are quite distinct from group therapy for it is the group that is being healed. The consultant is serving as a process facilitator in group relations. Perceptive listening varies in focus but remains crucial at this and all other levels, including the level of *community relations facilitation*. Enabled participative communication of many members can itself be a crucial process of discovery and illumination. Cumulative listening leads also to a sensing of blockages, tensions, polarities and dynamics of communal feeling. *Inter-group relations* between communities or organisations is another distinct level. People communicating across large-group boundaries react from within the engagement system of their total group, their subgroup within it, their role and ambitions in these contexts, and their anxieties about the Other. Often, needs have been satisfied and perceptions 'validated' by a status quo of opposition and conflict. New/deeper awareness around self-motives, interactive dynamics and the consequences of change are all part of movement in stressed large-group relations.

Helping to effect change in *relations between large people systems* is more complex still. Each such system differs in its structure, in the historical and current outlook of its people, and in their governmental system and leadership. In relations of conflict, each system almost certainly will include people whose experienced interests or life meaning are embedded in the conditions or process of conflict and the quest this entails.[4] Yet, the possibility of change exists — and is a topic to return to.

This total direction of thought has been distilled in a few propositions, of which the most pivotal is expressed as follows: *Therapy and helping processes over a wide range of levels comprise a single spectrum of which a unifying axis is the healing of relationship.* Another principle centres on the therapist-facilitator's resources and stance, emphasising counsellor 'literacy' in the realm of relational life, and an 'active responsiveness to the lived relational worlds of client persons and groups' (Barrett-Lennard, 2002a, p. 152). A further proposition acknowledges that each level of envisioned helping intervention introduces unique features, and effective facilitation is not simply another application of identical principles. Consider, for example, the level and phenomenon of community — next explored in its own right.

Community experience and process was a 'later' focus of serious interest to me, triggered by particular experiences against a background of interest in groups and in human relations studies as an interdisciplinary field. One relevant event was an extended leave experience away from my home base and in a young, elaborately planned city. The very attractive environment was not 'home' to most of its highly mobile middle-class inhabitants. No previous setting had

---

[4] I believe and have noted elsewhere (2002, p. 151) that 'large systems have interwoven currents and a dynamic momentum that gains energy and direction from many sources in interaction, and significant change in the stressed relations and posture of two such systems in conflict must require wider involvement than that of one or a few leaders on both sides'.

left me with such a strong sense of paradox; effectively, of beauty without heart. Missing was a quality of felt communal association and life. The following year (1975), I took part in a two-week *big* group residential workshop that amounted to a learning laboratory around the formation and meanings of community. That complicated experience, data gathered at the end of it, and some reflective processing, resulted in a conference paper that fed into later publications (Barrett-Lennard, 1979b, pp. 217–22; 1994).

But what is the phenomenon of 'community'; what are its primary characteristics? Clearly, a vital one is a felt *sense of community* existing in the subjective experience of members. This requires that members be effectively within reach of each other, with a language in common — often used in distinctive ways. A quality of interdependence in the relation of members is reflected, for example, in a division of labour or role in order to meet the varied needs of the community. A communal group acquires a code of conduct, overt or (more often) implicit, in which relations and dealings among members are the primary concern. A certain cohesion or organic quality also is implied.

A communal whole experienced by its members naturally influences relationships within it, relationships that in their turn co-determine the whole. The community is an expression and form of human relationship, a relational life form with its own type of 'consciousness' built up over time and mediated through the consciousness of its members. Many ingredient aspects of history, circumstance and present relationships internally and with its neighbours and larger society combine to make one community distinct from another. There is of course more than one way to view and seek to discover and understand a community, in its individuality.

A census-type approach might focus on origins of the community, its forms of leadership, governance and decision-making, its population characteristics, where members live and what they aspire to, what the community produces by way of goods and services, and broadly how it deals with neighbouring groups and systems — all of this useful for some purposes but not tuned to the study of community as relationship. In an approach used in some anthropological studies, the participant-investigator engages closely with members to understand their worlds of meaning, interrelation, valuing and belief. This 'inside view' can greatly enrich but does not replace an evolving systematic frame of reference belonging to the investigator. Redfield (1960, p. 82) has argued that effectively and creatively managing the union of inside and outside views 'is the central problem in studies of culture or of personality'. This position implies that empathic engagement has a fundamental role in coming to understand the ethos of a community.

Detailed accounts of the residential workshop that helped to spark my thinking in this area have been published (Barrett-Lennard, 1994; Rogers, 1977; Wood, 1984). *Some* of the mentioned criteria for community were satisfied from the start of the workshop. Members were in reach of each other, with natural points of contact. Importantly, however, most arrived as strangers to each other, so that their first-hand relationships started from zero. They had a common language (though difficult for some) and a variable familiarity with person-centred concepts. The living and meeting arrangements, and desire to come into each other's presence, made for a degree of built-in interdependence. The presumption that members brought a common code with them was tested, challenged and sometimes found wanting. Most important, the experience and sense of community had not yet happened.

The workshop was something of a paradox. It launched into 'community' meetings but with members not yet acquainted and with little idea of how to work together as one big group. Some core components of belief and value were treated as if not open to question although discovery through experience was a primary value. Personal empowerment was an expressed aim, but in the big meetings (130+ members) opportunity for overt expression was just a tiny window for each person (or no window at all for the less assertive). Data gathered at the end suggested that concurrent small-group meetings and one-to-one encounters were also basic to most people's sense of being together and coming into community. Some emphasised that they also needed time alone. The data lent support to my idea that a communal experience and relationship is founded in big part on networks of more personal relationship among the members. This view would imply that workshops where many are strangers at the start, but which proceed directly to intensive big group sessions, are effectively short-circuiting basic steps in the building of relationship in a community.

One outcome was that I began to formulate a theory of community (1979b, pp. 217–20; 1994; 1998, pp. 215–17) or, more exactly in present form, a theory of community as relationship. Initial propositions distil ideas about the basic nature of communities and why they form. Further elements encompass dynamic principles, such as how interdependence works in a well-functioning community. One proposition contends that formed communities (like persons) seek to maintain and enhance themselves, have an identity interwoven with relations among and self-definition of members, and 'satisfy human needs for affiliated belonging and presence with others'. Another proposition, about thriving communities, states that *when communities satisfy growth needs of constituents, beyond a period of initial development, they tend to behave in constructively responsive ways toward other communities, organisations and individuals.* Properties of 'a poorly-functioning or severely-threatened community' are also identified, the theory then speaks to the relation of a community to its host society, and the final proposition articulates a value stance: *A community is an emergent whole with a life of its own which normally it seeks to maintain. As a life form, it should not lightly be conceived, subverted or destroyed* (Barrett-Lennard, 2003, Chapter 6).

Communicide has been rampant in human history. When community systems are seen to have emergent life beyond the separate lives of the constituent members then to forcibly extinguish the heartbeat of a developed community becomes visible as a crime comparable with the taking of individual human lives. It is all too painfully clear that many communities throughout the world are suffering, bloodied by internal or external conflict, collapsing, dying of neglect by a host society on which they depend, or in visible process of destruction. Even in affluent societies, factors such as high social mobility, developments in entertainment technology, and belief that individuals make their own destiny in a basically competitive world, contribute to a culture in which strong human bonding in dynamic communities seems to be more the exception than the rule. All this links to issues and ideas about loneliness and alienation.[5]

Loneliness is an experience not a circumstance and, although some situations can trigger or feed into it, has very little to do with being out of the immediate presence of others. Indeed, one may have times of distinctly felt need to be alone, and actively seek solitude to sift through confused or uncertain feelings and ideas. In other circumstances, solitude can be the last thing a lonely person really desires. Feeling cut off, apart and different, and perhaps hungering for contact but unable to speak of what lies heavily within, are very familiar human experiences. The many faces of experienced separation and loneliness I see can be clustered in three groups or levels. One group, with variant forms, involves *self-estrangement*, or being 'out of touch on the inside'.

Inner dividedness is one clear form of self-estrangement. Our conscious self (or a main subself) avoids — may not be able to tolerate — awareness of desires, fears or other emotion and action arising from a more submerged part of the self (or another subself). Inner dialogue is restricted or frozen in argument. Another quality of estrangement results when a primary anchoring feature, or even the whole familiar context of one's life is lost or ripped away. An acute loss of meaning, with feelings of futility, impotence or anomie results. A more extreme form of estrangement involves the fracture or loss of a basic sense of self, which may happen in a breakdown or psychosis such as acute schizophrenia.

---

[5] My expressed interest on the topic of loneliness began with a talk in the late seventies, later revised for *The Ceshur Connection* (in the mid-1980s — see Appendix 1). Subsequent versions were shared with students in training workshops and, sometimes, with colleagues and clients. I procrastinated over regular journal publication but, finally, came back to my progeny and added another main part on 'recovering connection'. David Mearns asked me to give a public lecture at Strathclyde University (in mid-2000) and that lecture, and group presentations in Vienna and elsewhere, were the launch points of the newly expanded paper — then invited for European publication (Barrett-Lennard, 2001b). A further version is now a chapter in my twin book (2003, Chapter 8), and it ends with a summing-up of the crisis of *dis*connection and its potential outcomes.

Another variant involves persons who seem to float in a 'self-less' hollowness, with an implicit hunger for identity, for selfhood, to be a 'Me' with distinct qualities and a sense of direction that carries over from one situation and moment to another. This directionless quality can seem like a deficiency of will to those of us with strongly patterned selves.

Beyond these varieties of *self*-estrangement, there is the whole further level of *interpersonal loneliness*. This does not require self-estrangement although any of the mentioned patterns could contribute to it. Unfulfilled needs for affiliation, caring, respect or loving intimacy in its various forms can leave us acutely lonely or even with chronic hunger for close connection. A person is handicapped by inexperience in close relationships, for example, with siblings or other built-in childhood companions, with emotionally responsive parents or their near substitute, or with people met and mutually chosen in friendship. Without the background of such relationships a person tends to live in a world of strangers, not knowing from experience how to know them. Conditions of modern life lead often to associations that are engaged in not for their own sake but as a means to some outside goal for which the other is a conveyance. A flow of such contacts can coexist with profound loneliness, felt even if not discriminated.

Severe loneliness for close personal relationships tends also to work against a sense of belonging in a larger group or community. As earlier implied, I believe it to be within our nature to *hunger for community* beyond close and intimate relationships, a hunger possibly related to our tribal origins. Western mass culture clearly leaves many people with little if any sense of inclusion and belonging in a communal whole. The experience of community belonging makes possible the sense of living in a world in which every person matters and has his or her own distinct part. It is of course possible for people to bunch together in towns and organisations out of convenience or necessity, not to enhance the meaning of their lives. Social alienation also can lead easily to an exclusive concern with self or with a small 'life raft' of family or other personal allies. Altogether, the domain of loneliness is extremely broad, and its ramifying expressions and effects are of crisis proportion. What recourses might overcome these effects?

A vital shift toward resolving the epidemic of disconnection and alienation — especially of loneliness in its many guises — is an evolving public consciousness that these conditions are an illness infecting the whole culture. From this increased awareness action would tend to follow, with steps to conserve and nourish experiences of interconnection on many levels. These levels potentially extend from the individual person to relations between large people systems, and even within the whole living world. As earlier discussed, in the well-functioning person context-sensitive subselves are dynamic entities not shut off from each other but connected effectively in open dialogue.

Analogously, a well-functioning relationship entails an open responsive meeting and interplay of selves, each projected from a larger self-system but without sharp boundary in their interaction. Thus, communication can flow freely and expressively between the linked selves, within an ambience of transparency and trust. To help recover these qualities of connection within and between selves, widely available and easily chosen therapy and counselling resources are called for. Accessible and highly skilled resources to enable group and community healing are a further considered level. But these developments are not sufficient.

Our civilisation faces the huge challenge of learning to better manage relationships between large, self-interested people systems. There is great need not only to defuse explosive tension or conflict between such systems but also to discover how afterwards to bring about the actual healing of relations. However, I think it naive to assume a positive outcome on all of these mentioned levels. A distinct possibility is that superficial association, conflict and predation, and emotional isolation of people, will continue to build. Communities of belonging may seldom revitalise but, instead, suffer dilution, deterioration or extinction. Factors such as population increase and inequality, environmental deterioration and decline of natural resources can drive stressed relations and conflict between peoples. The human family may well become more divided, more people will be desperate individually and in collectives of varied kind and scale.

The other broad possibility I see is more hopeful. Although there have been ferocious and tragic local/regional wars, and a large war is raging in Iraq as I write these lines, no huge international war has engulfed our civilisation for over half a century. Most nations would see their self-interest as being to avoid at all costs such a huge, convulsive and uncontained conflict. Some forward steps can be seen in the field of education, in respect to economic security in some regions, in nations coming to the aid of others in the face of major *natural* disasters, and in a growing consciousness and concern for the environment and our impact on it. The United Nations, with its agencies, has survived as a significant symbol and context for negotiation, and a broadly humanising and often practical force. Expressions of competition, and the issue of whether winning out over others should continue as a mainspring of the world culture, can be questioned now. This questioning needs to grow and spread much further, so that failure in competition no longer demeans and demoralises individuals and, most of all, so that everyone retains a sense of inclusion.

Most serious inquiry is about discovering connections, and the broad aim of my coming book is to throw light on 'the connective tissue of human life, a tissue stretched in many contexts to tearing point' (2003, Chapter 8). I believe that a common factor running through the diverse circumstances, reactions and desires that perpetuate social illness is a failure of knowing, of seeing into or discriminating the connection of things. Issues of connection apply also within us as humans, given the complexity of our make-up. The differing configurations of self brought into play in diverse personal and social contexts not only satisfy varied needs but can express diverse codes. Or, as already implied, the person may be at home in each of their diverse realms of engagement, moving easily and without conflict through the natural versatility of their complex make-up from one modality and expression of self to another. Moving away from the former state and toward the latter is a freshly expressed but basic level of healing in person-centred and related therapies.

The experiential group process (Chapter 6) is another selectively valuable avenue, best suited to those who are in fairly open inner dialogue and desirous of more perceptive awareness and intimacy in their relationships. The members' ongoing relational lives naturally influence a group's process indirectly. Who offers the groups, for whom and with what aims and practice approach, all have vital bearing on informed choice by participants and the potential values (and valuing) of their experience. Other limiting factors that need to be overcome include expense and accessibility hurdles. Although costs are distributed among group members, they will still be out of reach for some unless underwritten or subsidised by sponsoring systems. Opportunity also depends on the availability of resource persons of wisdom, skill and integrity, to organise and facilitate the groups. Another factor is the furtherance of informed community awareness of the *actual process nature* and potentials of such group experience.

Organisations, especially those providing work life environments, can be viewed through the lenses of varied metaphors and associated mindsets. A classical one depicts the human participants as ideally working together like perfectly synchronised components of a machine (Morgan, 1986, pp. 19–38). Other images treat organisations as political systems, or as being like a living organism, or as having self-organising brain-like qualities (ibid.). Another major, widely applicable image is of the organisation as a culture. I believe that most organisations need to further confront the implications of being a context in which members live a significant part of their lives and from which they take home significant effects to their families and communities. A potential change outcome would be for the organisation truly to see itself as a people-resource, this linked to increased awareness of the critical need for wide-ranging human relations recovery and development.

Work organisations, at their best, provide a sense of bonding among their members, although this does pose some risk since loss of membership can be very hard to cope with where there is a general dearth of communal experience. This wider deficit requires growth in public consciousness of the crisis in community identification and sense of belonging for people both in 'developed' and 'under-developed' regions. As public discrimination evolves, there will be pressure for governments to take further steps to protect and support communities in their efforts to strengthen and revitalise. As part of this change, community impact assessment will become a regular practice when major new legislation or industrial-commercial developments are being planned. Communities felt from within to be at risk need to be able to reach out and obtain highly skilled help, as already mentioned, to recover their energy, resolve tensions, and bring into focus priority directions and accompanying strategies. For a deeply divided community, competent outside assistance may be crucial for members to be able to confront strongly felt issues together and engage in a healing quality of problem-solving.

Many multi-national organisations exceed the economies and influence of smaller nations, and their operations can be out of effective reach of individual governments. The possibility of 'bridling' such systems for the public good depends on the general improvement of relations of trust and open responsive cooperation between national governments. Resulting coordinated action could then forcefully influence the policies and culture of multi-nationals. This level of change would be enhanced by another: the needed evolutionary shifts in the general culture of organisations as human relations systems, such that the relationships and well-being of members became a natural and self-perpetuating priority.

Differences in living standards, ethnic affiliation and/or belief systems provide the backdrop to bitter conflict between peoples in regions across the world. When such conflict builds to violent clashes, the protagonist/enemy group diminishes in perceived humanity, fear and hatred are dominant feelings and the relation becomes devoid of empathy. In addition to tragic loss of life, grief, anger and impairment of relations beyond measure prevail among the survivors from recent and current conflicts. The healing of relations between the peoples involved is enormously difficult. Interchange between affiliated groups of nations or peoples who differ group to group in world view and circumstance are particularly difficult at the best of times. Effective management and improvement of relations hinges on a variety of factors, not least the human relations knowledge resources *effectively available* to powerful governments and international bodies. Further commitment of support to action research groups seeking to advance this knowledge base and develop strategies for its utilisation is an urgent priority.

In approaching the end of this chapter and book I will sum up priority developments mentioned or implied as though they *will* happen. First, I foreshadow that healing will no longer be compartmentalised in the way that it is now. Differing levels will be recognised but seen as interconnected on a single continuum, such as outlined. To date, they have been treated as basically different processes belonging to different areas of knowledge, although all parts of the spectrum are concerned with connection and relationship. A familiar level concerns the self and its varied configurations, which can live together in qualitatively very different ways. Each diverse or plural self also lives in direct relation with the diverse selves of others. Such relationships may deeply engage and satisfy the participants or connect only a limited part or configuration of self in each person, or be neutralising to parts of either person's self.

Continuing in positive vision, where couples and families want to and can seek help together, a choice of highly skilled and wise assistance will be open to them, including person-centred relationship counselling as a major avenue. This recognises and will not simplify the complexities of relationship. It will be oriented jointly to the We/Us system, the experiencing of each person and the larger relational contexts of their lives. Participants will be able to discover new depths in their own and each other's felt experience and come to see their twosome (or family, etc.) and its working as a whole. Some troubled relationships cannot regenerate and become fruitful, but the therapy will enable recovery from the grief, demoralisation or bitterness of failing or failed relationships.

Where tense conflictual relations between communities arise, and presuming that representatives from them become — with or without special assistance — psychologically and politically able to meet, skilled facilitator assistance will be forthcoming. Helpers well qualified to give this assistance are likely to be active also at the level of within-community facilitation. I have touched on the idea of a new breed of human relations specialists within organisations. Outside consultants who have special knowledge of dynamics and alternatives in organisational functioning will be a further resource, both in situations of conflict and to contribute more broadly to relational life quality within and between organisations — and the communities they draw on and impact.

The prospective mediator-helpers qualified to assist in managing and resolving conflict between large people systems will, in particular, have the experience-based perspective and resources to contribute uniquely to subsequent healing processes among and between the protagonist peoples. The emergence and utilisation of such helpers will be associated with a development of more preventive kind. My further book discusses a possible UN-based world conflict monitoring system, designed to detect and plan multi-level response to serious tensions before they erupt into warring conflict.

The training and becoming of relationship helpers with excellent resources *between them* to assist over the comprehensive range of levels and contexts envisaged will need to evolve as a high priority by self-interested governments and educational institutions. As well as being conversant in sense and theory with the whole spectrum of enabling resources and process outlined, each resource specialist desirably will have the capacity to work on more than one adjacent level. Some helping principles and capacities (in the sphere of active listening, for example) will be relevant at all levels, others distinct to the particular nature and complexity of the system involved.

Conclusion: Can significant change really happen?

If it is generally assumed that healing change in directions such as I have proposed may be a nice dream but is unrealistic in practice and, especially, if nearly everyone feels no capacity of influence, then significant change is unlikely to occur. Large historically rooted and entrenched systems do have a ponderous inertia, and little bits of fine-tuning can seem more realistic than a basic overhaul. Further, 'most of us are so bombarded with information, or distracted by entertainment and acquisition and/or occupied with survival that it's hard to step off the conveyer belt of everyday life, actively question where it is all going and then follow our emerging answers to try to make a difference. But, if we . . . collectively just tinker at the edges, there will be hardly any change and human affairs will stagger on essentially as they are doing now.' An implication is that the 'enormity of suffering in the human world, and the even more vast lack of fulfilment of people, will continue', and may well increase (Barrett-Lennard, 2003, Chapter 9).

Yet, change is happening. As I write this, the worldwide tidal expression of opposition to the war in Iraq is a new phenomenon in its dimension and in the shared agony of concern and fellow-feeling of so many. It has not stopped *this* war but governments have been put forcefully on notice that the destruction of war is felt by most peoples to be an intolerable and contradictory 'problem-solving' instrument, in almost all circumstances. The emergent response is a great and important movement *against* something. This book describes pro-active shifts and, at the end, proposes a framework that can connect a very wide spectrum of healing change. Earlier chapters have discussed the theory and processes of healing development on more familiar levels. Making these avenues both better understood and accessible to all, and working continually to refine them, remain major change issues and possibilities. The wide canvas of this chapter points in part to the prospective role of a largely new breed of highly resourceful, relational catalyst-helpers. But, will the emergence and utilisation of this new resource actually occur? What is realised of this and related dreams may well be too little or too late in coming to avoid further deterioration and disaster.

Supposing, however, the whole range and general thrust of development considered actually did occur. First, people would be safe from and with each other — their biggest present source of danger. Relationships between individuals and groups would be open, responsive and generally enhancing to human life quality. It would be a climate also for further discovering our own nature and our place in the larger scheme of things, especially within our planetary life system. Communities would strengthen, further develop their individuality, and fulfil their potential as a major source and context of belonging and meaning. Organisations would be, among their main functions, a people resource disposed to enhance and opposed to diminishing human life quality; and occupational working life would be an actualising context not just for a minority but for most people. Self-interest would not disappear as a dynamic in relations between nations and peoples but there would be a generally heightened concern to understand and know the other and discern connecting interests. There also would be new mechanisms and human resources to facilitate communication and problem-solving, an appreciation of diversity as enrichment, and a more equitable sharing of resources and knowledge.

Many kinds of steps, small but numerous as well as large, could help to tip the balance toward this latter alternative. This book and the complementary volume are such steps for me personally. They represent a devotion of energy and concern, effort to communicate clearly, and desire to contribute usefully — with an element of risk-taking that is always part of advancing something new. On balance, I see the possibility of motion and improvement in the appalling state of relations in our world. I believe that human consciousness *is* evolving, that human relations processes are a gradually increasing focus in the human sciences and that events and conditions *are tending* to be seen more in context. In short, there are some hopeful signs. To build on this hope, I believe it is crucial to deepen the visions we live by of personal and societal well-being. Somehow the energy to attend to, and to know and wisely cultivate our humanity as dynamically interwoven beings, needs to build. My broad best hope for this book is that it can flow with many other tributaries into a river of change that moves the human family forward.

Appendix 1

Journey notes — clippings from a life

The notes that follow are gleaned from experience in my own life journey but they do not aspire to be an autobiography. To make oneself the subject of a full life story, a life interwoven with the lives of others, would be a very demanding undertaking. I have no yen to devote all the necessary energy and (if I did) would need another book for it. Instead, I have assembled 'clippings' from my life, some drawn from previous accounts, others newly prepared. To establish the context for these varied glimpses I will begin by freshly sketching the broad progression of my journey.

Frame for a life — my life

A person's picture of self in context is a creative endeavour. The picturing depends partly on the stage and circumstance of life within which it is drawn; certainly, this is true in my own case. In preparing these notes I searched for, but could not find, an 'autobiographical sketch' I wrote (*c.* 1952–53) and submitted with my application to the psychology department of the University of Chicago. It interests me now that such a sketch (needing to be 'five pages or more', not merely a fact sheet) was a required element of formal application; and I worked very hard at my candid, self-revelatory statement. A considerably later personal statement (January, 1966) came to hand without difficulty, and I have drawn generously from it. But that too is from a stage nearly four decades past, and a fresh write-up of that earlier part of my life would not come to me now in the same form. Now at age 77, I feel greatly influenced in my development and thought by experiences since mid-life. This second 'half' has in many ways been as eventful as the first, and my consciousness has evolved. Nowadays I experience less 'have-to bes' than earlier, and I'm more at home with more of me than used to be the case. The things I have energy for have shifted in their balance.

As I think *now* of my life in terms of phases, the first stage spans my childhood, youth and university education up to the time of my marriage in 1948. Besides the transition into a life with my life partner, I had found (after starting university studies with a different focus) my career direction — in psychology and pointing to the helping field. Studying, foundation clinical training and discovery of Rogers, working and conducting research, taking first steps in practice, starting a family and laying the ground for another major transition, together occupied the next six years. At its end (1954), we pulled up stakes and headed for Chicago, for what I still feel was the most fruitfully formative phase of my adult life. It was a daring step, particularly from here and in those post-war days, but one that felt like an imperative for a life of meaning to really open up. Four and a half memorable years later — with my doctorate in hand — we moved to another 'country', still in the US but in the Deep South, and later went on from there to the deep southern hemisphere (Armidale, New South Wales). Although so distinct in location and history, each setting was a fairly small university town surrounded by farming country and equally *unlike* Chicago. Somehow as I look back from present time, our seven years in those settings feels like one two-step phase.

From the isolation of the New England tablelands of Australia I was drawn back to North America, and we went on to settle in Waterloo, Ontario. I was courted to go there in a new, adventurous and rapidly growing university, to head a beginning master's programme in applied psychology and with promise of developing doctoral studies in counselling (clinical was already initiated). Difficulties soon surfaced although the promise remained for some years, and creative good things happened. Then, with leadership changes, mischosen appointments and other crises, the innovative programme that I had poured so much of myself into — but was not then leading — became torn with dissension. Rather than all-out effort to resolve the problems, the institutional response was a decision to phase the programme out. I had tenure but afterwards had little base for my work, and the disillusionment I felt was not compatible with staying in that setting. After visiting appointments and some private work we decided to make a complete break and settle again in Perth. The protracted inner crisis of Waterloo began to lift as I was able to see that the problems we suffered were in some degree my own doing and responsibility. I had not fomented any conflict; *my* failure was in not properly discerning what was happening, seeing ahead, and acting firmly on what I saw. Then, but too late for any application in that context, scales fell from my eyes and the long-painful episode became a powerful learning experience (Barrett-Lennard, 1998, p. 363).

In mid-2003 it is 20 years since we returned to Perth to live — relative strangers on arrival, not to our families or the natural environment but to the culture and everyday ways of doing things. The confusing mix of strangeness and familiarity took some time to work through and beyond. Finding my way in independent practice, no longer centred in academia but still with serious scholarly interests, was a considerable challenge. Before leaving Canada, I had invited a dozen or more significant colleagues in various locations to join me as international fellows in a network Centre for Studies in Human Relations (Ceshur), a project that I continued to work on in Australia. Strange to say, up to that time (*early* 1980s) there was no context of affiliation of people sharing a substantial client-centred background *and* seriously contributing in their own right. In 1985 we began to produce a newsletter publication called *The Ceshur Connection*. My first issue editorial, still of interest I think, is reproduced in this Appendix. It was a time-consuming and significant expense to keep the Connection going and, after three years (and with the *Person-Centered Review* by then in full operation), we allowed it to lapse. John Wood produced the last issue, in Brazil.

I see two decade-long phases in this 20-year Australian episode. In the first phase I had a leased city office as a clinical psychologist-psychotherapist, was active with Ceshur and related overseas conferences (as feasible), regaining my confidence, experimenting with new forms of expression (especially poetry), doing limited professional writing — and becoming a grandparent! Then, but more obvious afterward, several things changed and in their combination heralded another phase. I gave up my city 'rooms' and established a full-scale office in our roomy home by then regularly occupied only by my wife and myself. My teaching activity developed to include a (person-centred) course unit in counselling offered each year for seven or eight years at Murdoch University. And, I decided and launched on an all-out effort to complete the book intermittently in progress since my last years in Waterloo — a project that ended with publication of the work in 1998. After some 'time out', and with more to say, I began another book. This later turned into two smaller volumes: this book and the 'healing of relationship' work. Two strands to my feeling about completing these three books in my seventies are 'better late than not at all' and 'hooray'. I'm lately more conscious of aging, do not have other big writing projects in mind but look to responsive follow-up on issues raised in these books, especially where they resonate with readers.

Perhaps our age-maturing process (my wife Helen's and mine), our evolving engagements with grandchildren and our wider family, more community involvement, and a natural tapering-down of professional initiatives, will lead me to distinguish another life phase. For now, this brief overview is complete. The closer-up picture that follows next is drawn almost verbatim from a personal talk I gave to a Unitarian fellowship group after we had left Australia for the second time and returned to North America. The footnotes are fresh additions, and I have left out any preamble and altered the sequence somewhat. Although framed in mid-life, the feelings and process I share in the first paragraph still seem essentially true of my experience.

Notes from 'A personal search'

Confusion, loneliness, pain, conflict, fear, felt inadequacies are very familiar to me in others and myself. Yet, I have been relatively fortunate in the persons and circumstances that have provoked and permitted me to struggle and suffer and search. For there seems typically to have been direction, purpose, hope and, I venture to think, gradual growth and movement toward increasing inner freedom, shorter periods of painful conflict and uncertainty, less loneliness, relatively more feeling of worth and assurance, and more genuine and sustained concern and sensitivity for other persons. With periodic setbacks and, I am sure, many remaining blind-spots, I have gradually become more open to my actual inner responses to persons and situations; and both more able and less compelled to convey what I do perceive in myself or in others. Subjectively, my search and struggle is not forced upon me as much as it used to be; I am able more to choose and pace myself, to decide to put myself in situations that I know will try me and change me rather than the alternative of repeating myself on familiar ground. I have found that some kinds of risks are worth taking.[1]

My childhood was spent on a farming property in Western Australia in a promising but isolated area that my parents had moved to just about the time I was born — as the sixth of seven children. The great depression of the early thirties struck when I was four or five years old and times were really hard. I was not able to go to school until the age of 13, but took lessons by correspondence and played my small but urgently needed and demanded part in the battle to which we were all committed. My experience in relationship was limited to my family (a self-contained social microcosm in its own right), any others employed on our property and to periodic contact with some neighbouring families and (infrequently) with relatives or friends further afield. There was not much time or encouragement from my parents, especially my father, to be concerned with my social-emotional well-being, and my heroes were mainly older brothers, up to half a generation ahead of me. I was shy, sensitive, physically robust, rather mixed-up about authority (my father) and the relationships that varied in my small word from tense and harsh to deeply nurturant and caring. Moral values such as honesty and loyalty were taken for granted. We rarely attended church because of the physical difficulties and because my parents' views tended to be agnostic — although my mother looked on our Church of England affiliation as part of the family heritage, in temporary recession like our economic situation.

My mother, especially, was deeply committed to ensuring her children's education against whatever odds. At age 13 I attended the nearest high school,

---

[1] One such modest illustration was this quite self-disclosing talk.

90 miles away, boarding privately, gradually learning but always rather naive and unsure of myself socially — although taking principal responsibility for the conduct of my life from the age of 14 or 15 on. The year before World War II ended, and with one older brother lost in that war and another returning from it, I went from school to the university in Perth. My ten years there were largely affirmative ones although they involved false starts, unlearning as well as positive learning, and a struggle especially during the end stages to meet expectations that ran counter to my personal needs, special interests and developing values. At that point (mid-1954), after working up to it for nearly two years, my wife and I pulled up our roots from the soil that had nurtured and then set around us, and sailed with our first, infant son to the distant, unknown and reputedly formidable city of Chicago. [2]

What took us, in our search for development and meaning, to Chicago specifically? Partly it was the University of Chicago, whose reputation easily reached to Australia. More particularly, though, it was to work with Carl Rogers and his colleagues in the Psychology Department and Counseling Center there. I was no longer satisfied at all with the kind of psychology I had been exposed to up to that time and it was not possible in Australia to obtain the specialised training and experience in psychological counselling and therapy that I sought. My still-in-use original copies of Rogers' three main books, to 1951, were all acquired by January 1952. To show further the kind of person he was and why he drew me so strongly let me quote briefly from Rogers' quite remarkable preface to the last of these three books, *Client-Centered Therapy*:

> I would willingly throw away all the words of this manuscript if I could, somehow, effectively point to the experience which is therapy. It is a process, a thing-in-itself, an experience, a relationship, a dynamic. It is not what this book says about it, nor what another book says about it, any more than a flower is the botanist's description of it or the poet's ecstasy over it. If this book serves as a large signpost pointing to an experience which is open to our senses of hearing and sight and to our capacity for emotional experience, and if it captures the interest of some and causes them to explore more deeply this thing-in-itself, it will have accomplished its purpose. And if it suffers that final degradation of becoming 'classroom knowledge' — where the dead words of an author are dissected and

---

[2] When we left Australia in mid-1954 it was a monoculture, except for the nearly invisible aboriginal people and some of the post-war immigrants from Europe — for whom the policy was one of assimilation into the existing Australian culture. Some change was in the wind in our later Armidale years, but it was not striking. In 1983 we returned to a multi-cultural society and a different world.

poured into the minds of passive students . . . then better by far that the book had never been written . . .

If then the purpose of this book is not simply to put dead words on paper, what is its purpose? . . . It is about a client in my office who sits there by the corner of the desk, struggling to be himself, yet deathly afraid of being himself — striving to see his experience as it is, wanting to be that experience, and yet deeply fearful of the prospect. The book is about me, as I sit there with that client, facing him, participating in that struggle as deeply and sensitively as I am able. It is about me as I try to perceive his experience, and the meaning and the feeling and the taste and the flavor that it has for him . . . The book is, I believe, about life, as life vividly reveals itself in the therapeutic process.

Now for a glimpse of my actual response to Rogers at that time — what I wanted to say to him, having read his books. I found this comment in my very first letter to him, dated November 1952:

I feel most deeply that only when the therapist is spontaneous and genuine in his warm, acceptant responsiveness to the client and his world, can the relationship be of maximum value to the client; and that this type of attitude may be learned but can never be taught, and exists in unique form in the context of each individual therapist's personality.

A further connection with these words occurs to me now. Four years later I chose for my doctoral research to somehow measure and experimentally test what we held to be the essential qualities of a therapeutic relationship — and this work laid the foundation for a strand that has continued throughout my professional life (as documented in Chapter 8).

Our first year and a half in Chicago, although it opened a new, promising-exciting world to us was also a difficult time.[3] There was the culture shock, the feeling of being trapped in a small oasis (the University) in a boundless, teeming,

---

[3] One troubling element followed me from Australia. Just before we left Perth, I had submitted a research thesis as the last step to complete my Master of Science degree in psychology. A huge amount of work had gone into this investigation, including the development and application of original questionnaire and other instruments for the study of satisfaction in work. From an extensive review of research in the same field, I hypothesised that differences in methodology fed into the diverse and sometimes conflicting results. My comparative study used five different sources of measurement, from very 'direct' to quite 'indirect', with the same sample of workers. The head (cont.)

throbbing, unknown city; our child fell sick and a residual, potentially serious symptom hung over us; it was not easy to make ends meet; there were difficult barriers to pass before I could really concentrate on what I had come for; and there were tough lessons of living to learn. We managed, our child gradually got better, a second son came and was also a joy to us; and I know that I moved into the most deeply and productively formative and releasing phase of my adult life. We even fell in love, with some qualification, with Chicago!

I will have to be briefer still in sketching our later experiences. On winding up my doctorate, a pressing and appealing offer came from the Deep South. We had decided to return to Australia (when we could afford to!) — in fact we were obliged to do so by my visa status — but felt that some time living in Alabama could add much to our understanding of the States and its people. We did learn, although our hearts were heavy with some of the things we could not fail to see, and I have not regretted our time in Auburn. In spite of our feelings of conflict over the political and racial situation I still feel sentimental about Auburn (called 'loveliest village of the plain', after Goldsmith's poem), where our twin girls were born. And we have a feeling for the South that goes beyond the branded conflict to the pain and hope and kindness and humanity of the majority of its people.

With mixed emotions, we returned to Australia in mid-1961. The temporary shock and initial readjustment was not unlike the way it had been on first coming to the United States. My appointment took us to the opposite end of the continent from our previous home base. It was a regular teaching position in the first provincial university in Australia, an institution young in years but old in the traditions and attitudes that shaped the essentials of its form, philosophy and atmosphere. The main tasks or 'duties' of my position were limiting and even conflicting for me. But there was also time and opportunity to do things outside this framework, on my own initiative; and I value very deeply what I did, with others, through this self-chosen work. By pursuing a course that was really my own, I was able to make a contribution

---

(cont.) psychology professor in Perth, in connection with my Chicago application had confidently predicted the completion of my degree. My supervisor, however, did not wish to see a draft write-up; thus, he said, to come at it more independently as an examiner. Six months after reaching Chicago word finally came that the thesis had been turned down. I felt a huge let-down. By then I was deeply into my doctoral programme and formally completing the previous degree was immaterial to Chicago faculty — some of whom had seen the thesis themselves. I did start serious work on a revision but was not able to finish it. The process leading up to formal thesis examinations was flawed, I learned that the next master's candidate submitted formally three times; then the system was changed. Essentially, my degree was earned but not awarded — and I still feel some pain over it.

that had far more impact and value for others than was possible in the hedged-in situation of my regular teaching. Out of this experience, and after much soul-searching, I decided to leave the position in Armidale. (As I put it, in 1966) we want and expect to return to Australia eventually, but our primary contract is with life, and the unfolding meaning that this has for us cannot be contained in any master plan for the future.

I will conclude by quoting from another paper of my own, written during our time at Auburn. It is called 'The mature person' (1962b) and expresses my own concept of what it means to be a freely and fully functioning human being. The first half of my paper deals with what I think are basic inner qualities of a mature person, and it concludes as follows:

> In summary, I have said that a mature person is open to his experience: meaning by this that all the processes comprising his inner being flow freely within him, registering according to their kind and without hindrance, in his conscious awareness. I have described him as congruent — implying that he functions as one consistent whole, that what he feels and thinks represents what he is, and that he discovers and identifies himself through his experience rather than imposing conformity on his self-awareness by means of a zealously guarded self-concept.
>
> Finally, I have stated that the mature person is spontaneously self-directing, that he feels responsible for what he is and does, that he trusts his own capacities to weigh and interpret the data of his experience, and that he looks to himself as the main source of purposeful and adequate decisions for his own behaviour.

The second part of my paper, concerned more with outward behaviour and relationships, includes these thoughts:

> The mature person is adaptable, original and creative, within the range of his potential capacities. He approaches each new situation equipped but not committed by his past experience. His own being has the quality of a continuously evolving pattern, a process that has direction but no end points, a state of becoming. He accepts this evolving nature of being and does not seek stability in the sense of fixed values, immutable purposes, ultimate understanding or completed development . . .
>
> He genuinely appreciates and values others as he does himself. He is comfortable and open with them because he is comfortable and open with himself. He is not guarded in a personal sense because he has nothing to hide. He does not distort himself to please others, nor

does he use them as scapegoats for self-dissatisfaction. He finds himself more fully with others rather than losing his own identity with them.

I hope that I can become more like my own picture of the way to be.

The line above is exactly where my personal statement ended, in January 1966. Only the footnotes are fresh additions. Before the 'mature person' passages I mentioned that, besides my regular teaching, I embarked on another very different activity; one that brought me into close contact with adventurous colleagues across Australia and from New Zealand. Effectively, it also brought Carl Rogers (by ship) all the way from California, as shortly described. The new context was a series of intensive 'residential workshops in therapeutic counselling', conducted along client-centred lines and involving participants from various fields engaged in personal helping professions or studies. The official announcement of the second workshop stated its aim as being 'to assist those taking part to further develop their capacities to engage in psychologically helpful relationships with other people', and it promised that 'every effort will be made to ensure that the specific content of the workshop experience grows out of the concerns and thinking of those who choose to engage in it'. To this end, provision would be made 'for regular intensive discussion meetings in small groups'. Remember that all this occurred 40 years ago and was without precedent 'down under'. Carl himself was still in Wisconsin, and not yet conducting such groups (although about to begin), when the first workshop took place and the second was planned. The announcement went on to refer to the inaugural workshop, in May 1963, noting that:

> It developed as an experiential learning process in which events occurring in the immediate discussion situation were increasingly focused on and used as a learning medium. Members explored together aspects of their experience and functioning as therapists, considered in relation to their own qualities as persons. Formal concepts of therapy were discussed but increasingly related to here-and-now processes in the group, which often vividly dramatised the meaning and significance of these concepts.

Since the prospective members would be mainly professionals, in residence but not meeting in experiential groups all the time, further resources were to be provided at the workshop and beforehand. Specifically:

> A specially prepared collection of recent books and articles and of tape-recordings and films of therapy interviews will be available for members' use. Copies of the articles not readily available in published

form will be provided for members to keep. It is planned to circulate the list of readings and some reprints to intending members, several weeks before the workshop begins.

Participants agreed to provide data for evaluation research of the workshop process and outcomes — results from which are outlined in my previous book (1998, pp. 294–9). The experiential group sphere, at the levels of practice, teaching and research, became a major focus of interest to me, especially over the next decade or so; and Chapter 6 of this book reflects my further experience and thought in this area. However, the Armidale phase had another significant dimension to speak of here, namely, the Rogers' visit to Australia and Carl's first-hand involvement. My informal account of that visit was prepared for a special issue of the *Person-Centered Review* (Volume 2, Number 3), which David Cain organised in memory of Carl's life. The record that follows preserves the subtitle and content of my PCR report, with a couple of extra footnotes.

Carl and Helen Rogers in Australia

In January 1965, Helen and Carl Rogers travelled by cruise ship from California to Australia. The long voyage included calls at several Pacific Island ports. Entering one of these, their vessel ground to a halt on a reef, tilting to an alarming degree. When finally freed, the ship steamed on for several hundred miles prior to any underwater inspection! But apart from this excitement and the ports of call, their shipboard experience, especially the society of their fellow travellers — largely affluent American tourists — was reported to be disappointing. The excursion altogether was one of Carl's lesser-known and most leisurely overseas trips.

Carl and I had corresponded closely in the preceding two years about our work and experience in the small-group field, which had developed simultaneously in our very different contexts as a primary focus of interest to each of us. I was located in a small, isolated university, even as seen from within Australia let alone from North America. My innovative work with groups, with most members coming from elsewhere into residence together for intensive two-week workshops, was partly a response to this isolation. I don't believe that the thought of a collaborative visit right there, from Carl, had ever crossed my mind. To my astonishment and delight, one day in mid-1964 a letter arrived in which he wrote, in part:

> Dear Goff. This is a hasty note to say that there is a slight likelihood that Helen and I might make a vacation trip to the South Seas and Australia at the beginning of 1965 . . .

If we did plan to do something like this would it be likely that there would be significant ways in which I could be in contact with groups of Australians interested in my work? . . . I suppose the thing I would like best would be to participate with you in a workshop if something of that sort were feasible.

Please understand that this plan is not definite . . . I am just raising the question with you to see what your initial reaction might be . . . What I would enjoy the most would be an opportunity for a continuing and deeper contact with some significant people in the field of counseling and psychotherapy (Rogers, personal communication, June 23, 1964).

My immediate reply began:

Dear Carl: I am extremely thrilled to hear that you and Helen might be visiting Australia early next year, and that you are interested in exploring the possibility of participating in a workshop with us. I find it difficult to imagine any piece of news coming out of the blue more personally exciting to me than this.

My reply foreshadowed a further response shortly, which turned out to be a six-page letter, the first half a rather detailed account of the residential intensive group workshop at the University of New England which had just taken place (May 1964). The second half of my response laid out a variety of suggested arrangements for the possible visit. This communication crossed another from Carl. Already, he and Helen had made up their minds:

We are getting increasingly excited too. As a matter of fact we have pretty well firmed up our plans, and they are as follows: We will be taking a Matson ship, and will arrive in Auckland on January 7 and then fly to Australia, probably Sydney, arriving about January 15 [and leave by ship February 8] (Rogers, personal communication, July 6, 1964).

The letters between us flowed thick and fast from the time of this mid-1964 correspondence until Carl and Helen's arrival in Sydney in January 1965. The ten-day workshop that he would lead in Armidale was carefully planned. It seemed best to limit it to one group, everyone working in the same group with Carl. We stretched to the largest group size that seemed to either of us to be workable at that time — 18 persons. I knew that there was a big potential interest and, rather than invite applications and then turn most people down, we agreed to fill the workshop membership by invitation. The specifics of preparation and planning were mostly in my hands. In typical style, Carl wrote:

> The prospects look more exciting as time goes by. I can't tell you how
> comfortable it is to have someone I know at the other end of the line
> making arrangements. It makes the opportunities look much more
> promising because they will be the kinds of opportunities which I
> can really meet most successfully (Rogers, personal communication,
> August 12, 1964).

The arrangements and opportunities as it turned out were to include, besides
the workshop, lecture presentations during short visits to Sydney, Melbourne,
Brisbane, and Canberra (about which I will say a little more, shortly, as part of
the story of Carl's visit).

In a lighter vein, I cannot resist sharing an anecdote that was part of Carl's
introduction to Australia. I travelled from Armidale to meet Carl and Helen
after they arrived in Sydney at the start of a weekend in which they had no
commitments. They were still in holiday spirit. I believe we went out to dinner
together and then, at Carl's suggestion, to a movie. The movie, if my memory
serves me, was *The Sound of Music*, then just out. Probably it was the next
morning when I accompanied them to collect their remaining baggage from
wharf storage at Circular Quay where their ship had berthed. (Some of their
belongings had come on by ship when they disembarked for a short visit in
New Zealand, and flew from there.) These belongings had to be declared and
cleared through Customs, in the usual way. But I need to digress for a moment.
In one of his letters Carl had written:

> I am going to try to bring a brand new film of therapeutic interviews
> by Fritz Perls, Albert Ellis, and myself, each interviewing the same
> client. The filming was done in early September, and I am not sure
> that it will be edited and available by December, but I am putting
> pressure on Dr Shostrom to try to get a copy for me so that I can take
> it to Australia (Rogers, personal communication, October 13, 1964).

Carl told me that at the last moment before they sailed from California,
Shostrom had made good and delivered the first copy to be released of *Three
Approaches to Psychotherapy*! There was the film, to judge by the three large
canisters, for us to take through Customs. In those days, one function of
Australian Customs was to serve as a kind of front-line guardian of public
morality. Films obviously beyond the dimension of home movies were one
main target of attention. They must often have made rather tedious viewing
for the patient officials who checked them. In any event, the Customs officer
cheerfully informed us that Carl's films could not be released right then but

could be collected, assuming all was well, in three or four weeks' time — by which time Carl and Helen would be on their way home!

Australian culture has an intriguing blend of a kind of independent-mindedness and strong egalitarianism, and a more subtle sort of acceptance that people do live in different worlds. The precise mores and legalities were novel to Carl. He hadn't expected to be told that he couldn't make use of his own film, and he was nonplussed. I had gone with him partly to help out with any such problems, and naturally stepped in at that point. I remember simply but carefully identifying myself, with accent and appearance to match, speaking quietly but firmly about Carl's work and standing, mentioning that films of his work already were in the Australian National Library, explaining his itinerary and the short time he would be in Australia, and pointing out that the films in any case would be used only with audiences of people in the mental health field. I could see from the face of the Customs man that he did not really imagine that Carl and I were trying to sneak by with some smutty movies. Probably too, his satisfactions came from 'mateship', not petty tyranny. He was looking for alternatives, given that he really didn't have discretion to release the films unchecked. The solution was ingeniously simple and characteristic for that era. Turning in another direction he said, in effect: 'I'm not sure what this is all about. I don't see any films. I haven't seen any; so what's the problem.' We picked up Carl's and Helen's belongings, including some curious round containers which had not been opened, and left.[4]

Carl's first official engagement was at the University of New South Wales in Sydney, on Monday evening, January 18th. He spoke there to an eager and responsive audience of some 700 people on the topic of personal communication — a highly communicative presentation published many years later (Rogers, 1980, pp. 7–26). His next talk, in Brisbane, brought forth a different reception, I was told. His audience was smaller, more specialised, and inclusive of members of the psychiatric establishment there. There appears to have been a polarisation of response, with dark mutterings on the negative side of 'naivete' and even 'charlatanism'. In Melbourne, he generously highlighted my own research in a talk on the therapeutic conditions and relationship, later published in the *Australian Journal of Psychology* (Rogers,

---

[4] There is also an intriguing sequel to the story of the films. I was in fairly close touch with a colleague in the film division of the Australian National Library — who was at once very keen to get hold of the new documentaries, and who was promptly in touch with the distributor in California. The 'uncleared' copy of *Three Approaches* brought in Carl's luggage never left Australia again. It was happily purchased with federal funds by the National Library, and was immediately in demand by other borrowers. Shostrom, I believe, was pleased to get a distant sale so soon, and very glad that he had been able to deliver the films just before Carl's ship sailed!

1965d). He was feted there and the talk went well. In Canberra, Pat Pentony — also active with me in the Armidale workshops — would have introduced him, probably to a more select audience.

Carl's last stop before the workshop had been in Brisbane, Queensland. There were no direct flights to Armidale and I remember that my wife and I drove the 60-odd miles to meet Carl and Helen when they landed near the little town of Glen Innes. There was no airport as such, simply a graded stretch of hard earth and a couple of small sheds. Although only a few hundred miles from Brisbane, the trip in an old DC3 aircraft, which had some problem with its landing gear, was rather an adventure for them both. We drove through farmlands and steep-hilled country, picnicking on the way. Another stop was made for Carl to take a photograph of a mob of sheep making a beeline for their watering place, in the late afternoon light. In Armidale, Carl and Helen were accommodated in one of the residential colleges of the university, along with nearly all other workshop members. Helen did not take part in the group sessions, and partly for this reason, she and my wife, Helen, saw a lot of each other over those ten days and their friendship deepened. Our children enjoyed her too and were impressed when she and Carl produced a book by their *neighbour*, Dr Seuss.[5]

The workshop group itself proved a tough one to work with. It never integrated fully, never reached the intensity and depth of process on a personal level that other groups I had worked with there had done. It was a memorable experience, notwithstanding, and there was a great deal of contact with Carl in and out of sessions. Constraints on the group's process grew perhaps from its structure: not only the mix of personalities as such but also the professional composition and individual purposes. From memory, six of the members were psychiatrists, six or more were clinical/counselling psychologists, and at least three were social workers by profession. All were fairly senior in their fields, established but advancing and ambitious. The few women had battled harder for their career positions than the men. All had gone to quite a lot of trouble to be there but it was not only their sense of need for further personal and professional development that drew them. Carl was a distinguished and famous visitor, founder and leader of his 'school', a world-renowned psychologist and

---

[5] Helen B-L particularly remembers another incident involving both Helen and Carl, during an interlude in the course of the workshop. Her account of it follows:

'The days of the workshop were very full and the Sunday in the middle was used for a group outing, but Helen insisted that we should have time away together, late on Saturday. We went, en famille, to a water-bird sanctuary, a few miles from Armidale. Carl's interest and pleasure colours the experience vividly in my memory: he was relaxed, entranced and delight-full, with the birds, water, sunset, children, friends — as always, so fully himself.'

therapist. To sit at his feet, even to challenge him, was an opportunity not to be missed. Thus, the initial motivation was less than ideal and the mix of members and complexities of size were a formidable challenge. And, Carl himself was still learning about groups, as we all were.[6]

Some research data were gathered during the workshop but not augmented, however, by any organised follow-up inquiry. The 'Australian data' referred to in Nat Raskin's (1974) reports of work done under the auspices of the American Academy of Psychotherapists were gathered at this time, from the workshop participants. All or most of the sessions were recorded. The tapes were given to Carl, and I am not sure what use if any he made of them. Perhaps United States Customs, in their turn, objected to a whole box of tapes of unknown content being brought in from Australia!

I am not sure that I actually saw Carl and Helen off on their voyage home. Carl's engagement in Melbourne followed the Armidale workshop. He also recorded a tape by invitation for the Australian College of General Practitioners — or its forerunner association. There is no dramatic conclusion to this account of his visit to Australia. In the circumstances, it did not start anything new here but furthered interest and developments that were already ongoing and left memorable impressions for many people who heard from him and, especially, those who took part in the workshop. I had already accepted a visiting position at Southern Illinois University for the next academic year and was provisionally planning to settle in North America on an extended basis. Before leaving Australia, I organised and conducted another workshop (May/June 1965), partly to keep faith with those who were seriously interested in the 'Armidale experience' but who did not have the opportunity to join the group with Carl.

Looking back, the fact that he was in Australia, engaged and involved, remains an expressive feature of his journey and a lasting symbol among others of his reach and influence.

This is where my account of the Rogers' visit ends, but it was accompanied by a poem also written for the Journal's memorial issue:

---

[6] I remember consciously avoiding stepping in as co-facilitator of the group. I wanted, for a change and with Carl at the helm, just to be a member with my own concerns like everyone else. But I had had a very active organisational role beforehand, invited everyone who was there, and had all the previous experience of initiating and leading workshops in the same setting. In retrospect I regretted not actively working to complement Carl's leadership within the group sessions, and came to feel that this could have added to their energy and salience. Carl had not spoken to me about what he had been going through in Wisconsin, which I think had undermined his assurance in some way, and left him in greater need of positive support and feedback. He had shone on stage in his Sydney lecture but the workshop was a situation more likely to play on any self-doubting.

A Legacy

In Memory of Carl Rogers

Carl, we are saddened by your death and leaving.
We remember you in person, and loved you in our ways.
Yet, our thoughts and feelings are not just ones of grieving.
From when we knew you first till now, we lived together,
Connected where'er we were, in this torn but precious world
         we share.
Your time with us is no mere flickering memory, it beats with life.
Who-and-how we are was further born because of you.
We learned to listen better, to ourselves and others,
To heed the cries and joys of being — and becoming,
To be more knowing of where to look, and how, and even
Why, to want to search but yet apply, to teach as we inquire,
To learn while giving what we know, to be receptive
To our nature and let experience flow — and find its truest voice.
Past, present and future are of one piece
In the larger skein that is our total journey.
The flowering of your past was once your future
Carl, a future that now flows surging into ours.

Notes from a Canadian setting

After Armidale, and an academic year interlude in Carbondale, Illinois (where my 'personal search' talk was given), the long and complex phase of our lives based in Canada followed. I had thought to say more about this up-and-down part of my life but anything like a complete account is not feasible here. What I experienced there ranged from the bizarre to the profoundly meaningful; from cherished aspects that enriched my life to those that were searing and life-diminishing in their occurrence. We arrived in Canada in mid-1983 — Helen pregnant with our fifth child — weary but soon excited, and full of hope for what lay ahead. We began to set up a new home, again, our youngest child arrived and was a joyful addition, and I was quickly inducted into my new job. My academic department proved a volatile context, to say the least.

The machinery was already in motion for the new applied master's programme that I came in to lead, and that side of things was demanding but fairly straightforward. Getting a fresh doctoral specialty off the ground — one of the inducements in recruiting me — was much more complicated and problematic, although students for me to supervise were already admitted! I was rapidly learning ways that the organisational structure, attitude differences, personal ambitions and other dynamics were working in the system I was part of. And there was another major 'wild card'. The department chairman had spent three and half years building psychology from a tiny unit into a major department of some 30 faculty, a large research facility and big graduate programme, etc. Now he was visibly burning out, drinking heavily and, by the middle of my first year, incapable of carrying on. I found myself thrust into the role of Acting Chairman (an added 'education' but with my individual priorities in abeyance) for 14 long months, while keeping the ship afloat and helping to recruit a new Head. In the meantime, the previous chairman died suddenly, alone and under mysterious circumstances. Such was the strange introductory phase of my career in Canada. But we were settled in a new home among friendly people, my family was flourishing, and we made lasting connection with a local Unitarian fellowship community.

A year later, the new doctorate in counselling was coming into view but still not a fully established integral programme within psychology. The focus was now defined as *counselling and human relations* and, within another year, it was formally launched under that heading. As expressed in the official brochure on graduate studies in psychology (printed November 1969):

> Doctoral studies in the counselling and human relations field are designed to prepare individuals in whom a synthesis of humanistic and scholarly-scientific values are coupled with potential to advance knowledge and practice relating to human facilitation, the study of complex experiential phenomena and the investigation and enhancement of human communication processes. The programme emphasizes the development of resources for facilitative intervention in dyadic, group, organizational, and community contexts; the study of man from a naturalistic or ecological perspective; the application and development of methodology suited to the investigation of complex, naturally-occurring experiential and interpersonal phenomena; and the investigation of social innovation and change.

Furthermore:

> In keeping with its broader objectives, the educational philosophy of the programme is to facilitate the integrated scholarly, professional

and personal growth of its carefully and mutually selected candidates. No special, major area examinations (outside the framework of individual courses) are anticipated, although it is the intention that relevant and helpful kinds of continuing evaluation and feedback will be provided and also received from candidates.

All of this was not very digestible within a large, ambitious psychology school, and the programme became increasingly autonomous. Before very long, with the headship of the programme rotated to a senior colleague eager for formal independence to materialise, the unit gained the status of a separate Department of Human Relations and Counselling Studies. In concept this was an exciting development with the mission to carry forward and further develop the vision just outlined. However, there were flaws in preparing for this independence, especially in respect to the faculty make-up of the fledgling department, and it became clear that not all members shared a common vision or value-system. In a word, personal attitudes, needs and differences undermined the enterprise, by means both deliberate and involuntary. After only four years, steps were taken to wind up a development that had been hard to bring into being, was full of promise and that ran into serious but not irremediable difficulties. My colleague, John M. Butler, recruited from Chicago, had suffered heart failure and died not long before the closure decision, leaving me as the only tenured faculty member. Closing down the programme and thus ending positions for the remaining faculty was, for institutional managers, a relatively 'easy' way of disposing of difficulties.

As implied, my eyes were opened in new ways through a difficult path of learning and healing. One of various steps (steps that included some further personal therapy) was to begin to set down some thoughts regarding processes about which I had been naïve before. I sought to bring into focus a type of influence process opposite in its nature to the enabling process and principles that held primary meaning for me. Inclusion of these ideas here is in context, and they may not otherwise be shared.

Toward understanding intended coercive action

These thoughts are forged from experience, not from studied background on their topic, a topic dissonant from my main interests. These interests involve strong personal belief in non-coercive, facilitative means of fostering change. However, I have to my sorrow been on the receiving end of sustained coercive tactics and, more often, have witnessed their application. I am prompted to set down observations born of damaging direct experience because to have known in advance what I only discriminated later would have been a positive resource. Such awareness would have reduced the destructive effects, certainly for me and possibly for others; and I believe that it is generally true that consciousness of things as they are contributes, at the very least, to the limiting of harm.

Coercive action intends to force a perceived opponent (person, group, or larger system) to bend or yield to the coercer's will. It is a form of intentional conflict in which the coercer works to mobilise or gain power and to change the presumed controlling forces in the person or group under attack. The scale can range from an individual relationship to a multi-national system. Adherents to coercive intervention may view their process as applying counter-power in a system already highly (and corruptly) coercive in its operation. The rationale then includes the aim of breaking down the existing order and replacing it with another. It is associated more with the idea of revolution than evolution although, in political terms it may be applied from the (far) right or (far) left.

I have thought about some of the 'rules' of coercive practice, especially as applied within an organisation that is relatively open and democratic or laissez-faire. Such a system typically has some implicit ethic or code but may have no strong central control or narrowly defined and set way of functioning. The coercive intervention may start from an injury felt by some member that feeds on natural complexity of motivation in others, on the ambiguity inherent in a 'loose' system and on the needs and ambitions of the 'injured' party. Communication is highly selective, and the stage is set for retaliatory action designed to upset and change the perceived existing order and powers of other members. If such a course is chosen deliberately, the following features are likely, in my experience:

1. The situation is dramatically represented and interpreted to potential allies in order to arouse concern and support for the initiator's cause. If little or no support is gained an openly coercive strategy may be aborted.

2. Threats or disturbance to the existing order of responsibilities and relations within the system are introduced, calculated to *invoke reactions* that are expected to increase the plausibility of the cause, further legitimise it, and win added support.

3. Linked to these steps is the development of a moral foundation based on social values such as democracy, 'fair play', or giving voice to some disadvantaged group, etc. The representation in terms of such values or movements is a tactic that links the coercer's position to sentiments widely held among those whose support is relied upon. Discrimination of this case from a case where the representation reflects quite genuine beliefs and motives can be quite difficult, especially to begin with. The repertoire of

actors on the extreme right often includes appeals to the desire for order, stability, and clear pathways, even 'freedom' under a tighter system of law or regulation.[7]

4. Coercive action does not gain momentum by searching for the truth, or sticking to it. Information must be slanted, reshaped, invented — to the outside limit of plausibility to constituents. Deception and covert action come to be seen as justified: tools of the coercer's enterprise. Some adherents to this enterprise are very likely to be used and manipulated by its leaders. The coercers, by and large, need to believe that the ends are of such profound consequence that a different order of morality is justified than that which applies in their personal lives, or most relations within their own group. The principle of ends justifying the means is implicit if not overt.

5. Finding forums to use as vehicles for visible protest and agitation usually is crucial. Open meetings, particularly if unwieldy and with few rules, or that are established to hear grievances, etc., are among the kinds of desired forum.

6. It may be necessary to mobilise many more supporters than those who discern and would subscribe to the methods or ultimate goals of the coercers. Gaining attention in the mass media may be one priority means to the goal since, to capture the attention of their audiences, media are highly responsive to carrying reports of sensational or dramatic occurrences. Sophisticated coercers can play and manipulate the media for covert ends.

7. A clear 'enemy' or adversary must be identified, which is plausible to supporters and perhaps to a larger constituency. If the adversary is an institution or other large system, this target often is personified by singling out one or a few of its most visible actors. Enemies may be avoided that are seen as overwhelmingly powerful, or extremely popular or revered.

8. Where the identified opponent or enemy is a group, one tactic is to work to sow discord among its members. Since people with common cause tend to pull together under threat, this long-used tactic may simply reveal the coercer's hand unless applied with covert finesse.

---

[7] The law in liberal-democratic systems does not for the most part (setting aside conditions of national emergency or response to criminal behaviour) support coercive action, and provides some safeguards against it. Coercers, where possible, may appeal to 'moral' principles not regulated in law or established policies or perhaps even protected by existing law or policies.

9. A further tactic is, by varied means, to attack and undermine the credibility of the target person or group, among the wider community of possible supporters. The 'enemy' may be slandered or treated/pictured in ways that provokes retaliation of a kind that helps to legitimise the campaign against them — as implied in point 2, above.

Coercive action can breed a response in kind, and finding non-coercive ways of resisting or counteracting such action is a difficult but crucial challenge. It needs to begin with an open-eyed awareness that coercive action is being resorted to, and a clear discernment of some of its 'rules' or principles, such as the points outlined. Public acknowledgement of the principles and resulting methods would tend to reduce effectiveness of the coercive process. Achieving clearly expressed understanding of where the coercer is coming from, in feeling and intention, can in some circumstances lead to an actual shifting of ground. Coercers do not always discriminate the method or pattern of their own actions, and *may* be susceptible to genuine 'consciousness-raising'. Where the coercer is, by policy or attitude, quite closed to any such communication, especially from the 'opposing' side, the person or group on the receiving end needs the capacity to avoid intimidation and respond from a position of strength and integrity that is apparent to more open observers and participants.

I do not mean to suggest that 'coercers' are a distinctive group or personality type. Most of us are capable of manipulative or otherwise destructive actions that are hurtful or even harmful to others. My concern here is with purposed coercive strategies as described, and with the potential for clear-sighted recognition of patterns that only 'work', or work best, when they are not seen through. Such awareness is one important step toward ways of responding that neither submit to the coercion or reinforce and perpetuate its pattern.

Coercive action, whether applied deliberately or unreflectively, is widespread and influential in our competitive culture — where some target groups or individuals fully expect it and may respond in kind. In this larger sense, overcoming the motivation for and methodology of coercion hinges on broader social change, including movement toward a more generally humane and subtly discerning consciousness. Regardless of wider change, I have learned something for myself through costly experience, and will be glad if it helps any reader with coercive experiences — of which we all are at some risk.

There was another, very different kind of sequel to my leaving behind the context of collegial affiliation within a university. The alternative was to initiate a close network of valued colleagues in diverse locations which, as I look back, was a kind of 'virtual department'. I asked 15 or so people, each an innovative and substantial contributor in his or her own right, to affiliate with me and each other as the core group of a network Centre for Studies in Human Relations.[8] One activity, as mentioned, was to start a newsletter-bulletin. The first issue included a vision statement (below) that I still resonate to and feel has interest beyond its origin. The same issue included another statement, under the heading 'Education and Ceshur — 1985', which followed up an earlier working paper for foundation members. This statement proposed a sequence of learning experiences grouped under broader headings and ranging through a number of 'cycles'. The envisioned international educational programme did not materialise, although it probably contributed to other initiatives, may still have merit, and would be more feasible in this age of easy Email and other Internet connection than it was at the time. (I would be happy to provide the outline to any interested reader.) Here is the more general vision statement, under its original heading and just with brief omissions and word changes to improve the flow.

Directions: A first issue editorial

The Ceshur Connection is conceived in its beginning as a forum for the exchange of information and ideas among members of The Centre for Studies in Human Relations (Ceshur), and for the sharing of this information and thought with interested non-member readers. The newsletter is both a quest and a pathway, as is the Centre itself, concerned with development and change from the levels of the personal and intimate to large-scale systems and movements. In a word, its potential concerns and aims mirror those of the Centre . . .

     People who see and feel the ubiquitous presence of human suffering and unfulfilled potential, and who have found or developed a thought and practice system that 'works' in their experience, tend not to place priority on research or intensive theoretical study. Indeed, such a focus in our perilous and needy world can seem like 'fiddling while Rome burns'. But putting out fires, important though it is, does not remove the causes of the blaze, or necessarily even reveal those causes. Further, excellence in firefighting (plus reliable insurance systems) may actually reduce incentive to find effective prevention. After all, it provides and contributes to employment and industry in a variety

---

[8] The member Fellows were David Bakan, Leif Braaten, Richard Farson, Eugene Gendlin, Gerald Goodman, Germain Lietaer, Pat Pentony, Nat Raskin, Rachel Rosenberg, John Shlien, Reinhard Tausch, and John Wood. Hedley Dimock (Canada), Les Harvey (Australia), Wolf-R Minsel (Germany), Alberto Segrera (Mexico) and Alberto Zucconi (Italy) affiliated as 'Regional Fellows'.

of fields, and tends to be a challenging and rewarding activity . . .

Those, whose primary commitment is to advance knowledge through research and other inquiry, often are persuaded that *this* focus has greatest urgency and importance. Painstakingly tested procedures, discoveries anchored in experiment or precise analysis, and sharply drawn impressions testable through observation, may seem the only route to empowering our capacity to effect known change; change that approaches the heart of human and social problems. It is true also that the excitement of the chase, of the process of uncovering, can be quite as strong as its counterpart in a practice context, and the various extrinsic rewards of a vigorous path of research inquiry can be very substantial. However, it too is a route that may lead to an exclusive quality of commitment, to a detachment from direct helping practice and other levels of healing or change-agency, and from the lived situations and pain of those who seek help. It also can lead to self-limiting orthodoxies that simply differ in particular kind from those the practitioner is vulnerable to.

The foundation members of Ceshur are an unusual breed in relation to these issues. Their/our interests and values embrace all of the mentioned levels, often in synergistic connection. A drive to explore, connect and know — and by and through so doing, to make a difference — is in our blood. Most of us have pioneered areas or lines of research inquiry and connecting developments in thought and practice. Equally, most have experimented and broken new ground on doing levels, and used research to test, or theory to illuminate, features of this practice . . .

Altogether, we have researched with persistence, discipline, passion and consequence [and] a great number of separate research studies have in one way or another flowed from our combined work. Notwithstanding its mass, however, on the whole this work has helped more to define and focus issues and point to what could fruitfully be done than to yield a great harvest of unequivocal findings and settled conclusions. This situation results partly from the variability in quality and understandably diverse particular interest of the research. It is also because 'we' have needed, and will need, to become more ingenious, subtle and knowing about doing research on the phenomena that interest us, and because the terrain of inquiry is both larger and more complex than we were earlier able to perceive.

Research can be a deeply engaging, absorbing, living process or an activity dragged along by external incentives, forced and painfully self-denying, a copied performance without spark or life. Ceshur fellows have been fortunate in coming to experience the first of these modes, but not without first-hand experience or observation of the latter. Most of us share the experience of a kind of birth of deep, self-propelling interest in research as this enterprise has shown a new face to us, effectively becoming an aspect of our own search for meaning. This seems, typically, to have happened in the unusually liberating circumstances of our own doctoral or other formal studies, or through work that followed soon afterward. Most often — then and later — we have pursued questions and hypotheses calling from our worlds of practice, our broader social concerns, or action projects in which the values of making a difference and illuminating its process have been conjoined . . .

We also experiment in a less formal sense as we practice, preferring not to only repeat ourselves but also to venture and try newly, with intuitive and observational processes in close interplay. And our scholarly and educational activities are integral aspects of the total practice of our profession and vocation. We almost take for granted the intellectual-experiential nexus which forms and re-forms from the differing levels of profound engagement in our work, levels in which 'subjective' and 'objective' are in fruitful interplay and partnership. These and other mentioned features bear directly on the nature of the Centre enterprise . . .

Ceshur, in sum and in reason for being, is profoundly concerned with research inquiry, education and practice, each mode helping to inform and enrich the others, no mode unaccompanied by an element of the others. No 'class distinction' prevails between these modes, all have to do with knowing, and each both depends on and contributes to crucial kinds of knowing. In effect, each is an integral aspect of a larger whole, and Ceshur is an expression of this whole . . . *The Ceshur Connection* provides a voice for each aspect, and carries the potential to further it.

There the editorial vision statement ends. Although Ceshur no longer links the former members, for most of them and other colleagues there are further developments of related vision, including the new journal, *Person-Centered and Experiential Psychotherapies*. These developments are living threads in a larger tapestry — for example, as explored in my last book (1998, pp. 342–52). My next step here is to conclude these varied clippings from my own journey with another change of pace.

Concluding note

Looking back over one's life poses interesting issues of personal and felt identity. Am I the same person as the young child I once was, 70 years ago, or even as the new doctoral graduate early in 1959, or as the grieving professor-person when programmes I had a large part in creating were being ended (and a dream extinguished) in the 1970s, or even when we first returned to Australia in 1983? My subjective answer is 'no' but 'yes'. On the Yes side is my continuity of memory and of long close relationships. The first document that affirms this continuity of being is a birth certificate, and a considerable sequence of other records is further evidence. In both law and custom I am the 'same' person, even as named in that long-ago register of birth. Yet my answer is also a clear No. I am wholly different as a self than the nascent self of my infancy, and have been in a process of becoming all of my life. My continuity of memory is not at all like that of a computer, for past events are viewed through a consciousness that has moved on. Thus their meaning and even their 'feel' and the elements that stand out have changed.

Memory of course is not just capricious or it would serve little purpose. It is many-layered, short-term and long-term, 'automatic' (underlying some perfected skills) and reflective, and mediated by symbols or by images. We have an information memory that can store a great deal of particular relevance and meaning to us, and do so with fair stability — especially given periodic reminders. As for personally and emotionally cogent happenings, in my case and perhaps in yours, these tend to be recalled in images coloured with feeling; and I have many such. Images often seem to come unbidden, and my inner life has many more 'non sequiturs' than I would venture to express in conversation or intentionally impose on the reader. I have had lengthy episodes of being painfully haunted by happenings that felt unbearable, that 'should-never-have-been'. One way my life quality has changed in recent years is that, although I can look and feel back (as in these notes), past events oppress me much less now than before this gradual change. More of the things that trouble me, like the recent war in Iraq, are out in front, happening now — at the point of most intense effect — not ghosts from the past.

Whither next, in my life? I am due shortly to travel to the Netherlands and nearby, for meetings with colleagues that I greatly look forward to seeing again — or meeting for the first time. There is little now that I *must* do professionally, and perhaps what I go on with will be more responsive than initiating. My means are modest but they suffice; I no longer *have* to earn my living — although extra earning helps. Family relations are integral to the meaning and depth of my life, and I also cherish the natural environment. I remain curious, always wanting to see and understand more. Perhaps I can continue to make a difference in my own way, less by effortful striving more by paying attention and responding to the eagerness of others and their shared concerns. I don't have the stamina of past times, and my living self and consciousness will come to an end in due course, as is the natural order. In the meantime I am absorbed, especially, with what keeps coming into fresh or fuller view.

Appendix 2

Relationship and self: Explorations in verse

Introduction

In the mid-eighties I began for the first time to venture into the medium of poetry. Occasionally, when I was reflecting meditatively and wished to express the meaning that was working in me, a poem seemed the most natural or feasible avenue. This medium carried implicit 'permission' to be subjective and expressive, to declare meanings and say in a brief space something that I could not economically (if at all) convey in prose. For me, the impulse to use poetry started when I was unable to go from Australia, where we had fairly recently resettled, back to Canada for the wedding of one of my daughters. What could I share or give her, not as a material gift but from my own person, that would be special and also unexpected? In an episode of indwelling, a poem began to form. It seemed to rise up in me almost of itself, and as its shape emerged, I decided to call it *Partners*. One of my sons was at the wedding, and he read out the poem on my behalf, at the reception and without warning of what was to come! The poem arose from a particular context and time in my life, and would not come to me in the same form now. This said, I sometimes surprise myself in imaginative storytelling with a grandchild (stories I make up on the spot), and I think that poetry like most self-expression comes out of relationship.

Encouraged by this first experience, I turned to the same avenue several times the same year (1985) — but have not done so lately. Like dreams, a poem can take its author by surprise, its content not thought of in the everyday trance of linear consciousness. In the case of some poems, I would ask myself afterwards 'Where did that come from?' or even, as the truth of it struck me, 'How did I know?' Then, as I 'listened', a connection with some potent experience or another (partial) explanation might occur to me. For example, in the case of the poem *InHuman Being* the situation in apartheid South Africa had been recently and vividly on my mind. I also had asked myself, at another time, 'What *really* caused the disappearance of that robust race of humans known as Neanderthal Man?' Some experiences also link to my poem *Deception* but they do not seem to account for the force and scope of the whole. Other longer pieces — *Love* and *Presenting to an audience* — did not come to me complete, all at once, but took some thought and working out. But the poems speak for themselves more eloquently than my prose. This selection does not repeat the verse in memory of Carl Rogers (Appendix 1) but it does start with another published poem that may be familiar to some readers.

The poems

A Person (1985)

One alone and many in one,
A community of I's in a Me made one
By thought, habit, a body familiar, law,
And consciousness of Other; of you distinct
From me, each of us a singular multiplicity.

Cannot I, the person that I call me, myself,
My name and writing now, does not this host
Of me have many tongues, voices that argue
Back and forth not listening, opposed desires?
Do I (and you) not have a hall of mirrored selves
Inhabited or remembered within, thus still with life
And varied/repeating presence? Are we not
As many as the seasons and settings of our lives,
An abundance answering to one name,
Multiple, uncounted but counting as one?

Is it any wonder if we neglect, deny members of this company,
Leave blind a hunger, disown some voice inside or acted self;
Else risk and work, perhaps with helper, to become a one
That is not only some or part, but *all* of us — befriended.

Relationships (1985)

Are relationships with others mere additions,
In principle, straightforward compositions
Robust in case of likeness, weak or jagged otherwise,
Based on individual traits, yours and mine,
Which add and cancel out when we combine —
All in arithmetic order, could we but realise?

Or, is our joining more a kind of fusion
In which the chemistry of each, in interaction,
Gives rise to something new: a whole we scarce
Could know until it happened, not like one of us
Extended but a species new in form and kind?
From two, one twosome, with energy and mind
Born from our conjunction, living as a We
And Us — or Them to others — which you and I
Will always parent and be partly governed by.

Partners (1985)

One and one equal three,
One, the other one, and two-in-one;
The third a We of partnership,
Friendship, love and motion of its own.

Love not felt alone by either one
But sparking, flowing, growing, bonding
But unbound, a symphony of endless
Variation on its theme; of voices
Calling and answering, dancing
In the dawn and day and unlit night;
Of sharing in play and work and striving;
Of quick-flashing cut and burning
Anguished pain; of fearfully,
Carefully listening, hoping, saying,
Touching, reaching, rushing in the wonder
Of oneness with another —
Friend, foe, partner, lover.

Paradox of Change (1991)

When you want me *not* to be the me you see
my inner self armours with encasing shield.
When you can accept me, prize me unjudging,
my warméd self unfolds its blooms, or sprouts
    fresh shoots.

If I myself require me to be another way
I then perform that way, the best I can —
divided: me within spurring, watching,
prompting the outer me wearily acting
    as insisted.

When another touches me with their clear
knowing of feelings alive within, beneath
the fumbling or withheld expression of my
words, my eyes moisten and easing runs
    thru my body.

If the other deftly points to contradictions,
division, the traumas of my life, picking at
the scars I wear, I smart and shrink away,
not wanting to surrender my troubled self —
    my only self.

InHuman Being (1991)

Groups like ourselves, but different,
Linked and apart, races we invent
In whom we see our own reflection
Distorted, deviant, tainting our perfection;
Mutant alter egos silently infecting
Our kind, our culture, our one direction.

Thus, we *think*, surely it is our right,
Our duty even, to use protective might
Against the 'lesser' beings and misshapen
Groups who would erode and threaten
By existing, the fullness and purity
Of our system, knowledge of reality,
Abundant living — for we who belong —
And a future this way, right or wrong.

Point of View (1994)

What do we prize most — riches, honour, beauty, learning,
our heritage from family, community or other belonging,
friends, a mate, children, the persons we hold most dear?
Or, is there something beyond, expressed in all of these:
Our own point of view, the way we understand the world,
our compass, through storm and swirl of circumstance
to landfalls sensible to ourselves.

Knowledge, viewpoint, wisdom; related but not one.
Viewpoint, a stance stemming from life's experience,
a way of putting contradictory happenings together,
is both conclusion and approach. Lacking viewpoint
we lose our way; threatened, we fight to defend it.

Yet, though oft we guard it, our viewpoint is alive
and on the move when not attacked or dismissed.
It came into being, and this coming can continue.
Ideas open, outlooks grow, when view and holder
are seriously received, with wish to understand,
responded to in sharing search, back and forth —
knowing found in being known.

Freedom and Belonging (1987)

To cleave or not to, how to belong
Yet be free, how to sing one's *own* song
Partnered, merging in relationship unity,
Or, be true to self within community?

What is a self, mine or yours; why say
*In*dividual when a person is many
And a twosome or group can be one whole,
Of one mind or motion, even one soul.

I am me in many layers at once —
Inside, outside, intelligent and dunce.
No addition A plus B can form the We
Born and flowing through You and Me.

Look we can at freedom *for* — not only
Freedom from — then see all the opportunity,
        passion and purpose
Which springs from our togetherings,
Bringing gift of body whole and wings
        to freedom.

Deception (1989)

To know or not to know, to seek truth
or to shun it, to speak the known
or conceal it, all are within our scope.
Deceit is an option, a choice to blind
the other and, in the end, ourselves,
inventing an image against our seeing —
a chimera which diverts honest vision
and leaves *us* prey to our own delusion.
Purposed untruth weaves a web without
boundary, a net that twists and tangles,
turning to entrap the teller and wrap
the believing victim in dark illusion.

Deception cripples deceiver and deceived.
Skilled deception is a skill that kills,
squeezing the soul in a vice of belief
and disbelief, tearing at singleness of self
with teeth, teeth which then spit forth
dismembered beings, part-selves haunted
and in fear of other parts, connected
by a consciousness without identity —
no hand within, no lit communing self,
the heartbeat lost though limbs still live.

Lies, white or black, can be lethal, first
to confidence and trust, to the valued 'we'
or 'us', then, to the inner person fogged
now with double vision — Yes but really No —
bent by secrecy, by shame, else by defiance,
ready for conspiracies unspoken, to pretend.

To live a lie building on itself is not to live
it is to die, to perish in our inner soul —
e'en if acting as though we still were whole.

On Presenting to an Audience (1988)

We easily speak to the audience we bring within us,
our eye turned in, to stage and actors set beforehand;
no need to search our way, the path is planned and clear.
Else, we begin by looking, listening, letting awareness come
of *this* peopled group unmet before or not the same today,
each member living and distinct within, with purpose
unexpressed until we care to know it; our presentation
then transformed, responsive sharing, minds meeting.

Oft we come with our speech fashioned, complete
for the purpose, our thoughts and words rehearsed,
ready-made, wound to unwind in clock-like precision.
We talk from mouth and mind of self working before,
a self whose living presence now, in this new moment,
is withheld, unshared. By differing choice, we come
equipped but not committed by forethought,
prepared in our knowing, curiosity, desire to share;
written words but a resource, part of a larger pool
to draw from in slaking the thirst we *find* together.

I, for one, easily point outside myself: to events,
circumstance, the shape of things or measurements,
to careful analysis and interpretation, to the arrow
of my thought more than the bow from which it springs.
I/we tend to share meanings distilled, not forming,
given not coming, holograms of thought traced afore
and beckoned for replay by inner fingers, quivering.

Why less easy to live in our words, to engage freshly
as we share, not copying what we thought before but
thinking as we go? If worried about losing our way
let's say it. (Ghostly fears haunt from behind, oft
fading when held before.) Thought can further stretch
and grow in fresh expression. This happened as we wrote,
then surely will again, in live encounter with other minds
— your minds, your inquiring selves, you also searching.

Overtaking the Future (1988)

We are sowers in our deepest nature,
Seeding the future in *all* our ways:
As we wrestle with happenings past,
As we strive to control the present,
As we work to realise possibilities,
Even as we dream and share our visions.

Through the being and growth of children,
In the procreation of ideas and of learning,
In being participants in nature, or overlords,
In friending and sharing, competing or warring,
In striving for power, fortune or distinction;
In all our creating and whenever we destroy,
Knowing it or not we are cropping the future —
And in the harvest our journey is revealed anew.

Love (1987)

What means it to love? Is it feeling
one's life flow brimming, merging
with the bright motion of another?
Is it sharing, listening, hearing, finding
that the other also sees what we behold?
Is it joining in a We, for each one of us
enlivening, transforming Me; or, a bonding
of lived loyalty, lasting, without possession;
or, desire to be one flesh, in passionate embrace —
unison of white heat, wondrous shock, centred calm?

What about love of one's child,
fruit of one's seed, miracle of nature?
Wonder, tenderness, compassion, empathy —
are these not also primary faces of love?
Consider, too, the longing love of a child
for its parent: life-giver, protector, guide,
glad or reluctant hero, partner even
in the sharing, learning world of play.

Observe the love of brothers and sisters,
sometime foes or rivals but with felt unspoken
pledge, caring given unearned, without decision,
the common heritage a wellspring of belonging.
Follow in thought to the oft-unspoken love
of one's friends (not given by birth but chosen),
to loving fellowship in groups of like belief or action,
or the ambient embrace of any larger community
that our selfhood drinks from and flows into.

Can we not also love creatures differing
from ourselves in kind, animal friends
drawn to us as we to them, responsive
and aware, fellow-children of that
same nature which spawned *our* kind?
Where it sleeps, shall we awaken love
for all this natural world, our planet,
precious inheritance, lifeline to futures
bounteous and sown still with life?

What of love for a befriending god or
for a spiritual world unseen but pregnant
with mystery and meaning, for a cosmos
beyond touch or present time but in reach
of mind, for the questing spirit in humankind?
In English, one little word — universe of meaning.

References

Barrett-Lennard, G. T. (1962a). Dimensions of therapist response as causal factors in therapeutic change. *Psychological Monographs, 76* (43, Whole No. 562).

Barrett-Lennard, G. T. (1962b). The mature person. *Mental Hygiene, 46,* 98–102.

Barrett-Lennard, G. T. (1963). Significant aspects of a helping relationship. *Mental Hygiene, 47,* 223–7. Also in *Canada's Mental Health,* Supplement No. 47, July-Aug., 1965.

Barrett-Lennard, G. T. (1965). Professional psychology and the control of human behaviour. *Australian Journal of Psychology, 17,* 24–34. Also in J. T. Hart and T. M. Tomlinson (Eds.), *New directions in client-centered therapy* (442–52). Houghton Mifflin, 1970.

Barrett-Lennard, G. T. (1973). The intensive group experience: Process description and guidelines. *Canada's Mental Health, 21*(1). Supplement (whole) No. 73.

Barrett-Lennard, G. T. (1974). Experiential learning groups. *Psychotherapy: Theory, Research and Practice, 11,* 71–5.

Barrett-Lennard, G. T. (1975). Process, effects and structure in intensive groups: A theoretical-descriptive analysis. In C. L. Cooper (Ed.), *Theories of group processes* (59–86). London: Wiley. (Preferred source is the *corrected,* soft-cover reprinting, 1976.)

Barrett-Lennard, G. T. (1976). Empathy in human relationships: Significance, nature and measurement. *Australian Psychologist, 11,* 173–84.

Barrett-Lennard, G. T. (1978). The Relationship Inventory: later development and adaptations. JSAS *Catalog of Selected Documents in Psychology, 8,* 68. (MS 1732.)

Barrett-Lennard, G. T. (1979a). A new model of communicational-relational systems in intensive groups. *Human Relations, 32,* 841–9.

Barrett-Lennard, G. T. (1979b). The client-centered system unfolding. In F. J. Turner (Ed.), *Social work treatment: Interlocking theoretical approaches* (177–241). New York: Free Press. Second Edition.

Barrett-Lennard, G. T. (1981). The empathy cycle: Refinement of a nuclear concept. *Journal of Counseling Psychology, 28,* 91–100.

Barrett-Lennard, G. T. (1984). The world of family relationships: A person-centred systems view. In R. F. Levant and J. M. Shlien (Eds.), *Client-centered therapy and the person-centered approach: New directions in theory, research and practice.* New York: Praeger.

Barrett-Lennard, G. T. (1985). The helping interview in counselling and psychotherapy. *British Journal of Hospital Medicine, 33,* 287–90.

Barrett-Lennard, G. T. (1986). The Relationship Inventory now: Issues and advances in theory, method and use. In L. S. Greenberg and W. M. Pinsof (Eds.), *The psychotherapeutic process: A research handbook* (439–76). New York: Guilford Press.

Barrett-Lennard, G. T. (1988). Listening. *Person-Centered Review, 3,* 410–25.

Barrett-Lennard, G. T. (1990). The therapy pathway reformulated. In G. Lietaer, J. Rombauts and R. Van Balen (Eds.), *Client-centered and experiential psychotherapy in the nineties* (123–53). Leuven, Belgium: Leuven University Press.

Barrett-Lennard, G. T. (1993a). The phases and focus of empathy. *British Journal of Medical Psychology, 66,* 3–14.

Barrett-Lennard, G. T. (1993b). Understanding the person-centered approach to therapy: A 'reply' to questions and misconceptions. In D. Coghlan and E. McIlduff (Eds.), *The person-centered approach and cross-cultural communication: An international review, Vol. 2* (99–113). Linz: Sandkorn. Center for Cross-Cultural Communication, Dublin.

Barrett-Lennard, G. T. (1993c). Viewing the person in context: A systemic model of change. *Network, 8*(2), 13–25 (Australian Psychological Society).

Barrett-Lennard, G. T. (1994). Toward a person-centered theory of community. *Journal of Humanistic Psychology, 34*(3), 62–86.

Barrett-Lennard, G. T. (1996). Therapy and groups in context: A study of developmental episodes in adulthood. In R. Hutterer, G. Pawlowsky, P. F. Schmid and R. Stipsits (Eds.), *Client-centered and experiential psychotherapy: A paradigm in motion* (185–98). Frankfurt am Main: Peter Lang.

Barrett-Lennard, G. T. (1997). The recovery of empathy — toward others and self. In A. C. Bohart and L. S. Greenberg (Eds.), *Empathy reconsidered: New directions in psychotherapy* (103–21). Washington, DC: American Psychological Association.

Barrett-Lennard, G. T. (1998). *Carl Rogers' helping system: Journey and substance.* London; Thousand Oaks, CA; New Delhi: Sage.

Barrett-Lennard, G. T. (2001a). *Draft Relationship Inventory resource bibliography.* Annotated bibliography listing approx. 400 studies organised in ten groups. (Periodically updated, and prepared primarily for investigators using the RI.)

Barrett-Lennard, G. T. (2001b). Levels of loneliness and connection: Crisis and possibility. *PERSON. Zeitschrift für Klientenzentrierte Psychotherapie und personzentrierte Ansätze, 5*(1), 58–64.

Barrett-Lennard, G. T. (2002a). The helping conditions in *their* context: Expanding change theory and practice. *Person-centered and experiential psychotherapies, 1*(1 & 2), 144–55.

Barrett-Lennard, G. T. (2002b). Perceptual variables of the helping relationship: A measuring system and its fruits. In G. Wyatt and P. Sanders (Eds.), *Rogers' Therapeutic Conditions: Evolution, theory and practice. Vol. 4: Contact and Perception* (25–50). Ross-on-Wye: PCCS Books.

Barrett-Lennard, G. T. (2003). *The primacy of relationship: Healing revisited in an altered world.* Manuscript book, under publisher review.

Blatt, S. J., Quinlan, D. M., Zuroff, D. C. and Pilkonis, P. A. (1996). Interpersonal factors in brief treatment of depression: Further analyses of the NIMH Treatment of Depression Collaborative Research Program. *Journal of Consulting and Clinical Psychology, 64*, 162–71.

Bohart, A. C. and Greenberg, L. S. (Eds.) (1997). *Empathy reconsidered: New directions in psychotherapy.* Washington, DC: American Psychological Association.

Bohart, A. C., O'Hara, M. and Leitner, L. M. (1998). Empirically violated treatments: Disenfranchisement of humanistic and other psychotherapies. *Psychotherapy Research, 8*, 141–57.

Bozarth, J. (1998). *Person-Centered Therapy: A revolutionary paradigm.* Ross-on-Wye: PCCS Books.

Bozarth, J. D. and Wilkins, P. (Eds.) (2001). *Rogers' Therapeutic Conditions: Evolution, theory and practice. Vol. 3: Unconditional positive regard.* Ross-on-Wye: PCCS Books.

Bozarth, J. D., Zimring, F. and Tausch, R. (2002). Client-centered therapy: Evolution of a revolution. In D. Cain and J. Seeman (Eds.), *Humanistic Psychotherapies: Handbook of research and practise*, (Ch. 5). Washington DC: American Psychological Association.

Butler, J. M. (1958). Client-centered counseling and psychotherapy. In D. Brower and L. E. Abt (Eds.), *Progress in Clinical Psychology Vol. 3: Changing Conceptions in Psychotherapy*. New York: Grune and Stratton.

Brodley, B. T. (1990). Client-centered and experiential: Two different therapies. In G. Lietaer, J. Rombauts and R. Van Balen (Eds.), *Client-centered and experiential psychotherapy in the nineties* (87–107). Leuven: Leuven University Press.

Butler, J. M. (1974). The iconic mode in psychotherapy. In D. A. Wexler and L. N. Rice (Eds.), *Innovations in client-centered therapy*. New York: Wiley.

Byrne, B. (1983). Trainee uses of reciprocal peer supervision and of faculty supervision in psychotherapy training. *Dissertation Abstracts International, 44*, 111A.

Cholden, L. (1956). Observations on psychotherapy of schizophrenia. In F. Fromm-Reichmann and J. L. Moreno (Eds.), *Progress in psychotherapy*. New York: Grune and Stratton.

Clarke, K. M. (1991). A performance model of the creation of meaning event. *Psychotherapy, 28*, 395–401.

Cline, E. W. (1970–1971). Confirming behaviour of school executives. (Doctoral dissertation, University of Florida, 1969.) *Dissertation Abstracts, 31*, 1067A.

Cooper, C. L. (1969). The influence of the trainer on participant change in T-groups. *Human Relations, 22*, 515–30.

Cramer, D. (1985). Psychological adjustment and the facilitative nature of close personal relationships. *British Journal of Medical Psychology, 58*, 165–8.

Cramer, D. (1989). Self-esteem and the facilitativeness of parents and close friends. *Person-Centered Review, 4*, 61–76.

Cramer, D. (1990). Disclosure of personal problems, self-esteem, and the facilitativeness of friends and lovers. *British Journal of Guidance and Counselling, 18*, 186–96.

Cramer, D. (1994). Self-esteem and Rogers' core conditions in close friends: A latent variable path analysis of panel data. *Counselling Psychology Quarterly, 7*, 327–37.

Elkin, I. (1994). The NIMH treatment of depression collaborative research program: Where we began and where we are. In A. E. Bergin and S. L. Garfield (Eds.), *Handbook of psychotherapy and behavior change*, 114–39. New York: Wiley.

Emmerling, F. C. (1961). A study of the relationship between personality characteristics of classroom teachers and pupil perceptions of these teachers. *Dissertation Abstracts, 22*, 1054–5. (University Microfilms No. 61–3002.)

Farber, B. A., Brink, D. C. and Raskin, P. M. (1996). *The psychotherapy of Carl Rogers: Cases and commentary*. New York and London: Guilford.

Fenichel, O. (1945). *The psychoanalytic theory of the neurosis*. New York: Norton.

Fretz, B. R., Corn, R., Tuemmler, J. M. and Bellet, W. (1979). Counselor nonverbal behaviors and client evaluation. *Journal of Counseling Psychology, 26*, 304–11.

Gendlin, E. T. (1961a). Experiencing: A variable in the process of therapeutic change. *American Journal of Psychotherapy, 15*, 233–45.

Gendlin, E. T. (1961b). Initiating psychotherapy with 'unmotivated' patients. *The Psychiatric Quarterly, 34*(1), 1–6.

Gendlin, E. T. (1962). Client-centered developments and work with schizophrenics. *Journal of Counseling Psychology, 9,* 205–11.

Gendlin, E. T. (1964). Schizophrenia: Problems and methods of psychotherapy. *Review of Existential Psychology and Psychiatry, 4,* 168–79.

Gendlin, E. T. (1967). Therapeutic procedures in dealing with schizophrenics. In C. R. Rogers, E. T. Gendlin, T. J. Kiesler and C. B. Truax (Eds.), *The therapeutic relationship and its impact: A study of psychotherapy with schizophrenics* (369–400). Madison, Wisconsin: University of Wisconsin Press.

Gendlin, E. T. (1968). The experiential response. In E. F. Hammer (Ed.), *The use of interpretation in treatment: Technique and art.* New York: Grune and Stratton.

Gendlin, E. T. (1969). Focusing. *Psychotherapy: Theory, Research and Practice, 6,* 4–15.

Gendlin, E. T. (1974). Client-centered and experiential psychotherapy. In D. A. Wexler and L. N. Rice (Eds.), *Innovations in client-centered therapy* (211–46). New York: Wiley.

Gendlin, E. T. (1981). *Focusing.* New York: Bantam Books. Revised Edition.

Gendlin, E. T. (1996). *Focusing-oriented psychotherapy.* New York: Guilford Press.

Gendlin, E. T. and Beebe, J. (1968). Experiential groups: Instructions for groups. In G. M. Gazda (Ed.), *Innovations to group psychotherapy,* (168–79). Springfield, Illinois: Charles C. Thomas.

Giesekus, U. and Mente, A. (1986). Client empathic understanding in client-centered therapy. *Person-Centered Review, 1,* 163–71.

Gilmour-Barrett, K. C. (1973). Managerial systems and interpersonal treatment processes in residential centres for disturbed youth. Unpublished doctoral dissertation (in psychology), University of Waterloo, Ontario.

Gomes, W. B. (1981). The communicational-relational system in two forms of family group composition. Unpublished master's thesis, Southern Illinois University.

Gross, W. F., Curtin, M. E. and Moore, K. B. (1970). Appraisal of a milieu therapy environment by treatment team and patients. *Journal of Clinical Psychology, 26,* 541–5.

Gurman, A. S. (1977). The patient's perception of the therapeutic relationship. In A. S. Gurman and A. M. Razin (Eds.), *Effective psychotherapy: A handbook of research* (503–43). Oxford: Pergamon.

Halkides, G. (1958). An experimental study of four conditions necessary for therapeutic change. Unpublished doctoral dissertation, University of Chicago.

Haugh, S. and Merry, T. (Eds.) (2001). *Rogers' Therapeutic Conditions: Evolution, theory and practice. Vol. 2: Empathy.* Ross-on-Wye: PCCS Books.

Holland, D. A. (1976). The Relationship Inventory — Experimental Form OS-S-42: A validity study. Unpublished honours BA thesis (psychology), University of Waterloo, Ontario.

Jaeger, T. K. (1989). Principal/teacher interpersonal relations and school climate. *Dissertation Abstracts International, 49,* 3571A.

Jahoda, M. (1958). *Current concepts of positive mental health.* (Report to the Joint Commission on Mental Illness and Health.) New York: Basic Books.

Kantor, D. and Lehr, W. (1975). *Inside the family: Toward a theory of family process.* San Francisco: Jossey-Bass. (Third printing: 1977.)

Katz, R. L. (1963). *Empathy: Its nature and uses.* Glencoe, Illinois: Free Press.

Kelly, G. A. (1955). *The psychology of personal constructs.* New York: Norton.

Kohut, H. (1977). *The restoration of the self.* New York: International Universities Press.

Kohut, H. (1984). *How does analysis cure?* Chicago: University of Chicago Press.

Kurtz, R. R. and Grummon, D. L. (1972). Different approaches to the measurement of therapist empathy and their relationship to therapy outcomes. *Journal of Consulting and Clinical Psychology, 37,* 106–15.

Leijssen, M. (1990). On focusing and the necessary conditions of therapeutic personality change. In G. Lietaer, J. Rombauts, and R. Van Balen (Eds.), *Client-centered and experiential psychotherapy in the nineties* (225–50). Leuven, Belgium: Leuven University Press.

Levant, R. F. and Shlien, J. M. (Eds.) (1984). *Client-centered therapy and the person-centered approach: New directions in theory, research and practice.* New York: Praeger.

Lietaer, G. (1976). Nederlandstalige revisie van Barrett-Lennard's Relationship Inventory voor individueel-terapeutische relaties. *Psychologica Belgica, 16* (1), 73–94.

Lietaer, G. (1979). De beleving van de relatie door client en therapeut in client-centered en psychoanalytisch georienteerde therapie. Een empirische bijdrage. *Tijdschrift voor Psychotherapie, 5,* 141–60.

Lietaer, G. (1984). Unconditional positive regard: A controversial basic attitude in client-centered therapy. In R. F. Levant and J. M. Shlien (Eds.), *Client-centered therapy and the person-centered approach: New directions in theory, research and practice* (41–58). New York: Praeger.

Lietaer, G. (1993). Authenticity, congruence and transparency. In D. Brazier (Ed.), *Beyond Carl Rogers* (17–46). London: Constable.

Lietaer, G. (2001). Unconditional acceptance and positive regard. In J. D. Bozarth and P. Wilkins (Eds.), *Rogers' Therapeutic Conditions: Evolution, theory and practice. Vol. 3: Unconditional positive regard* (88–108). Ross-on-Wye: PCCS Books.

Lietaer, G. (2002). The client-centered/experiential paradigm in psychotherapy: Development and identity. In J. C. Watson, R. N. Goldman and M. S. Warner (Eds.), *Client-Centered and Experiential Psychotherapy in the 21st Century: Advances in theory, research and practice* (1–15). Ross-on-Wye, England: PCCS Books.

Lindsay, J. S. B. (1976). Balance theory: Possible consequences of number of family members. *Family Process, 15,* 245–9.

Marques-Teixeira, J., Pires de Carvalho, M. M., Moreira, A. M. and Pinho, C. (1996). 'Group effect?' Implementation of the Portuguese translation of the Barrett-Lennard Inventory on five group types. In R. Hutterer, G. Pawlowsky, P. F. Schmid and R. Stipsits (Eds.), *Client-centered and experiential psychotherapy: A paradigm in motion* (585–98). Frankfurt am Main: Peter Lang.

Mead, G. H. (1934). *Mind, self, and society.* Chicago: University of Chicago Press.

Mearns, D. (1997). *Person-centred counselling training.* London; Thousand Oaks: Sage.

Mearns, D. and Thorne, B. (1999). *Person-centred counselling in action* (Second Edition). London: Sage.

Mearns, D. and Thorne, B. (2000). *Person-centred therapy today: New frontiers in theory and practice* (see 101–19, and 172–95). London; Thousand Oaks;

New Delhi: Sage.

Mente, A. (1990). Improving Rogers' theory: Toward a more completely client-centered psychotherapy. In G. Lietaer, J. Rombauts and R. Van Balen (Eds.), *Client-centered and experiential psychotherapy in the nineties* (771–8). Leuven, Belgium: Leuven University Press.

Mente, A. and Spittler, H-D. (1980). *Erlebnisorientierte Gruppenpsychotherapie: Eine wieksame methode der klienten-zentrierten behandlung von verhaltensstörungen.* Vol. 2. Paderborn: Junfermann.

Mitchell, K. M., Bozarth, J. D. and Krauft, C. C. (1977). A reappraisal of the therapeutic effectiveness of accurate empathy, non-possessive warmth, and genuineness. In A. S. Gurman and A. M. Razin (Eds.), *Effective psychotherapy: A handbook of research* (482–502). Oxford: Pergamon.

Morgan, G. (1986). *Images of organisation.* Beverley Hills; London; New Delhi: Sage.

O'Leary, C. J. (1999). *Counselling couples and families: A person-centred approach.* London: Sage.

Prouty, G. F. (1994). *Theoretical evolutions in person-centered/experiential therapy: Applications to schizophrenic and retarded psychoses.* Westport, Connecticut: Praeger.

Prouty, G. and Pietrzak, S. (1988). The pre-therapy method applied to persons experiencing hallucinatory images. *Person-Centered Review, 3,* 426–41.

Purton, C. (1998). Unconditional positive regard and its spiritual implications. In B. Thorne and E. Lambers (Eds.), *Person-centred therapy: A European perspective* (23–37). London: Sage.

Quintana, S. M. and Meara, N. M. (1990). Internalization of therapeutic relationships in short-term psychotherapy. *Journal of Counseling Psychology, 37,* 123–30.

Rank, O. (1936/1945). *Will therapy* and *Truth and reality.* New York: Knopf.

Raskin, N. J. (1974). Studies of psychotherapeutic orientation: Ideology and practice. *AAP Research Monograph,* No. 1. Orlando, FL: American Academy of Psychotherapists.

Raskin, N. J. (1985). Client-centered therapy. In S. J. Lynn and J. P. Garske (Eds.), *Contemporary psychotherapies: Models and methods* (155–90). Columbus, Ohio: Charles E. Merrill.

Redfield, R. (1960). *The little community.* Chicago: University of Chicago Press. (Phoenix Edition, including *Peasant society and culture* in same volume.)

Rice, L. N. (1974). The evocative function of the therapist. In D. A. Wexler and L. N. Rice (Eds.), *Innovations in client-centered therapy.* New York: Wiley.

Rogers, C. R. (1939). *The clinical treatment of the problem child.* Boston: Houghton Mifflin.

Rogers, C. R. (1942). *Counseling and psychotherapy.* Boston: Houghton Mifflin.

Rogers, C. R. (1946). Significant aspects of client-centered therapy. *American Psychologist, 1,* 415–22.

Rogers, C. R. (1947). Some observations on the organization of personality. *American Psychologist, 2,* 358–68.

Rogers, C. R. (1949). The attitude and orientation of the counselor in client-centered therapy. *Journal of Consulting Psychology, 13,* 82–94.

Rogers, C. R. (1951). *Client-centered therapy.* Boston: Houghton Mifflin.

Rogers, C. R. (1953). Some directions and end points in therapy. In O. H. Mowrer (Ed.), *Psychotherapy: Theory and research* (44–68). New York: Ronald.

Rogers, C. R. (1954). Some basic hypotheses of client-centered therapy. Mimeographed, privately circulated article.

Rogers, C. R. (1955). Persons or science: A philosophical question. *American Psychologist, 10,* 267–78.

Rogers, C. R. (1957). The necessary and sufficient conditions of therapeutic personality change, *Journal of Consulting Psychology, 21,* 95–103.

Rogers, C. R. (1958). A process conception of psychotherapy. *American Psychologist, 13,* 142–9.

Rogers, C. R. (1959a). A theory of therapy, personality, and interpersonal relationships as developed in the client-centered framework. In S. Koch (Ed.), *Psychology: A study of a science, Vol. 3: Formulations of the person and the social context* (184–256). New York: McGraw-Hill.

Rogers, C. R. (1959b). A tentative scale for the measurement of process in psychotherapy. In E. A. Rubinstein and M. B. Parloff (Eds.), *Research in psychotherapy* (96–107). Washington, DC: American Psychological Association. *Psychotherapy with schizophrenics* (3–19). Baton Rouge: Louisiana State University Press.

Rogers, C. R. (1961a). *On becoming a person: A therapist's view of psychotherapy.* Boston: Houghton Mifflin.

Rogers, C. R. (1961b). The process equation of psychotherapy. *American Journal of Psychotherapy, 15*(1), 27–45.

Rogers, C. R. (1961c). A theory of psychotherapy with schizophrenics and a proposal for its empirical investigation. In J. G. Dawson, H. K. Stone and N. P. Dellis (Eds.), *Psychotherapy with schizophrenics* (3–19). Baton Rouge: Louisiana State University Press.

Rogers, C. R. (1962a). The interpersonal relationship: The core of guidance. *Harvard Educational Review, 32,* 416–29.

Rogers, C. R. (1962b). Some learnings from a study of psychotherapy with schizophrenics. *Pennsylvania Psychiatric Quarterly,* Summer issue, 3–15. (Republished, 1967, in C. R. Rogers and B. Stevens, *Person to person: The problem of being human* (181–92). Lafayette, California: Real People Press.)

Rogers, C. R. (1963a). The actualizing tendency in relation to 'motives' and to consciousness. In M. R. Jones (Ed.), *Nebraska Symposium on Motivation, Vol. 11,* 1–24. Lincoln: University of Nebraska Press.

Rogers, C. R. (1963b). The concept of the fully functioning person. *Psychotherapy: Theory, Research and Practice, 1,* 17–26.

Rogers, C. R. (1964a). Freedom and commitment. *The Humanist, 24*(2), 37–40.

Rogers, C. R. (1964b). Toward a modern approach to values: The valuing process in the mature person. *Journal of Abnormal and Social Psychology, 68,* 160–7.

Rogers, C. R. (1965a). Dealing with psychological tensions. *Journal of Applied Behavioral Science, 1*(1), 6–24.

Rogers, C. R. (1965b). Audio-recorded address given at the University of New South Wales, Sydney, January 18th. (Rogers, 1980b — listed below — is very similar in content.)

Rogers, C. R. (1965c). Filmed interview in *Three approaches to psychotherapy* (edited by Shostom, E.) Santa Ana, California: Psychological Films.

Rogers, C. R. (1965d). The therapeutic relationship: recent theory and research. *Australian Journal of Psychology, 17,* 95–108.

Rogers, C. R. (1966). Client-centered therapy. In S. Arieti (Ed.), *American handbook of psychiatry, Vol. 3* (183–200). New York: Basic Books.

Rogers, C. R. (1967). A silent young man. In C. R. Rogers, with E. T. Gendlin, T. J. Kiesler and C. B. Truax (Eds.) (1967), *The therapeutic relationship and its impact: A study of psychotherapy with schizophrenics* (401–16). Madison, Wisconsin: University of Wisconsin Press.

Rogers, C. R. (1969). *Freedom to learn.* Columbus, Ohio: Charles E. Merrill.

Rogers, C. R. (1970). *Carl Rogers on encounter groups.* New York: Harper and Row.

Rogers, C. R. (1975). Empathic: An unappreciated way of being. *The Counseling Psychologist,* 5(2), 2–11.

Rogers, C. R. (1977). A person-centered workshop: Its planning and fruition. In *Carl Rogers on personal power* (143–85). New York: Delacorte Press.

Rogers, C. R. (1978). The formative tendency. *Journal of Humanistic Psychology, 18* (Winter), 22–6.

Rogers, C. R. (1980a). *A way of being.* Boston: Houghton Mifflin.

Rogers, C. R. (1980b). Experiences in communication. In C. R. Rogers, *A way of being* (5–26). Boston: Houghton Mifflin.

Rogers, C. R. (1980c). Client-centered psychotherapy. In H. I. Kaplan, B. J. Sadock and A. M. Freedman (Eds.), *Comprehensive textbook of psychiatry.* Baltimore: Williams and Wilkins. Third Edition.

Rogers, C. R. and Dymond, R. F. (Eds.), (1954). *Psychotherapy and personality change.* Chicago: University of Chicago Press.

Rogers, C. R. and Farson, R. E. (1957). *Active listening.* University of Chicago: Industrial Relations Center (and, University Library).

Rogers, C. R., with Gendlin, E. T., Kiesler, T. J. and Truax, C. B. (Eds.) (1967). *The therapeutic relationship and its impact: A study of psychotherapy with schizophrenics.* Madison: University of Wisconsin Press.

Rogers, C. R. and Wallen, J. L. (1946). *Counseling with returned servicemen.* New York: McGraw-Hill.

Rosen, H. H. (1961). Dimensions of the perceived parent-relationship as related to juvenile delinquency. Unpublished Master's thesis, Auburn University, Alabama.

Rowan, J. and Cooper, M. (1999). *The plural self. Multiplicity in everyday life.* London; Thousand Oaks; New Delhi: Sage.

Seeman, J. (1989). Toward a model of positive health. *American Psychologist, 44,* 1099–1109.

Shlien, J. M. (1961). A client-centered approach to schizophrenia: First approximation. In A. Burton (Ed.), *Psychotherapy of the psychoses* (285–317). New York: Basic Books.

Shlien, J. and Sanders, P. (Ed.). *To Lead an Honorable Life: Invitations to think about Client-Centered Therapy and the Person-Centered Approach.* Ross-on-Wye: PCCS Books.

Snyder, M. (1992). The meaning of empathy: Comments on Hans Strupp's case of Helen R. *Psychotherapy, 29,* 318–22.

Snyder, M. (1994). The development of social intelligence in psychotherapy: Empathic and dialogic processes. *Journal of Humanistic Psychology, 34*(1), 84–108.

Sundaram, D. K. (1976). Psychological adjustment as a function of interpersonal relationships: A field study. Unpublished doctoral dissertation, Columbia University. Abstract in *Dissertation Abstracts International,* 1977, *37,* 5380–1B.

Taft, J. (1933). *The dynamics of therapy in a controlled relationship.* New York: Macmillan.

Thornton, B. M. (1960). Dimensions of perceived relationship as related to marital adjustment. Unpublished Master's thesis, Auburn University, Alabama.

Toman, W. (1976). *Family constellation: Its effects on personality and social behaviour.* New York: Springer. Third Edition.

Townsend, M. E. (1988). Self-disclosure and psychological adjustment: Towards an understanding. Unpublished honours bachelor thesis (psychology), Monash University, Melbourne.

Turner, F. J. (Ed.) (1979). *Social work treatment: Interlocking theoretical approaches.* New York: Free Press. Second Edition. (Barrett-Lennard chapter: 177–241.)

van der Veen, F. and Novak, A. L. (1971). Perceived parental attitudes and family concepts of disturbed adolescents, normal siblings and normal controls. *Family Process, 10,* 327–43.

Wampler, K. S. and Powell, G. S. (1982). The Barrett-Lennard Relationship Inventory as a measure of marital satisfaction. *Family Relations, 31,* 139–45.

Wargo, D. G. and Meek, V. C. (1970/1971). The Relationship Inventory as a measure of milieu perception in rehabilitation center students. *Rehabilitation Counseling Bulletin, 14,* 42–8.

Wexler, D. A. and Rice, L. N. (Eds.) (1974). *Innovations in client-centered therapy.* New York: Wiley.

Wilkins, P. (2000). Unconditional positive regard reconsidered. *British Journal of Guidance and Counselling, 28*(1), 23–36.

Wilkinson, G. R. (1972). The application of differentiated small group processes to developmental learning in an educational setting. Unpublished doctoral dissertation, University of Waterloo, Ontario.

Wood, J. K. (1984). Communities for learning: a person-centered approach. In R. F. Levant and J. M. Shlien (eds.), *Client-centered therapy and the person-centered approach: New directions in theory, research and practice* (297–336). New York: Praeger.

Wyatt, G. (Ed.) (2001). *Rogers' Therapeutic Conditions. Evolution, theory and practice. Vol. 1: Congruence.* Ross-on-Wye: PCCS Books.

Wyatt, G. and Sanders, P. (Eds.) (2002). *Rogers' Therapeutic Conditions: Evolution, theory and practice. Vol. 4: Contact and Perception.* Ross-on-Wye: PCCS Books.

Index

U

unconditional positive regard 23
unconditionality of regard 8, 95, 97, 99,
        103, 105, 106n, 108, 109, 110,
        119
University of Chicago 29, 94

V

van der Veen, F. 98, 196

W

Wargo, D.G. 106, 196
wellness 2
Wexler, D.A.   23, 196
Wilkins, P. 3, 110, 196
Wilkinson, G.R. 74, 196
Wyatt, G. 110, 196

PCCS Books

The largest list of Client-Centred Therapy and Person-Centred Approach books in the world

Client-Centred Therapy and the Person-Centred Approach
Essential Readers
Series edited by Tony Merry

Client-Centred Therapy: A revolutionary paradigm
Jerold Bozarth

Experiences in Relatedness: Groupwork and the person-centred approach
Colin Lago & Mhairi MacMillan (Eds)

Women Writing in the Person-Centred Approach
Irene Fairhurst (Ed)

Understanding Psychotherapy: Fifty years of client-centred theory and practice
C.H. Patterson

The Person-Centred Approach: A passionate presence
Peggy Natiello

Family, Self and Psychotherapy: A person-centred perspective
Ned L. Gaylin

Contributions to Client-Centered Therapy and the Person-Centered Approach
Nathaniel J. Raskin

Rogers' Therapeutic Conditions: Evolution, Theory and Practice
Series edited by Gill Wyatt

Volume 1: Congruence
Gill Wyatt (Ed)

Volume 2: Empathy
Sheila Haugh & Tony Merry (Eds)

Volume 3: Unconditional Positive Regard
Jerold Bozarth & Paul Wilkins (Eds)

Volume 4: Contact and Perception
Gill Wyatt & Pete Sanders (Eds)

PCCS Books

The largest list of Client-Centred Therapy and Person-Centred Approach books in the world

The Tribes of the Person-Centred Nation: A guide to the schools of therapy associated with the PCA
Pete Sanders (Ed)

Idiosyncratic Person-Centred Therapy: From the personal to the universal
Suzanne Keys (Ed)

The Client-Centred Therapist in Psychiatric Contexts: A therapists' guide to the psychiatric landscape and its inhabitants
Lisbeth Sommerbeck

To Lead an Honorable Life: Invitations to think about client-centered therapy and the person-centered approach
John Shlien

Learning and Being in Person-Centred Counselling (second edition)
A textbook for discovering theory and developing practice
Tony Merry

Person-Centred Practice: The BAPCA Reader
Tony Merry (Ed)

Trust and Understanding: The person-centred approach to everyday care for people with special needs
Marlis Pörtner

Classics in the Person-Centered Approach
David J. Cain (Ed)

Client-Centered and Experiential Psychotherapy in the 21st Century:
Advances in theory, research and practice
Jeanne C. Watson, Rhonda N. Goldman & Margaret S. Warner (Eds)

Pre-Therapy: Reaching contact-impaired clients
Garry Prouty, Dion Van Werde & Marlis Pörtner

Voices of the Voiceless: Person-centred approaches and people with learning disabilities
Jan Hawkins

Freedom to Practise: Person-centred approaches to supervision
Keith Tudor & Mike Worrall (Eds)

Visit our website for news of the latest releases www.pccs-books.co.uk

UK customers call 01989 77 07 07 for discounts